Probationary Inspector Diaries 1982-86

Alain Allen

PI236 Publishing, Hong Kong

Copyright © 2022 by Alain Allen

All rights reserved. No part of this publication may be reproduced, distributed or transmitted in any form or by any means, including photocopying, recording, or other electronic or mechanical methods, without the prior written permission of the publisher, except in the case of brief quotations embodied in critical reviews and certain other non-commercial uses permitted by copyright law.

PI236 Publishing, Hong Kong

Book Layout ©2022 PI236 Publishing

Cover Image by Martin Lovatt

Probationary Inspector Diaries 1982-86/Alain Allen 1st ed.

ISBN: B0B4G4VMR9

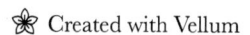

❦ Created with Vellum

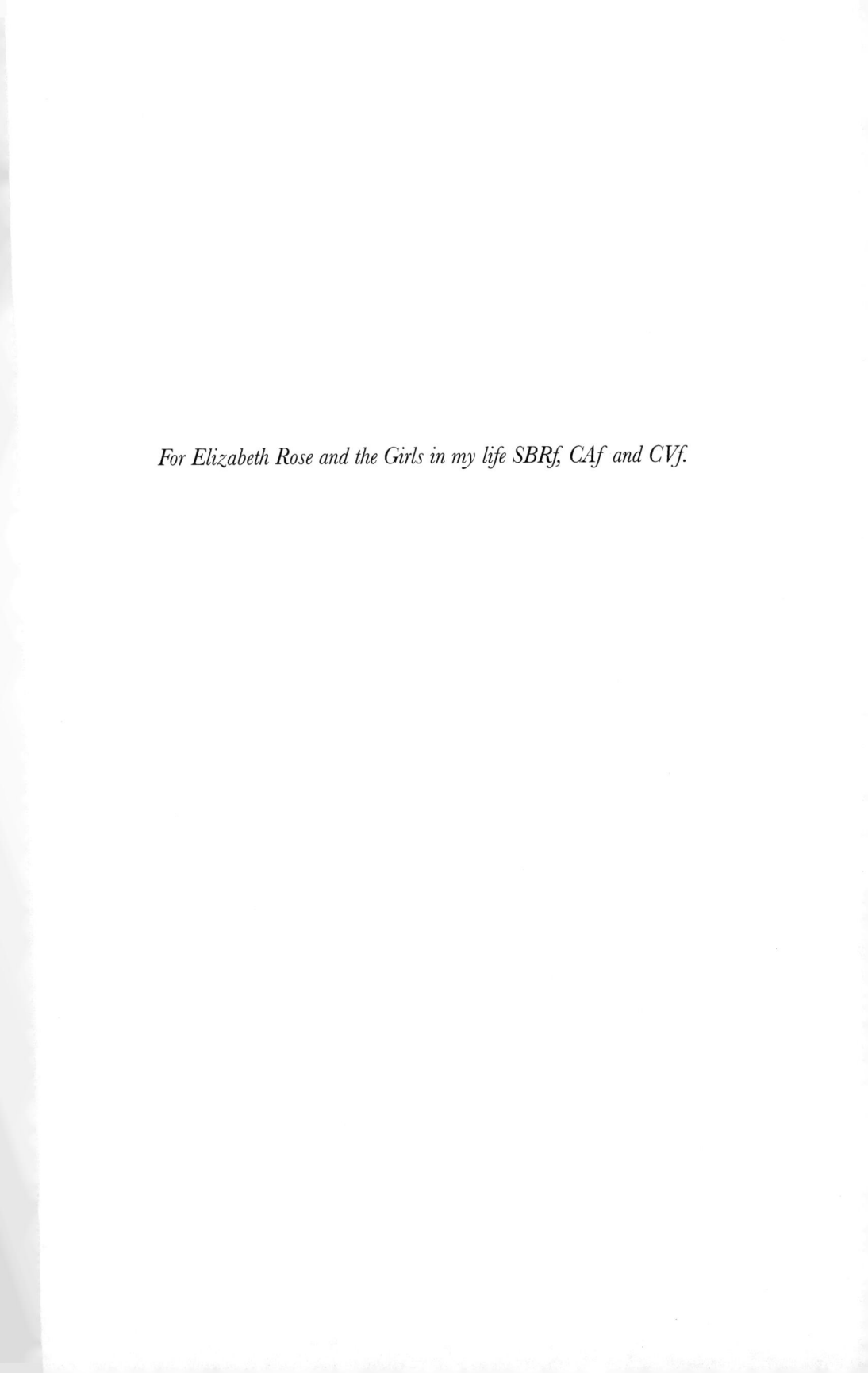

For Elizabeth Rose and the Girls in my life SBRf, CAf and CVf.

Contents

Glossary of Terms Used	8
What to Expect	14
Preface	16

Part One
1982

1. June to December 1982 Pre-Posting to Hong Kong	23
2. The Summer of 1982 Newcastle Upon Tyne	30
3. Germany, The Windermere Marathon & Hung like a Shire Horse	37
4. Preparation for & Trip to India	44
5. Final Week Count Down in the UK before Flying Out to Hong Kong	52
6. Trip to Hong Kong, the Longest Weekend & Meeting The Emperor	55

Part Two
1983

7. Introductory Stage Day 1 and Week 1 Police Training School	65
8. Cantonese, Two Admin Officers & the Introductory Stage	71
9. Arrival of the New Intake & the Junior Stage	82
10. Intermediate Stage & The Emperor's "Interview"	88
11. Leadership Camp	92
12. Social Life as It Existed & Life After Studies at PTS	97
13. Senior Stage, PTS Passing Out & The Emperor's Sinister Trick	100
14. Victoria Mortuary, Cocktail Night & Assault by The Emperor	107
The Photographic Record	115
15. First Posting to Kwun Tong Police District, Ngau Tau Kok Police Division	130

16. The Force Swimming Gala at Tai Wan Shan Pool, Hung Hom	136
17. Beat Incidents	139
18. Social Life at Work & off duty from Sept 1983 to Jan 1984	158
19. Shift Duties in NTK Division	161
20. Activities Off Duty	164
21. House Warming and Meetings with SDKSf	166
22. Scuttlebutt	172

Part Three
1984

23. Back to Police Work & the Events of January to April 1984	179
24. Meetings with SDKSf January to May 1984	182
25. NTK Police Station after the Taxi Riots	184
26. Standard Two Inspectorate Professional Exams	186
27. Attachment to DIS KT DIST January-April 1984	187
28. Inspectors Continuation Training Mid Way Through DIS KT Attachment	190
29. Return To DIS KT DIST	193
30. Trip To Peking (Beijing) Easter 1984	195
31. Peking Photograph Development	200
32. Patrol Sub Unit Commander NTK Division	202
33. Visit of SDKSf at my Workplace	204
34. Unexpected Call and Visit by SDKSf	206
35. Sighting of The Emperor, Ho Man Tin	208
36. Visit of Son and Cousin of my Mother's Friend	209
37. Three Weeks for Wedding in the UK June 1984	211
38. Visit to See SDKSf After UK Trip	215
39. The Long Letter from SEPf	216
40. Flat Hunting with RJm	218
41. Special Duty Squad One Kwun Tong Police District	220
42. Visit of Mother and her Friend Mrs. T October 1984	225
43. New Quarter Ming Court Boundary Street	228
44. Occurrences While Visiting Rick's Café	230
45. Work in SDS 1 KT DIST Continues	234
46. Christmas Week Dinner in Food Street Causeway Bay	236

Part Four
1985

47. SDU Selection Monday 7th January 1985	241
48. Back to OC SDS 1 KT DIST	244
49. The Golden Dragon (Gam Lung) Ballroom Jordan Road.	247
50. Splitting KT into Two Districts KT & Sau Mau Ping (SMP)	249
51. Coast of China Marathon	253
52. Sau Mau Ping Estate Block 20 Operation	255
53. Raid on Ngau Tau Kok Lower Estate & CAPO Complaint	258
54. Raid in Lei Yue Mun with CID Action Squad NTK	260
55. Sighting of The Emperor, Shatin Inn	263
56. The End of being OC SDS 1 SMP DIST	264
57. The Philippines Vacation with RJm & HNm	267
58. PTU Company Training: First Day	272
59. The Forming of PTU G COY 4/85: Officer / NCO Cadre Training	275
60. The Forming of PTU G COY 4/85	278
61. Kowloon West PTU Golf COY Regional Attachment Incidents	283
62. Problematic Police Division of Shek Kip Mei	285
63. Golf Company Life	289
64. Special Duty Unit Selection Again	299
65. End of SDU Selection Dinner	308
66. British Military Hospital for Nose Operation	309
67. Return to PTU Golf COY 4/85 KW	312
68. Visit of the last of the Three "A"s from Peking KAf	314
69. Sighting of SDKSf and Invite to Her Flat October 1985	315
70. RJM Leaving Party and Leaving Night	316
71. End of PTU Golf COY 4/85 KW & Transfer to MESUC SMP DIV	318
72. Social Activities November 1985 to April 1986	320

Part Five
1986

73. Last Standard Two	325
74. Two-Week Holiday in Thailand	327
75. Return to MESUC SMP DIV	330
76. Last Sighting of The Emperor as MESUC SMP DIV	331
77. Vacation Leave: India	332
78. Vacation Leave: Nepal and the Annapurna Circuit	336
79. Vacation Leave: Return to India	339
80. Vacation Leave: Maldives Bolifushi Island	341
81. Vacation Leave: Sri Lanka	343
82. United Kingdom: 7 Weeks Leave	345
83. Vacation Leave: USA	348
84. Vacation Leave: Japan and back to Hong Kong	351
Photos 1986	353
Acknowledgments	355

Glossary of Terms Used

A, B, C Shifts: Morning, Afternoon and Night shifts.

ADC CRM: Assistant District Commander Crime at the rank of Superintendent.

ADO: Assistant Duty Officer, is normally a sergeant.

ADVC ADM: Assistant Divisional Commander, normally a Chief Inspector of Police rank.

ADVC OPS: Assistant Divisional Commander Operations at the rank of Chief Inspector of Police

Amah: Domestic helper who cleans flats and arranges laundry.

AO: Administrative Officer, a rank in the Civil Service.

BRV: Bullet Resistant Vest

Brian Slevin Trophy: Trophy named after an ex-Commissioner of Police given to the best Inspectorate officer of the intake.

CAPO: Complaints Against Police Office. An internal police unit which handles complaints against Police.

CCR: Crime Complaint Register used to record crime.

CDMI: Chief Drill and Musketry Instructor, previously a retired Regimental Sergeant Major.

CID: Criminal Investigation Department.

CIP: Chief Inspector of Police.

Commandant: Position in charge of a training establishment at the rank of Chief Superintendent.

CPTI: Chief Physical Training Instructor.

CX: Cathay Pacific.

DC: District Commander normally at the rank of Chief Superintendent.

DDC: Deputy District Commander normally at the rank of Senior Superintendent.

DDGA: Dangerous Drug General Authorization. A power used by an Inspector to raid a premise without a warrant.

DIS: District Intelligence Section is a crime unit.

DIST: District, a police formation normally comprising two police divisions.

DJ: Disc Jockey

DMI: Drill and Musketry Instructor at the rank of Inspector.

Dowman Road Race: A running race named after a retired Commissioner of Police called Dowman run annually over a distance of 12Km.

DOO: District Operations Officer normally at the rank of Chief Inspector.

Duty Officer (DO): Normally, a Station Sergeant or Inspector of Police ranked officer is responsible for the Report Room.

DVC: Divisional Commander, normally at the rank of Superintendent.

ENT: Ear, Nose and Throat.

EU KW: Emergency Unit Kowloon West. A police unit that handles emergency 999 calls.

Foxtrot Oscar: Eff Off.

FSD: Fire Services Department

Gam Mo Jai: Golden-haired boy

GSMEAC: Method of briefing using titles of Ground, Situation, Mission, Execution, Administration, Communication and Command.

Girlie Bar: Alcoholic premise that has topless girls dancing on a bar in bikini bottoms.

HHH: Hash House Harrier is a running group that undertakes a set course off-road.

HISQ: Ho Man Tin Inspectorate Service Quarters for single inspectors.

ICAC: Independent Commission Against Corruption, an independent body that handles reports of corruption.

I/C: In Charge.

2 I/C: Second in charge.

IDD: International Direct Dialing phones.

J Block: A letter given to a building at PTS used for Inspectorate Officer barrack accommodation.

JPO: Junior Police Officer is a collective name for all ranks below Inspector.

KT: Kwun Tong an area of Kowloon.

MRB: Miscellaneous Report Book used to record non-crime reports.

Mess: Officers eating and drinking room.

Names: These use initials, and sex is denoted by f for a female and by m for a male. On occasion, pseudonym initials are used.

Intake Director: This is a Chief Inspector of Police in charge of Probationary Inspector classes headed by other Chief Inspectors called squads.

Mamasan: The boss woman who controls other women, normally for the purposes of sexual activities.

MESUC: Miscellaneous Sub Unit Commander normally handling death enquiries.

MGC: Model of MG car with 2998cc engine.

MOU: Memorandum of Understanding

MP Car: Mobile patrol vehicle.

MTR: Mass Transit Railway like the Underground in London but more modern.

NPO: Neighbourhood Police Office

NTK: Ngau Tau Kok an area of Kowloon, Hong Kong.

PC: Police Constable

PE: Physical Education.

PI: Probationary Inspector wearing one shoulder pip within the first three years of service.

PI 236: Probationary Inspector Squad number 236.

POL 159: A police form for recording the first information about an action.

POL/MIL: A Police-Military unit at Police Headquarters.

POP: Passing out parade.

PRC: Peoples Republic of China

PSRC: Police Sports and Recreation Club for all ranks but mainly junior police officers on Boundary Street Kowloon.

PSUC: Patrol Sub Unit Commander normally at the rank of Inspector.

PTI: Physical Training Instructor.

PTS: Police Training School, Wong Chuk Hang, Hong Kong Island.

PTU: Police Tactical Unit (Riot Police)

PTU Cadre: A four-week training course for COY HQs, Platoon Commanders, and NCOs.

PTU COY: Police Tactical Unit Company comprising 170 men.

PTU COY CDR: Police Tactical Unit Company Commander at the rank of Superintendent.

PTU COY 2 I/C: Police Tactical Unit Company second in charge.

PTU HQ: Police Tactical Unit Head Quarters, a training establishment.

RAF: Royal Air Force.

RC: Regional Commander at the rank of Assistant Commissioner of Police

RCCC: Regional Command and Control Centre dealing with radio communications, 999 calls and tasking.

Red Tab: Chinese officer who speaks English denoted by red cloth behind the number on the shoulder.

Room Boy: Civilian who collects all uniforms on a daily basis to be taken for laundry at the station laundry. He also polishes shoes and boots.

SB: Security Bureau is a secret unit.

SDS: Special Duty Squad investigating drugs, gambling and prostitution.

SDU: Special Duties Unit, which is a police anti-terrorist unit based on the SAS.

SKM: Shek Kip Mei an area of Kowloon

SOBTW: Staff Officer Basic Training Wing with the rank of Superintendent.

Standard 1 Professional Exams: Taken to pass out of PTS.

Standard 2 Professional Exams: Taken in the first three years of service to become a confirmed inspector.

Standard 3 Professional Exams: Taken within the first five years of service to be advanced to Senior Inspector.

SSGT: Station Sergeant is the most senior non-commissioned officer rank.

THA: Temporary Housing Area of prefabricated huts.

Third I/C: the third person in charge of a subunit.

Typhoon Signal 8: A very strong wind signal.

Typhoon Signal 10: An extremely strong wind signal.

UI: Unique identifiable number is given to each officer.

W D General: Warning for Dismissal for any offence as opposed to a specific offence.

YMCA: Young Man's Christian Association.

What to Expect

These diaries cover:

- The Probationary Inspector's life in the UK before Hong Kong
- Mention of the Falklands War 1982,
- A trip to India via Afghanistan were he comes in direct contact with anti-Western sentiment when taking photographs while landing in Kabul 1982,
- Coming in contact with an Islamic fanatic on a train journey between Madras to New Delhi 1982,
- Befriending fellow travellers who were residents of Bhopal also on the same train journey,
- Early electronic manufacturers in Bangalore,
- The commencement of the talks on the Handover of Hong Kong and how he is treated by his Chinese Probationary Inspector Intake Instructor cum Course Director, known as The Emperor, intent on returning him to the UK 1983-85,
- Relationships with his fellow Chinese subordinates who he treats like his family being so far from home,
- Coming into hostile contact with the Tamil Tigers in Sri Lanka while on a trip back to the UK in 1984,
- A trip to the Communist Peoples Republic of China also in 1984 while the guest of a British Embassy secretary/political assistant involved in the Handover Talks,
- A trip to the Philippines for Rest and Recuperation (R n R) and discovering Boracay which was just opening up 1985,

- Nightlife in the melting pot of Hong Kong during the 13 year count down to the return to the PRC 1997,
- Learning of the Chernobyl disaster while trekking in Nepal in 1986 and
- Returning to the UK, which hadn't changed since he left four years earlier, and last but not least
- Life on the Front Line as a Probationary Inspector on the streets of Hong Kong 1983-1986 dealing with incidents he comes across.

The book is the most in depth depiction of the life of a Probationary Inspector of the Royal Hong Kong Police (RHKPF) during the 36 months of his first tour of duty contract between 1982 to 1986. The book covers his nine months of training as well as how he tackles the law and order issues that existed at that time in the Hong Kong melting pot, which was a much different place than it is today. Everybody wanted to better themselves be it legally or illegally and were prepared to pay the ultimate price be it failure or imprisonment. Life was frantic with everyone working hard and playing hard, grasping opportunities as quickly as they could in what was a 24-hour city always on the go!

This book is published on the 40th Anniversary of his arrival to Hong Kong. The year 2022 also happens to be the 25th Anniversary of the handover of Sovereignty over Hong Kong to Mainland China in 1997.

Preface

This book tells the story of a Probationary Inspector of the Royal Hong Kong Police Force between the 30th of December 1982 to the 11th of August 1986. The book also includes his last six months in the UK after finishing his degree prior to travelling to Hong Kong and the final four and a half months of his first tour leave, prior to returning to Hong Kong for his second tour of duty for another 30 months.

It is of note that Hong Kong was still a British Colony in 1982, and talk of its return to the Peoples Republic of China (PRC) didn't begin formally until 1983, with a Memorandum of Understanding (MOU) being finalised in mid-1984. The MOU, when completed, stated that the whole of Hong Kong would return to the PRC on the 1st of July 1997 despite this date originally only referring to the end of the 99-year lease of the New Territories that had been signed in 1898. This lease basically referred to everything north of Boundary Street in Kowloon. According to the rumours at the time, if all land south of Boundary Street was retained by the British, the PRC, who it was known wanted all of Hong Kong back, would stop all provision of water and food supplies. It was estimated that what remained of British Hong Kong wouldn't last more than a few months, and great costs would be incurred until it capitulated. It was further rumoured that the UK economy wasn't performing well at the time and was therefore not in a position to afford to keep Hong Kong. This left the Prime Minister at the time, Margaret Thatcher, in an unenviable position in her negotiations with the PRC on the handover of sovereignty of Hong Kong in 1997. Luckily the PRC knew the value of Hong Kong with its ties to big business as well as the value and attraction of its common law system. Further, the PRC wanted it to be handed over as a going entity, and hence this resulted in the concession that it wouldn't change for fifty years under the PRC policy of One Country Two Systems developed by Premier DENG Xiaoping.

That's enough of the history lesson other than to state that Hong Kong was a real melting pot with the local population all wanting to better themselves both legally or illegally as well as the many ex-pats, both high and low, working for big businesses or in other jobs of a transitory nature such as bartenders and the like. A fair few others were in the military services land, sea, and air on postings to Hong Kong, and the local airline Cathay Pacific employed air hostesses from many South East Asian countries from the age of 18, all of which could speak English. The Hong Kong Government also employed many ex-pats as Administrative Officers as well as in the Disciplinary Services such as the Correctional Services, Fire Service, and the Royal Hong Kong Police Force, which had by far the greatest number of ex-pats.

The Royal Hong Kong Police Force had nine-month training courses starting every two months at the Police Training School situated in Wong Chuk Hang at the bottom of Brick Hill. The training courses that commenced every two months were made up of squads of probationary police constables as well as probationary police inspectors with both local direct entry and Force entry inspectors, as well as up to 13 ex-pat inspectors in three squad intakes amounting to 30 inspectors. The ex-pat inspectors were generally degree holders, although officers could join with two A levels at the age of 18 if found suitable. Generally, the ex-pat inspectors were mainly all sportsmen, with sports such as rugby, football, cricket and hockey being of the most value to be selected and being Scottish also helped.

As can be seen, many ex-pats, no matter what they did, were all in their early twenties and were outgoing. This resulted in the few discos that existed at the time, such as The Front Page and Rumors on Hong Kong Island and Rick's Café, Hollywood East, Canton

Disco, Hot Gossip and the Cavern in Tsim Sha Tsui Kowloon, all being packed, no matter what day of the week let alone at weekends. The fact that one's tenure could be finite, be it tied to a police contract or military posting, added to the caldron of excitement that existed at all social venues, let alone a sense that things were temporary and good things had to be enjoyed and grasped as soon as possible. There were also other areas of Hong Kong, such as Wan Chai, that had girlie bars (topless) for fast action and discos such as Crossroads, Neptunes and the rest that attracted less well-paid bar staff and domestic helpers, let alone off duty ladies of the night. In its heyday, the bars of Wan Chai was the rest and recuperation (R&R) hot spots for the military either based in Hong Kong or who were US servicemen deployed in Vietnam on R&R in Hong Kong.

It can be said that Hong Kong had a 24-hour all-action edge to it, which made it an exciting place that seemed to be temporary, where everyone worked hard and played hard, and nearly everything went. This feeling only increased when talks on the future of Hong Kong began, and by mid-1984, the thirteen year count down to the Handover of Hong Kong had commenced.

To those ex-pat probationary inspectors at the Police Training School and those having passed out to Police Districts, life was lived as a continuation of being a student with money, albeit workwise, there were some responsibilities to be shouldered, and a set disciplinary system not to fall foul of if all was to run smoothly. Learning was done on the job, and studying for professional Standard 2 and 3 exams was done in one's own time. Probationary ex-pat inspectors mainly lived in single officer quarters either in the Hermitage on Kennedy Road Hong Kong Island or in the quarters at 19 Ho Man Tin Hill Road Kowloon, both of which were a taxi flag fall from the nearest nightspots. These quarters were often likened to rabbit hutches with little if any privacy because if you turned on the lights of your flat, people could see you were home. This, more often than not, meant there would be a knock at the door with someone wanting a cup of tea and a gossip, or go for a beer and hit the night spots!

Sports and fitness were also taken seriously, and discovering all the nooks and crannies of Hong Kong was done on days off and public holidays. This often resulted in ex-pat inspectors having visited parts of Hong Kong that local officers had not visited; such was the fault of the time-consuming custom of getting an education and the size of the local family budget. Ex-pat officers also had more free time as all their laundry, be it uniform or plain clothes, was done by either the room boy at the station or the amah on each floor back at their quarters. The attitude of 'work hard and play hard' was the mantra, and when this was coupled with the sky-high testosterone levels and hot to trot rose lip maidens and light-foot lads, the atmosphere was electric. There was an edge to the early to mid-1980s in Hong Kong, and the attitude was to enjoy now like there was no tomorrow! This story is true, and no apologies are made for including the warts and all other occurrences as they did happen!

Alain

Part One

1982

Chapter 1

June to December 1982 Pre-Posting to Hong Kong

The alarm went off at 06:00hrs, and I immediately got out of bed as I had done for the past two weeks. It was early June 1982, and it was the last day of the final exams of my degree, with the Long Essay Paper kicking off at 14:00hrs that same day.

I quickly went through the six essay questions that I had prepared in skeleton format and ensured that all the parts learned the night before could still be remembered. By 08:00hrs, I grabbed a bite to eat and then had a quick shower, having decided to visit a close course friend, who lived in Lovaine Hall of Residence at Newcastle Polytechnic, to see what essay question he had chosen to do. I was at his flat by 08:45, having driven there on my motorcycle. Over a cup of tea, we discussed what the likely essays we would answer were, with mine being Econometrics and his being Economic Principals. I was back home by 10:00hrs and hard at it, rote learning my subject skeleton and then remembering what meat to add, so it was properly filled out to an acceptable level.

By 13:15hrs, I was done and then, on my motorcycle, took the route I had taken for the past two and a half weeks from Croydon Road, Fenham up to Brighton Grove across to Hunters Road and then onto Claremont Road. This road had two roundabouts to throw my bike around to get rid of the cobwebs of the morning, and at the same time raise my heartbeat and then onto the Civic Centre at Barras Bridge. I turned right at the City Baths and parked up on College Lane just behind the examination hall. I dismounted and had a last look at my skeleton answer, remembering it all and then entered the examination hall, saying hello to those that I knew.

The examination started on time and lasted for three hours, during which unusually no one left despite some pens falling silent with nothing more being written after two and a half hours. The invigilator gave the ten-minute warning, and then when three hours had passed, he declared the exam finished and that everyone could leave. At that moment, there was a crescendo of noise by all the students and a loud round of applause, as that marked the end of our final exam and, ultimately, student life at Newcastle Upon Tyne Polytechnic.

This was my second third year, having left in March of the previous year to deal with a family matter that was growing and had begun to envelop me as well as swamp me at that time. The matter got sorted with me standing by the strength of my convictions and moving out of the family home in June of that year, before deteriorating relations with my stubborn father could explode, with the chance of blows being traded. I moved into rented accommodation and found work doing a six-night, 12-hour day work week in a cotton mill that paid enough for me to afford to finish my final year, purchase a second-hand Suzuki 400cc motorcycle after trading in my Honda CB 200, and still have some pocket money left during my new final year.

On arrival back to Newcastle Upon Tyne, I found accommodation in Croydon Road at an address that two girls from the Poly Swimming Club that I had been the captain of had occupied the year before. They had left after finishing their courses, but one of the tenants who had a young son was still there, and there were two other students, one English doing Chemistry and the other was

Iranian doing Politics while also avoiding the draft for the army in his home country.

I settled down into the new final year class as I knew some of the students and all of the lecturers. There were also two students from my year, both of which had taken a year out, with one joining a band and the other getting over some serious illness.

About two months into the final year, I had settled down and had a solid routine with swimming and water polo two nights a week, and on other days I managed to fit in three runs. The runs were with the medics I was friends with from swimming who lived on Dilston Road, better and more warmly known as the Dilston Boys for short as a sort of joke. Three were from Newcastle, with the most handsome one being nicknamed Rob the Dog and the other two the L Brothers, with the fourth being an engineering student from Cockermouth called Curly because of his twisted hair. All three medics were in relationships, with the eldest L Brother's girlfriend being a sister at a local hospital called RAf. By November, I had developed a close friendship with a girl from Lincolnshire of German origins on my course, and life was good with studying also going well. There was also no animosity from the stance I had taken with my family's domestic arrangements, albeit things were still estranged with my father.

Christmas came and went, and the Tyne froze over for the second time in four years while I spent the New Year in Sleaford. On return to Poly, life settled down and the swimming and running were good outlets to let off some steam with the ever-increasing study schedule and compilation of a dissertation of 10000 words. There was even talk of running the Great North Run and ultimately the Windermere Marathon as a long-term goal. In February, an old girlfriend [PJf] from school came to visit me for four days. Which somehow, I managed to balance with all my other entanglements with no damage done. Visits to Durham, Whitley Bay and the Big Market kept me from the places I usually frequented. In that month, I also crewed for a friend of mine in a two-man dinghy competition near Dunston Straits on the Tyne, which had only just reopened after freezing over. During the competition, we capsized twice, with me somehow managing to walk on the bottom of the dinghy until it righted and stayed dry through the first capsize. Whilst my friend from Embsay near Skipton [MIm] got thoroughly wet, much to my good luck and amusement. He was wearing a wet suit while I had jeans, Green Spot sports shoes, a jumper and a windcheater. The second time I wasn't so lucky and got stuck under the sail until I released myself, totally wet and miserably cold. We got the dinghy righted and set off around the course, having four more laps to do. After the second lap, as the wind was gusty and sailing was sporadic, I began to shiver uncontrollably and could hear my bum beating a beat on the wooden side of the dinghy I was sitting on. To put it mildly, things weren't going good. So, I suggested we retire from the race as I couldn't do another two laps. On getting out of the boat on the side of the Tyne, I found that I couldn't feel my feet and had real problems knowing when they touched the ground, which made dragging the dinghy up to its resting place very difficult. On securing things away, I had a very interesting motorcycle ride back to my digs. At least I could hear the revs of the bike engine when I changed gear which helped a lot, as I certainly couldn't feel my feet. Immediately on getting into my digs, I got changed into warm, dry clothing and sat in front of the gas fire trying to thaw my feet out while at the same time being ever aware of chilblains. After about two hours, just as I thought that I should go to the hospital, I started to get feeling back in my feet. After another 30 minutes in front of the gas fire, I saw my feet return to normal.

During the warming process, I thought of two winters earlier when I had gone to Embsay Reservoir sailing on Boxing Day, basically watching how my friend sailed his single-person dinghy. After about an hour, he asked if I wanted a go as he would shout instructions from the side of the reservoir to tell me what to do. Needless to say, after about 30 minutes, I capsized and shouted for instructions on what to do, especially in righting the dinghy. My friend told me to hang on and went inside the clubhouse, re-emerging with a camera in hand. He shouted that he wanted photographic evidence of me going for a swim on Boxing Day, which was certainly outside the normal sailing season. I remember the Tyne was much colder and that I should, at some time in the future, invest in a wet suit.

As March came and went, I had handed in my dissertation, which had been neatly typed up and had begun to draft up a study programme plan which would take me to my final exams. Lectures had more or less stopped, except for revision topics and my attachment to my friend from Lincolnshire was put on hold if not ended. As for the next 12 weeks, there were more important things to do. I would have eight exam papers and I chose six topics to prepare for. With each paper, I made sure I had skeletons for each question and the meat memorised to fill out the answers. I decided I would study at the University Library as I would see fewer people that I knew and therefore, there would be less distractions. A tight schedule would be kept with 18-hour days planned during the exam weeks and no swimming or water polo, especially after the sixth week of study.

April arrived quite quickly, and I had already laid a solid foundation for my studies. However, on the 2nd of April 1982, the Falkland Islands War was declared, which made me feel very patriotic and want a slice of the action. One of the Uni students [WIm] from the swimming club got his call up papers as he was studying engineering and had managed to get a sponsorship from the Royal Navy with him being destined to become a sub-mariner. He would report for duty immediately after he had finished his final exams in June.

Life went on with the daily study schedule, but I would still go for two to three runs a week in the evening with the medics, who were in their final year, from Dilston Road. The run was for about 10km, with the end of the run going uphill on the Great North Road next to the Town Moor before heading back to Dilston Road and Fenham. I still remember having vivid discussions with Rob the Dog running up the Great North Road hill, which Curly couldn't believe. He said as much between sharp intakes of breath while also mentioning our fitness for still having the ability to talk. The preparations for the Great North Run were coming along nicely, and it was after one of these training runs that Curly and I decided to enter the Windermere Marathon.

The daily routine of morning, day, and night was set with studying. This was only interrupted when I went for a run three nights a week, but it was immediately back to studying as soon as I got home after the run. At 10:00PM each night, I would take 30 minutes out of my schedule to watch the news and learn what was happening with the Falkland Armada and War. On one Saturday night, the Dilston Road medics invited me to a "white coat party" (doctors) party at one of the nurses' homes which went really well, as I met a State Registered Nurse from Windy Nook in Gateshead called [MDf], and we hit it off like a house on fire. This was given the blessing of Rob the Dog, as he stated that she must like me very much as he had never seen her become so attached at other such parties. Life was good, and relationships all fitted in with my studying schedule.

Employment wise, I had applied for pilot training in the RAF, also to become a Merchant Marine Officer with the Blue Star Ship Management Ltd, as well as the Royal Hong Kong Police as a course friend from the year earlier had joined, together with many other job applications being made. It is of note that I had, at the age of 17, while in the 6Th Form at school, undertaken the four-day aircrew selection tests at Biggin Hill but had been advised to go back a year later for further consideration. I didn't go back as by that time, the A level results envisaged didn't materialise, so I lost the Plessey Scholarship and my place at Bath University to do Electrical Engineering, ending up at Newcastle Upon Tyne Polytechnic doing Economics. I thought rather than go back after a year, I would go back with a degree. I also had an interview at a career day at the Poly with a Royal Navy interviewer, who apologised for his manner after five minutes of seeing me, having had a torrid time with the candidate before. He ended the interview by stating that he looked forward to seeing me at Dartmouth

Studies progressed, as did the running and my relationship with my friend from Windy Nook. During one of my last days at swim training, I gave a lift to a girl from Heidelberg studying English at the Poly to her digs as we had become good friends. She stated that she and the other exchange students would soon return to Germany. Having developed a close bond through swimming, we exchanged addresses promising to visit each other at some time.

Studying continued, and from about five weeks out from the exams, I was doing 18-hour days, getting up at 06:00hrs and going to sleep at midnight listening to the Phil Collins tape "In the Air Tonight". I would only have breaks for meals, the 'News at 10' and weekend drinks on Saturday nights after a run with the lads or seeing the nurse from Windy Nook. If I remember correctly, a Barry Manilow Concert on TV immediately after the news was also fitted into my revision schedule one night.

The exams came, were endured and completed with me having no doubts that I had passed every paper. The only thing left was to enjoy the summer, get some employment, go for interviews for future careers and train for the Great North Run and Windermere Marathon. The exam results would be out in four weeks, and that was something to look forward to, to find out why I had worked so hard for four years.

Chapter 2

The Summer of 1982 Newcastle Upon Tyne

Midway through June, I decided to stay in Newcastle to work until I sorted a job out. As I still had two months on my student accommodation lease to go, I also had to look around for alternative digs. Training for the Great North Run increased as it would be held on the 28th of June, and my running friends and I had all been successful in our applications, despite 50,000 runners applying for the 20,000 places.

One day while at the Poly, I spotted a job advertisement for a credit traveller that would last the whole summer, and despite not knowing what it was, I noted that it gave you the use of a minivan and was for six days a week. I rang the number on the advertisement and secured an interview, which would be held at a small department store on Pink Lane in the West of Newcastle that same day. I immediately went home and got changed into a suit with a tie and went for the interview at 14:00hrs. During the interview, I had my driving license checked and the job was explained to me. Basically, as the North East of England around Newcastle was a coal mining area, there existed many pit villages. People living in the villages didn't get the chance to go to Newcastle that much, and hence the department store sent out credit travellers with catalogues that had all sorts of household items that could be bought and paid for weekly, fortnightly or monthly. As it was summer, the normal credit travellers would go on leave and I would be filling in doing the set rounds of the holidaying credit travellers. I would have the use of a minivan and could claim the cost of petrol bought back from the department store at the same time I deposited the collected cashback daily in the morning before going out collecting. The area covered was huge from Berwick Upon Tweed in the North to Carlisle in the West and as far South as Darlington and the whole of the coastal area in the East. I stated that I would like the job and started the next day as the pay would more than pay for accommodation and food as well as give me the chance to save some money.

The day of the Great North Run arrived, and the Dilston boys and I lined up in the City Centre together with 20000 other people with the atmosphere being electric. The elder L brother had arranged for his nursing sister girlfriend [RAf] to pick us up at the end of the run, so there was no need for a change of clothing. Mind you, there was no such thing as depositing clothes, as runs such as this were still in their infancy and as such were rudimentary. One thing that we hadn't done during our training runs had been to run the course. Hence, this deprived us of knowing which landmarks to look out for, so we had to depend on the roadside mile markers. The run started, and we left Newcastle City Centre and went over the Tyne Bridge to Gateshead and then on a meandering course passed Gateshead Stadium. The run ended up in South Shields at the seafront, where we were all given a bottle of water and a banana, both of which had never tasted so good. All of us finished under two hours, which was the time we were aiming for, having never run more than eight miles in our training runs.

Just after the Great North Run, I went for a provisional job interview for the Royal Hong Kong Police in Manchester. Which if successful, would see me attend a formal interview in London. I travelled by motorcycle, and a friend provided accommodation overnight so I could shower and attend the interview in a suit. At the end of the interview, I was informed that they would put me forward to London, who would then contact me and provide train tickets to London with meals being covered. After the interview and on my way back to Newcastle, my motorcycle had a problem with the electric starter, which caused the bike to come to a halt near Whitefield. I contacted a friend [WVGm] who lived in Bury as I knew he was good at electrics, and he came out and got me going again after some soldering on the wires of the electric starter. I thanked him and was on my way, thinking this had been the first time back to Manchester and not having been home.

On return to Newcastle, I continued with the credit travelling job and on some occasions, would go out with the actual credit traveller the week before his leave commenced so he could introduce me as his temporary replacement while he was on leave. I remember going to a house in Ashington, which the credit traveller advised me that they normally served a full meal when he went, and he said that he would let me eat it while he had a cup of tea. On entering the house, after all formality's food was served and when my plate arrived, it looked like I had been given the whole roast. Anyway, I ate everything as it would be rude not to and felt rather full, even the next morning. The people at the house were the salt of the earth and nothing was too much trouble.

On another traveller's rounds, I had been advised that a customer at a certain house in an area of Newcastle called Battle Hill Estate was never home and if after two knocks no one answered, I should leave as the people were quite rough. I called for the first two weeks and despite hearing noise in the house, no one answered, so I left. On my third visit, I again heard noise and decided to knock at the door until someone answered. After ten minutes, a bloke answered who looked like a right bruiser, very rough and ready and asked what I wanted. I stated where I was from and having heard a noise in the house, wanted to make sure everyone was OK. He answered that his mother wasn't home, so I asked if he could let her know I had called. However, I got no answer.

The marathon training continued with Curly setting out all the training runs with increasing distances as we got through the summer. I particularly remember one run up to Ponteland in the North of Newcastle near the airport and back on a long route to Fenham. On arrival in Ponteland, Curly said we should get water from Rob the Dog's parents' house, which we did, who were amazed at the distance we had run with no water! On another long run, we stopped to pick blackberries to supplement our water intake as we were so thirsty. The marathon was on the 31st of October and we already knew there would be water stops and bananas and heat blankets at the end.

Midway through July, [WIm] arrived back from Dartmouth and was full of the stories he had heard from fellow officers who had been to the Falklands with the war finishing on the 14th of June 1982. One particular officer told him that he was allowed to take any kit over and above his issued kit if he could carry it, so he took a camera. He described the officer as an oversized rugby player that if you pointed him at a brick wall and told him to go through it, he would. Apparently, during one battle running for cover, he fell over but couldn't get up, only then to realise he had been shot. On being pulled to a safe position, he asked his men to get his camera from his backpack so he could take some "Happy Snaps"! Another story being told was that two soldiers had searched the dead body of an Argentinian and found a letter from his girlfriend with an address. The two soldiers took a photo of them with the dead soldier all smoking cigs and sent it to the girlfriend with a note which, when the proverbial hit the fan, an International Incident was just averted. There was another story about a navy helicopter pilot who went down in the South Atlantic and broke his back, kicking the windscreen out to escape from being drowned. He stated that this pilot had been awarded his South Atlantic Swimming Badge and become a member of a very unique club.

The interview for the RAF at Biggin Hill was also during July, but on arrival after the medical, I was informed that my right eye was slightly short-sighted and hence I would not be considered for aircrew. I was then given the option to withdraw, which I did, and returned to Newcastle Upon Tyne.

About two weeks after this, I attended the Royal Hong Kong Police interview at Grafton Street London. I was interviewed by three people, with one [TPm] being a serving Superintendent officer in charge of recruiting in the UK, a Hong Kong Government official and the last one being a retired police officer. The interview went well; however, the retired police officer wanted to know more about my boyhood dream of flying for the RAF and how and why I was interested in joining the Royal Hong Kong Police. I noted that with every answer I gave, he tried to press his point home that the Police was really my second choice. I answered all his queries while at the same time standing my ground. Eventually, the serving police officer in charge of recruiting cut the retired officer short. I was then asked to wait in the waiting area and listen to whether I had been called for a medical. A short time later, I was called to go for a medical on Harley Street, which I passed with the doctor stating that I should enjoy going to Hong Kong and despite being right-handed, I could use my left eye to aim when firearms training. About two weeks later, I was officially informed I had been accepted and was asked to choose a joining date, which I did. I opted for the 30th of December 1982 due to the Windermere Marathon I had entered and the time needed to sort out my UK affairs. I filled in a large amount of paperwork, including forms for buying a suitcase, which would be reimbursed, and I also had the option of receiving one month's salary in advance, which I opted to do. The sale of my motorcycle would pay off the advance even though I had been informed that instalments for the first three months of salary in Hong Kong would be deducted to settle the advance.

The remnants of the UniPol (University-Polytechnic) water polo team entered a summer water polo league with away games as far away as Carlisle, and the social life was ongoing as disco music was all the rage.

Songs like Come on Eileen were very popular and were played in every pub, with some pubs even having music video machines. I got my results for my degree and got a creditable 2:2, being told by staff I would have got a 2:1 if I had taken the degree a year earlier. The day I got informed, a few of us retired to the Poly staff room and got very drunk on lots of wine, with staff taking my crash helmet off me so I couldn't drive home. Anyway, I got home somehow despite being blind drunk and hit the sack for a short sleep as I was going for dinner with the nurse [MDf] from Windy Nook. About two hours later, she woke me up and realised what state I was in, so we still had dinner but not too much to drink. Things were a bit stop and start, as she had an old boyfriend who was still interested. A few weeks later, I came home from a party and found her in my bed at my digs, as she had been let in by one of my flatmates. On knowing that I had been to a party where I could have gone off with someone, she stayed the night. A few weeks later, after a trip to Greece with her girlfriends, she came back, and that was the end of that. I had an early morning trip to walk the beach at Whitley Bay to get rid of the cobwebs of the relationship and life continued with my credit traveller work, training for the Windermere marathon and preparation to go to Hong Kong.

The graduation ceremony for my degree was scheduled for August. My mother and twin brother could only come if my father came. Otherwise, no family member would attend. I accommodated this arrangement, but the existing relationship with my father put a damper on the day and after they had left to return to Manchester, I couldn't help thinking I had been used and he had won the battle that day. Subsequently, I didn't attend any of the celebrations scheduled for that night, instead choosing to have a quiet night in my digs.

In August, I moved into [WIm's] house on Brighton Grove agreeing to do some painting while he was at Dartmouth in exchange for rent. I was also asked to make sure that all his tenants had moved out and any damages paid for out of their deposits.

In the middle of September, I had to leave [WIm's] house quite quickly as his new tenant didn't want a stranger in the house even if it had six bedrooms, no matter what work was being done. I ended up in the elder L Brother's girlfriend's nurses' quarters as they had a spare room. It was at this time that my friend from Heidelberg came back to Newcastle to see some friends, including me and we had dinner. During which, I was told I was welcome to visit her at any time in Heidelberg and I stated that I would try and do that.

I quickly found a room for the Autumn term from the Poly Accommodation Board, which saw me still living in Croydon Road but in a different flat with two female students. I moved in first to a single front bedroom, thinking the girls would have the two doubles, but when the named tenant arrived, I was told her future flatmate had taken it and I could have the back double bedroom. On meeting the main tenant [ERf], I was very pleasantly surprised as she had a great tan, having just come from a holiday in Ibiza. If I do admit it, I was quite taken by her and we soon became very good friends. Life went on with the credit travelling and the training for the marathon increased. At the end of September, my right foot was beginning to ache and on advice, I changed to trainers from Green Spot shoes as the trainers were much better and healthier.

Chapter 3

Germany, The Windermere Marathon & Hung like a Shire Horse

Midway through September, Curly and I put our heads together and put in place a training routine for the Windermere Marathon that would see us stop any long distance runs by the 14th of October. We would do three 10km runs during the week and over the next three weekends, we would do a 20km, 25km and 30km run. It was certainly hard going but for the last two weeks before the marathon, we would do just four 10km runs and no running for the last six days.

On sorting out the running, I decided to go to Heidelberg by motorcycle between the 15th of October and arrive back in the UK on the morning of Friday 29th of October. I let Curly know of my plans and stated that on arrival back in Newcastle, I would see him in the evening of the same day and we would travel to Kendal on Saturday the 30th of October by motorcycle.

I quickly let my friend in Heidelberg know my intended travel plans and she said she was looking forward to seeing me. I then booked the North Sea ferry to depart South Shields, Newcastle on Saturday 16th of October and return overnight on Thursday 28th of October. The rest of the marathon training went well, albeit the back-to-back long runs were hard going, especially the last one on Friday the 15th of October, as Curly had taken a day off work. After the run, I had time to wash and dry all my running kit and pack my backpack for the motorcycle trip to Germany.

The next morning, I arrived at the South Shields North Sea Ferry Terminal at 08:00hrs and was on the 1000-person ferry by 09:00hrs with the crew instructing me to secure my motorcycle properly, as the trip was going to be rough. I lashed my bike down properly and then went to find a spot which I could claim in the middle and lower part of the ferry, as I believed this would be the most stable. I then went up to the passenger deck to watch land slip away but couldn't as the rain was horizontal and when it hit the face, it was like getting smacked. The wind was that powerful. In the galley, I spotted two motorcyclists and asked if I could sit with them over a cup of tea. They told me they were brother and sister from Hamburg and had been touring around Scotland for two weeks which they found interesting, especially the single-track roads. On hearing that I intended to drive from Esbjerg in Denmark directly to Heidelberg, they suggested that I stay with them for a night on the way down back in Hamburg, as it was a very long drive. I agreed and the sister, who was a teacher, would put me up as her brother was a baker and had very early starts. They said we should meet the next morning two hours before arrival to Esbjerg in the galley as they had their own cabin for the night. It was of note that at that time, not many people were in the galley despite 1000 people being on board, but I spent most of the day there as all the Danish female crew were all blonde-haired and rather good looking.

As the day unfolded, the movement of the boat became more noticeable and by 21:00hrs, I went to claim the spot I had seen earlier and got my sleeping bag out and slept there for the night using my backpack as a pillow.

The next morning, I went to the galley early for some breakfast and it was empty. I did notice the waves outside through the portholes were rising almost as high as the galley, and the ship was noticeably rocking and rolling. Before my breakfast arrived, I went to the toilet and on entering, they were in a right state with many toilets being full of vomit which explained why no one was in the galley. The two Germans arrived after about an hour and after they had eaten, it was almost time to go below deck to get our motorcycles ready for the trip to Hamburg.

We set off at about 11:00hrs after docking and the roads were relatively quiet and scenic, even seeing the sign for LEGOLAND. On arrival in Hamburg, after about four hours of riding on relatively empty autobahns, I rang my friend in Heidelberg to let her know I would arrive the next night as I was splitting the trip up because of the distance that had to be travelled. The night soon arrived and after we all had a long dinner, we returned to our respective residences and turned in for the night. In the morning, my female German host prepared a hearty breakfast and by 11:00hrs, I was on my way to Heidelberg taking the advice on the best route going via Hanover, Kassel, Frankfurt, and Mannheim. I had a couple of stops for petrol and a coffee but other than that, I soon got used to cars overtaking me on the inside with me being in the outside lane. I soon discovered that Ausfahrt meant exit and left and right in German were almost the same as English. At about the midway point of the trip, I was occasionally woken up by cars going pass me at about 200km per hour on the inside and then I saw a sign which I didn't know what it meant. I soon found out it was a noise-making structure on the ground of the autobahn as the concrete/tarmac was sliced horizontally and vertically, so people falling asleep would wake up. What it meant for me on my motorcycle was that I had to slow down very quickly in order to stop my handlebars from gyrating, which I had to grasp very strongly to keep level which came as quite a shock.

I arrived at the railway station in Heidelberg at about 21:00hrs and my host [KMf] was waiting in her purple Volkswagen Beetle together with her two friends, who I had also got to know in Newcastle Upon Tyne. On arrival back at KMf's flat in Dossenheim, we had drinks and some food and I handed over the leather they had requested I bring for them from the Priory in Newcastle, which they would use in their handicraft hobby. I was introduced to KMf's flatmate [Bf] and I noted that the student accommodation in Germany was much better than in the UK. Domestic arrangements were sorted with me sleeping on a spare mattress in KMf's room. Pretty soon after that, I was off to sleep absolutely knackered from the trip on strange roads that demanded a high level of concentration and attention.

The next morning after breakfast, I was given a quick familiarization of Heidelberg University and also Heidelberg City as KMf knew I wanted to do some running and play some water polo at the University Water Polo Club. During the next 10 days, I picked up quite a bit of German and met many friends of friends, not to mention did some sightseeing in the Black Forest, the Castle called Heidelberg Palace and the hill railway station that gave panoramic views of Heidelberg City. The bars we went to were great as you only paid for your drinks when you were about to leave. The city centre was beautiful with many gifts and meat shops to walk around which had great smells. On one occasion, we all went for a sauna and before I went, I was informed it was a mixed sauna with women on one side and males on the other, so I said I would bring my trunks. On arrival in the changing rooms, I could hear female voices nearby and when I walked into the sauna, I spent the first 30 minutes looking at my feet to avoid an embarrassing moment, as there were naked women sitting opposite me. I soon got used to the surroundings, which I learnt to enjoy thoroughly, especially the cold-water plunges!

Very soon, my stay in Heidelberg came to an end and I was sad to be leaving, especially as my friendship with KMf had blossomed and I had got to know many new contacts. I would miss the vistas of the River Neckar and Bismarckplatz at the centre of the city, as well as listening and singing along to Chris De Burgh's "A Spacemen Came Travelling" and the Scorpions "Still Loving You" when driving to social events. A particularly hard physically demanding dry ski training session at the University Ski Club would be something I also wouldn't forget!

Germany, The Windermere Marathon & Hung like a Shire Horse   41

Breakfast for my last morning was fresh fruit, German bread and meats as well as nue wine as it was that time of year. After this, I was escorted to the start of the autobahn, where I said my long goodbyes and hugs to my host and set off for Hamburg, having confirmed arrangements the night before with my Hamburg host.

At a stop on the way up to Hamburg, while having a coffee at a service station, a German Truck driver sat opposite me and asked in German whether it was cold on my motorcycle. I tried to answer and between our broken German and English, I stated it wasn't cold as I was wrapped up and he said at this time of year, most Germans had put away their motorcycles until the following summer.

On arrival in Hamburg, my host greeted me in a friendly manner and was surprised at how much German I had picked up in 10 days. After a great dinner together with her brother and good conversation, I went out like a light as I had an early start the next morning to catch my ferry from Esbjerg to Newcastle. I made the ferry just on time after another hearty breakfast and friendly goodbyes, during which I gave my Hamburg host my contact address in Hong Kong.

The ferry to Newcastle was much smoother than on the way out and I even had time for a sauna. However, disappointingly it wasn't mixed! On arrival to Newcastle in the morning, I got home and did my laundry while letting Curly know I was back. I also rang work that I would be in first thing Monday morning. Arrangements for the Saturday night accommodation in Kendal were also confirmed and all that was left to do was get my running gear ready and mentally prepare for the marathon, which I knew would require a lot of effort. On travelling to Hamburg, I noted that Frankfurt was approximately two marathon distances away from Heidelberg, so I now had an idea of how long the run would be, not to mention the effort needed.

Saturday arrived and I picked up Curly, put our running kit in my top box on the bike and arrived in Kendal midafternoon, after about a two-to-three-hour trip. Our hosts for the night met us and on arrival at their house, we got our sleeping arrangements sorted out and were informed that we would have a pasta dinner to give us energy for the run the next day. We also had a drive around the course, during which we noted a number of hills on a route that basically went anti-clockwise around Lake Windermere. We settled early into bed and had a solid night's sleep, albeit thoughts were always on the task at hand. After a light breakfast and getting hydrated, we went to the start point where I met a swimmer [FTm] I knew from my home town Bury, who was a member of Bury and Elton Swimming Club.

The race started in overcast conditions and by the halfway point, there had been some drizzle, but things were going well. At about the 20-mile mark, I stopped at a water point, feeling really hungry. I noticed one of the support staff was eating a sandwich, which I asked if I could have a bite of. I was told in succinct terms that eating while running would be no good for me. Such was the thinking at the time, which is different from now. The last five miles were hard going and I think I hit the wall but the endpoint came in sight and both Curly and I ran in together. Upon finishing, we quickly grabbed a banana and a bottle of water, having completed the run in four hours and 20 minutes. We were pleased with the time and more pleased we had finished running the whole course. At the presentations, all finishers were given a medal, each made from slate. Soon after, we returned to our host's house and got things ready to leave to go back to Newcastle. Prior to leaving, I had a bath and when I submerged myself in the water, my nipples gave off a shooting pain as both nipples were chapped due to the drizzle and sweat of my shirt rubbing against my nipples during the marathon. I now knew how women felt when breastfeeding and they all have my total admiration. Other parts of my body felt similar due to chaffing. However, after the bath, everything was good to go.

On getting on my motorcycle, I had problems getting my leg over the saddle and I could tell that I had exerted myself. We said goodbye to our hosts and decided to have a break on our ride back just the other side of Carlisle in a place called Warwick Bridge, where we could get a pint. On arrival, Curly dismounted and I more or less fell off the motorcycle as the weather had become cold and my legs were beginning to freeze up. The bike got put on its stand. I then walked into the pub in a very laboured manner finding an empty table while Curly got us a pint each. On entry, as we were strangers, the pub went quiet while the locals examined the new patrons. I went to the bar for the second pint order and still walked in a laboured manner. I put my order in and while waiting, another customer aged about 50 and dressed like a farmer also made an order. During the wait, he asked where I was from and then noted that when I walked in, I walked in like I was hung like a shire horse with a set of huge balls! I was astonished at his frankness but quickly replied yes, I imagined I looked like that as I had just run the Windermere Marathon, to which he started to laugh and the tension eased. At the end of the second pint, it was time to straddle the motorcycle, which was truly comical, and we headed back to Newcastle, arriving at about 23:00hrs. I had difficulties getting up the stairs to my bedroom after putting the motorcycle away but the next morning, all was well apart from feeling a bit stiff.

During the month of November, I had itchy feet for another trip and one country that I wanted to go to was India. I gave it deep thought as I was still missing Heidelberg, but I got on with my credit traveller rounds. During the month, I noted a few nice pubs in villages that I visited and then revisited with the Dilston Road boys at the weekends. After much thought, I decided to go to India from the 27th of November until the 19th of December, finishing work on the 26th of November and set about what I wanted to see, what airline I would go on and get everything else ready for going to Hong Kong. During the month, I got my first pair of eyeglasses. Which when first worn, caused me to walk very carefully as I felt dizzy, but the brain soon adjusted. Going to India meant that I would miss out on seeing Dire Straits in concert live at the City Hall, but that was good news for the elder L brother's girlfriend [Raf], who immediately bagged and tagged my ticket.

Chapter 4

Preparation for & Trip to India

I got a map of India and decided to visit New Delhi, Bombay and Goa. I checked for cheap flight tickets in the Sunday papers and chose a cheap foreign flight bucket shop in East London to buy my ticket and noted they only accepted cash. I made a booking and was informed the airline chosen was Ariana Airlines, an Afghanistan airline that flew from Paris, but the price included a flight from London. Pretty soon, the last day at work approached, after which I was taken for a few drinks to celebrate and say goodbye.

On the morning of the 27th of November, I slowly got out of bed with a bit of a sore head but soon got going packing my backpack in record time, which I hadn't done the night before. I then ran down to the main railway station in Newcastle and just made my train with very little time to spare. On the way to London, I studied my map of India and put together a schedule for visiting different locations but had already decided to stay at the YMCA in New Delhi on arrival. However, I had not made a booking.

On arrival in London, I made my way to the bucket shop and before handing over my cash, I was informed that the airline I was travelling out to India on would be grounded and banned from flying to the UK because of selling cheap tickets. As my dissertation was on North Atlantic Air Routes, I asked whether the airline was a member of IATA and that it was given a positive response, noting that other IATA airlines would recognize my return air ticket to get me back to the UK? I parted with my cash and was given two tickets and an itinerary flying British Airways from London to Paris and Ariana Airlines to New Delhi via Kabul.

I made my way to Heathrow and on arrival, soon checked in and got a boarding pass with a seat number. On departure, I noted that the plane was only half full. However, all the passengers looked European, with only a few none European faces. We soon arrived at Charles De Galle Airport, after which I made my way to the Ariana Airline desk. I showed my ticket and was given a boarding pass for New Delhi with no seat number. I then made my way to the advertised departure gate, and as soon as I arrived, I noted many passengers who were of Indian and Arabic origin. Many of them were carrying excess hand luggage, the quality of which made my Berghaus backpack look like it was first class.

I soon spotted another European face who I started a conversation with. It turned out he was from Yorkshire and was travelling to Kashmir for four months to do some carpentry. He had been there two to three times before, mainly during the winter and advised that we should get a seat together on the plane as it was free seating and there would be a mad rush to get the best seats. What he said turned out to be true and after we got our seats, we settled into our flight. I noted the inflight food and drinks service had to be paid for and that at least two passengers had started up their primus stoves to brew their own tea in the aisle ways of the aircraft, with the airline staff saying nothing.

After a very short night, we were informed to get ready for arrival in Kabul. I got my camera ready and took photographs of the capital city, more interestingly, the anti-aircraft guns at the side of the runway we landed on. At this point, I was roughly asked what I was doing by another local passenger, who accused me of being a member of the press. I didn't like the tone of his voice, so to avoid any problems, I put my camera away.

On arrival at the airport terminal, all transit passengers were told to wait in the terminal lounge, where we got a rough and ready rice dish to eat. After further chatting with the carpenter, he said we should share a room on arrival in New Delhi at a place he had stayed at before as it was quite cheap. Thinking it would be late when we got in, I took the offer and this meant that I could check out the YMCA the next morning. The carpenter asked whether I was a member as it was required in order to book a room. After a five-hour wait, we were on our way to New Delhi and on arrival, I was struck by the amount of people everywhere as well as the wooden shanty structures they called home. It was certainly an eye-opener, as was the number of people trying to sell us all sorts of goods. We got to the small hotel in the centre of New Delhi and turned in for the night, saying our goodbyes the next morning.

On arrival at the YMCA, I joined the organization and booked in for four days. I would need some time to sort out my return trip home due to the grounding of the airline I had arrived on. I also noted that the Asian Games were on and asked where I could buy tickets which I would do after I had sorted out my return ticket. I first tried British Airways but they were full, so I tried Pan Am and arranged a booking for Saturday the 18th of December, direct to London. I asked if there would be a problem and the Indian clerk swore blindly that everything would be alright and there would be no problems. Once this was done, I went to see if I could buy tickets for the Asian Games, which I managed to do for athletics and the water polo competition. On the way back to the YMCA, I walked passed the Old Delhi Railway Station, which had many food stalls outside. The stalls looked really seedy and I made a mental note that I wouldn't eat there as everyone looked like vagabonds up to no good, despite it looking very busy.

On arrival back at the YMCA, I asked where I could get an evening dinner and they pointed me in the direction of a shopping centre on Connaught Circus. Eventually, I found somewhere that fitted my backpacker budget. It was a Chinese food shop, so I ordered a diced pork chilly. The dish turned up and the top of the dish was full of green chillies that looked like the ones you get on kebabs in the UK. I dug in and took my first bite, soon realizing the chillies were not the same as in the UK but were extremely hot. I grabbed my breath but continued to eat the whole dish, as I was on a shoestring budget. When I had finished, I asked for a hot coffee to drink to see if I could put out the fire in my mouth. The coffee arrived and after my first sip, my mouth exploded as it was like putting water on an oil fire. I noted the food stall sold ice cream, so I asked if I could have a portion. When it arrived, I ate it immediately as this reduced the temperature in my mouth. On finishing the ice cream, my mouth exploded even more than when I drank the coffee. I paid my bill and walked back to the YMCA breathing through my mouth to try and cool it down. On arrival, I immediately went to sleep as my mouth, despite being hot, was bearable. After about four hours of sleep, I woke up with severe pains in my kidney area and had the need to go to the toilet. While on the toilet, I soon noted that if food was hot and spicy on the way in, it was much hotter on the way out. I just about survived my trip to the toilet but promised myself to have strange food in moderation for the rest of my trip.

In the morning, I had boiled eggs, toast and porridge plus tea at the YMCA for breakfast. After which, I made my way to the Asian Games water polo competition. After watching many games and getting to speak to a group of people my age from Bangalore, they asked if I wanted to join them for dinner, which I did. However, on arrival, I noted it was at the food stalls at the Old Delhi Railway Station, so I was quite wary. The dinner arrived consisting of many Indian dishes and surprisingly, the food was very good, so I ate quite a bit. After dinner, I said I would meet them again the next day at the athletics. After the athletics the next day, I obtained a telephone number for my new acquaintances and stated that I might see them in Bangalore with them offering to put me up if I did. I then went to the Old Delhi Railway Station and booked a ticket to Bombay the next afternoon. Once this was done, I returned to the YMCA to sleep for the night.

The next day arrived and while getting on the train to Bombay in 2nd Class Reserved, I noted that my bed bunk wasn't obvious. Upon asking my fellow passengers, they stated that at night time, the seat we were sat on would be the bottom bunk and the back of the seat could be pulled out and hung for a 2nd middle bunk. The 3rd upper bunk would be where bags were placed overhead during the day. The train had a food service with staff coming around the cars, and food could also be bought from train stations we stopped at such as coffee, chai (tea) and small snacks through the barred windows of the train.

After a poor night's sleep, I arrived in Bombay and visited the Tourism Office and noted that accommodation was expensive, so I decided to do two sightseeing trips only. I bought my rail ticket from the magnificent railway station called Victoria Terminus or VT for short to go to Goa. The two tourist trips took in the aquarium, if that was what you could call it and a couple of museums. The museums were great, apart from being ambushed outside one by a snake charmer with a large cobra in a rattan container, which appeared when he lifted the lid as I walked past, much to my consternation.

At about 21:00hrs, I boarded the train to Vasco De Gama and looked forward to a few days on a beach and swimming in the Arabian Sea. Again, I chose 2nd Class Reserved and settled in for the 15-hour journey having my section of the cabin to myself. At first light, I was amazed at the scenery and the waterfalls as well as the forests we passed through. At one station, a boy about 16 years old boarded looking like Stig of the Dump or Huckleberry Fin, who I noticed didn't have many possessions, let alone money. When I bought some chai and snacks at a railway station we stopped at, I also bought him something to eat and drink, if only to keep him friendly. On arrival at Vasco da Gama, I marvelled at all the street markets and noted many of the inhabitants looked of European origin, obviously from their Portuguese history, not to mention the many churches I could see. I found a resort to stay at, about 30 minutes from Goa by cycle rickshaw and settled into my new surroundings. In the evening, I had some food, which was much different from New Delhi and Bombay, which was very enjoyable. During the next two days, I did some sunbathing and got quite tanned. However, I noted that during the night, when I went to urinate, it was a little painful. My urine was very dark coloured, which I put down to not drinking enough and being dehydrated. Buying water wasn't recommended because it couldn't be trusted, so I drank more soft drinks to solve the problem. On my third day of sunbathing, a girl [Cf], my age from Switzerland, approached me and asked if she could join me and also asked me to look after her bag when she went swimming. During our conversation, I found out she started her Indian trip with her boyfriend and another male friend but after an argument, they had split up and gone their separate ways. I was gobsmacked, as travelling in India as a male was a challenge and a major challenge for a lone female. We sunbathed for the next three days and ate during the evening while Cf relaxed and felt safer. I mentioned that I had an invite to go to Bangalore and asked if she wanted to join me. However, she said she would spend another week in Goa before flying home. I gave her my contact details in Hong Kong and she said she might visit, having caught the travel bug.

The next day, I took the train to Bangalore, arriving the following morning. I had real problems with the telephone number I had been given and couldn't get through to anyone despite the operator stating there should be no problem. Eventually, I gave up and noted that if anyone said there would be no problem, then that meant there would be a problem. I found somewhere to stay and booked a tourist trip for the next morning, which included breakfast. During the sightseeing trip, I had a Masala Dosa for breakfast, which I ate after asking how it should be eaten. Also, during the trip, a couple of local shop owners noticed my electronic mini timekeeper and alarm gadget and even offered to buy it as they said they had seen nothing like it and Bangalore was just becoming an electronic manufacturing centre. I stayed another day and then travelled to Mysore and explored its tourist sites spending just one night as I decided that I should get back to New Delhi 4 days earlier than my flight just to ensure there was no problem, having been told there would be no problem.

I booked my ticket, which went via Madras, and then direct to New Delhi, taking just over two days on the train such was the size of India. My tickets stated I had the same seat for the whole journey, so I readied myself for a long session of reading James Clavell books. There was a 3-hour wait in Madras for the New Delhi train, which I made the most of to eat some good train station food, which consisted of soft-boiled eggs, toast and great tea. Once on the train to New Delhi, I soon made friends with my fellow passengers in 2nd Class Reserved and got on with my reading. After about four hours, a late twenty-something aged male got on and said I was sitting in his seat, which I objected to. However, on checking, I noted I should be seated two seats across, so I got up and moved. The male released a verbal barrage about how his religion was better than any Western country and that he was on his anti-westerner pilgrimage to Afghanistan. Little did I know how in the future, this sort of fundamentalism would affect the whole World. My fellow passengers consisting of a couple of families told me to ignore him and set about talking to me while isolating him, despite the odd few hostile glances from him. After about another 24 hours, the two families got off in Bhopal and two years later, I couldn't help but think if they had survived the Union Carbide gas tragedy.

On arrival in New Delhi on the 13th of December, I went straight to the YMCA and booked one night's accommodation. After which, I went to the Pan Am Office to confirm my flight for the 18^{th,} but they had no record of my booking. They checked that date and it was full, but they did have one flight on the 14th that went via Frankfurt, so I booked that and decided to get off in Frankfurt and see my friends in Heidelberg. On arrival in Frankfurt on the 15^{th,} I noted how cold the weather was, so I quickly travelled to Heidelberg and went to KMf's flat, arriving at about 12:00hrs, absolutely tired. I had no sleep on the flight mainly because I talked to one of the stewardesses the whole night. In those days, doors were not locked, so I left an Indian newspaper in KMf's letterbox with a note that said I was visiting and hoped she wouldn't mind if I got some sleep in her bed. At about 18:00hrs, I was pleasantly woken up by KMf, who was showing her flatmate [Bf] what the storks had brought back all the way from India and dived into conversation about my adventures. The next three days went very quickly and we had a great time with KMf even showing me how to mischievously kick a lamppost so that its overhead light went out. On Sunday the 19th, I took the train from Heidelberg to London via the car ferry and was up and about to see the White Cliffs of Dover on the morning of the 20th. Once in London, I got a ticket to Newcastle Upon Tyne and made the 21st a day to get my plans together for packing up my room and seeing my friends in Glasgow and Skipton.

Chapter 5

Final Week Count Down in the UK before Flying Out to Hong Kong

On Tuesday the 21st, I rang around many car hire companies, but they all had no cars to hire, so I had to make a long-distance phone call. I arranged to borrow a mini, which had to be picked up in Manchester. The rest of the day was spent making plans to see my water polo friend and his wife in Glasgow on the 23^{rd,} staying overnight and leaving on the 24th. The second appointment was to visit my friend [MIm] from Skipton on the 26th, leave on the 27th to go to Manchester and return the car I had borrowed. I then picked up my motorcycle before going to my mother's house. Putting it in the garage, cleaned up and ready for sale. The rest of the day was spent packing all my study books and clothing, apart from what I was going to wear and take with me to Hong Kong. One thing that would be going with me was my twin deck ghetto blaster, as I could not do without my music. Bank details were also obtained so that I could remit money back to the UK.

On the 22nd, I rode my motorcycle to Manchester down the A1M and when I stopped outside Leeds for petrol while filling up, I saw a car skid off the main road. Later on, going over the Pennines, my glove became frozen and wouldn't wipe the snow from my visor, so I lifted it up and noticed the whole motorway was covered in a thin layer of snow. I proceeded cautiously and on dropping down a few hundred feet in height, the motorway was clear. I arrived at the house, where I would pick up the car only to find out it was in another garage. We then travelled to the garage, I connected the battery and parked my motorcycle. I spent the night at a friend's house and then travelled up to Glasgow, just in time for a bite to eat and a few pints.

On the 24th, as there had been a lot of snow, we went gully jumping in the Trossachs. This took the whole day as well as a couple of drinks, after which I said my goodbyes. In the evening, I headed back to Newcastle but thought I would call in at my flatmates ERf's parents' house in Ravelston Dykes in Edinburgh and have a quick drink. On arrival, I was told she was at the carol service at the City Centre Cathedral, so I went and waited outside the only exit. Luckily, I spotted her and she had a friend in tow. She was flabbergasted to see me and we had a few drinks, after which I was invited to stay at her parents for the night.

I had intended to leave early Christmas day but was talked into staying for Christmas lunch, which I did. Eventually, I left at about 18:00hrs after being escorted to the start of the A1M. Before I left, I said my long goodbyes and hugs promising to write. I arrived back in Newcastle at about 22:00hrs, having had a great trip listening to a Grace Jones tape that ERf had given me. Before going to bed, I did some more packing, knowing that I had little room in the mini to carry much stuff and was also wary that I had to be in Skipton by 13:00hrs for lunch.

The packing the next day went well and I was sad to leave my room and flat, remembering all the good times I had in Newcastle during the last four years. This became final when I dropped the flat keys through the letterbox. Lunch went well in Skipton and the pints in the evening were very enjoyable as I wasn't going to be leaving until the 27th. The next morning, I set off at about 10:00hrs and arrived in Bury to drop off all my stuff I wouldn't be taking to Hong Kong at my parent's house and packed them away while my father was at work. The stuff I would be taking, basically one suitcase was left in the front room while I went to drop off the mini and pick up my motorcycle. I stayed at a friend's house for the next two nights and picked up my suitcase on the 29th. After parking my clean motorcycle in my parent's garage, I gave my mother the paperwork for its sale with the recommended price.

My brother gave me a lift in his car to Manchester Piccadilly, and I got the 15:00hrs train to London Euston still using my student travel card, which had stood me in good stead over the last year. Once at Euston, I headed to Victoria Railway Station, and as I was entering the station, I heard a guy shout at me if I needed accommodation for the night as he saw that I was pulling a suitcase. I turned around to look in the direction the shout came from and saw a male about 50 years old in a slick city suit, obviously under the influence of drink, looking like he was looking for a rent boy. So, in my best Lancastrian accent, I told him to piss off. Once on the train to Gatwick, I got to thinking that I was glad to be leaving the UK but there would be many friends I would miss. Once at the airport, I grabbed a bench to sleep on for the night as I hadn't booked a hotel, knowing I could grab a good wash and shave the next morning. This would allow me to get changed into my suit, ready for the 10:00hr check-in at the Cathay Pacific Airline counter, which was the meeting point. By 22:00hrs, I was ready to sleep, which I did lightly as I had my suitcase to look after, looking forward to the new day.

Chapter 6

Trip to Hong Kong, the Longest Weekend & Meeting The Emperor

On the morning of the 30th of December 1982, I was up at about 06:30hrs at Gatwick Airport. So, I grabbed a light breakfast, after which I went for a good wash, shave and change of clothes. At 10:00hrs, I went to the Cathay Pacific check-in counter and noted that there were about 11 other males my age and a guy I recognized from Grafton Street who was taking a roll call and handing out boarding passes. At 10:30hrs, we headed to the boarding gate and were wished a good trip by the guy from Grafton Street, who then left. I didn't recognize any of the 11 other guys but as we boarded, I noted that we were sitting in Business Class and I was sitting next to a very tall bloke who introduced himself as [SEPm], who seemed outgoing. We were all offered a pre-flight drink by very attractive and attentive Asian stewardesses and a packet of almond nuts. This service was much different to the budget airlines I had previously travelled on as everything was free. The seat we were given reclined to an almost horizontal position but not quite, which I guessed would be good for sleeping. After take-off, we were offered further drinks and snacks and were also given a menu for lunch that would be served prior to our transit stop in Bahrain.

I got talking to SEPm and he had many similar habits to me, such as motorcycling and sports. He told me of the motorcycle that he had restored, which on its maiden run out with his girlfriend, he had hit a drunk that had suddenly dashed out in front of him. The drunk was killed and the collision also ended up breaking his girlfriend's nose, while he had to sort out the damages himself. He also stated he wasn't prosecuted. He then described how he had ridden across North Africa, sleeping in the deserts during his trip. I informed him of my trip to India and he seemed intrigued, stating that was one country he wished to visit.

Just prior to our arrival in Bahrain, I noticed a guy from our group, very similar looking to me, ring the bell for the stewardess to come and take away two sick bags, as he had drunk too much Guinness. This guy later became part of my squad at the Police Training School (PTS) and was known as [HNm]. In Bahrain, we all looked around the duty-free shops and then, as a group, introduced ourselves, with four or five people stating that they had their interview at Grafton Street on the same day. There was one guy called [LCAm] who had a brother already in the Royal Hong Kong Police, who was about 19 years old, and the rest were graduates apart from a SGT from the Welsh police called [GPm]. Others included the son of a military officer who was called [WFLJm], a language teacher aged about 27 called [PSm], a law student from Birmingham called [CJm], and a guy called [TMRJm], who was a bit gobby. He was also full of himself, stating he had been at Manchester University but had been a nightclub manager afterwards. He stated that he already knew how to speak Cantonese, having been self-learning for six months. Another guy called [MBm] was from my home town of Bury and a Lancastrian called [MPm], who had been in the territorials, all of which seemed outgoing, positive and looking for adventure. The last two were a guy called [DBm], who had been to Stonyhurst School and had been in the Paratroop Regiment or so he said, and one other who would be joining us in Hong Kong called [GRm].

Trip to Hong Kong, the Longest Weekend & Meeting The Emperor   57

Once our transit in Bahrain was finished, we boarded and the lights in the cabin were dimmed after we had been told we would be woken up for breakfast. I had two more Bloody Mary's with a beer chaser and listened to some chart disco music on the inflight entertainment while trying to get some rest. This didn't come naturally, as it was only about 20:00hrs UK time. Breakfast came and went, and on hearing we were going to land at Kai Tak Airport, we were told that the best view would be from the right side of the aircraft. The plane lurched to the right and before it straightened up, we marvelled at how close the rooftops that we could see from the cabin windows were. Once landed, we got our carry-on bags and boarded a bus for the terminal building, noting that it was early morning, quite cool and that the airport only had one runway. There was also an odd smell which we were told was the nullah, whatever one of those was, plus the smell from the nearby tobacco godowns. The hills surrounding the airport look magnificent, as did the close tower blocks of nearby Kowloon City, which were interesting, to say the least, and totally alien to anything in the UK.

Once in the terminal building, we were met by three males who were all Chief Inspectors, in their early 30s, comprising of two ex-pats and one local, who was apparently the Intake Director, who seemed quite aloof called [GKLm]. The other two were doing all the talking, making sure some people even fastened up their ties. They stated that they had already cleared immigration for us and all we had to do was pick up our bags and board a police bus that was waiting for us. Once on board the bus, we were told we would travel through Kowloon and take the vehicle ferry to Hong Kong Island before arriving at the Police Training School (PTS). At PTS, we would be shown our sleeping accommodation and be given an hour to unpack and shower before reporting to a classroom to fill in all sorts of administrative forms needed for our stay in Hong Kong. As we travelled to the car ferry, we went past many areas, the names of which escape me. I do remember one of the CIPs [CSm], later to be known by us as the "Slug", as he was thought to be smarmy. He did point out the New World Apartments overlooking Victoria

Harbour, which had some single inspector quarters. On arrival at the Jordan Road Ferry Pier, we boarded the ferry and parked the bus. We all got off to look at Victoria Harbour and take in all its wonders.

While I was pondering the harbour, I noted that I started to feel a bit tired, as I had been up for nearly 18 hours plus, having slept rough at Gatwick Airport. I was suddenly asked by the third CIP [CJm] what I thought so far, to which I answered that I expected that the weather might have been a bit hotter. He just shrugged his shoulders, stating that it was nearly Chinese New Year, which was usually the coldest time of year.

On arrival at the Police Training School, we were shown where we would be sleeping, which was an open dormitory with sections of four beds section with 12 beds in total per floor. When I was given my bed, I quickly put my clothes away in my wardrobe and put my Ghetto Blaster on my chest of drawers. I saw a single bar fire halfway up the wall, wondering when that would be used. Knowing that we had an hour and that I had used 10 minutes to square away my things, I laid down on my bed for a rest, asking the others to wake me up when they left, despite adjusting my clock and setting the alarm. I quickly fell asleep as I needed to rest.

I was woken up by the last guy leaving the dormitory and quickly got up, went to the toilet and went out to find the rest of the intake about 100 meters in front of me. On arrival at the classroom block, I was the last one to enter and was greeted by the "Slug" that it was good that I could join the rest of the intake who were just settling into their desks and chairs. We were given forms for the Immigration Department, the Hong Kong and Shanghai Bank, payment of salary and Police Officers Mess signature cards, not to mention a whole host of other forms that took about two hours to fill in.

Once the form filling had finished, we were informed that the first week would be busy with our local counterparts joining us the following Monday. I was informed that I would be the intake prefect

Trip to Hong Kong, the Longest Weekend & Meeting The Emperor 59

for the first week by the Course Director [GKLm] (later christened 'The Emperor' because of his aloof manner), who insisted on using my surname as though he was practising how to pronounce it. It was Mr. Allen would lead the intake and collect uniforms from the barrack, Mr. Allen would lead the intake to the barbershop, Mr. Allen would lead the intake to morning roll calls, Mr. Allen would lead the intake to the classrooms and the gym and Mr. Allen will ensure the intake will walk in step and not speak.

I had never heard my name mentioned so many times before in such a short period of time and it was a bit perturbing. Especially when the briefing ended, when I was informed most mistakes were made the first week, and I could expect extra uniform inspections and or gatings. The ex-pats were then informed which CIP would be their squad instructor and I ended up getting [GKLm], the Course Director. On reflection, I guess being the last one in the classroom meant that [GKLm] had lost a bet with the other two CIPs, better known as "face" in Chinese culture and I would receive his attention as a result. The admin work came to an end and we were taken to the Officers Mess, where the rest of the training school staff were waiting together with other Probationary Inspectors. Introductions were given to the Commandant [FJm], Deputy Commandant [DDm], and the Staff Officer Basic Training Wing (SOBTW) [WPm], as well as drill instructors. We were then allowed to get some lunch but informed we had to be back at the bar by 14:00hrs.

During the lunch, the other four senior intakes all chatted with us and explained that as the next day was a public holiday, there would be no passing out parade as that was held last Saturday. In the afternoon, we could expect some mess games, which could get rough and then when we were released at whatever time in the evening, the intake immediately above us would take us out to show us the Hong Kong nightlife.

Dead on 14:00hrs, we were all in the mess waiting as that was my first task as squad prefect, so I was determined not to fall foul of any rule I didn't know. Immediately on entering, we had beer races against all the other intakes, which meant we consumed at least four pints, plus the extra ones for senior intake members who stated that they didn't drink. This caused us to lose all the races and have to drink a shot of whatever a senior staff member thought would be a good drink. After this, we did bottle walking, which again, if you hadn't practised, was hard to win. Then relay races commenced, where you would run the length of the mess, pick up a mop, and putting your head to the mop handle, spin around six times in a circle before trying to run back to the start point with everyone running into furniture and walls.

After this, you had to drink a half pint of beer and put your empty glass on your head before the next runner could go. Finally, there was some mess rugby, which had very few rules, which meant it got pretty rough, very fast. After this, the evening came to an end and the intake above us split us into groups to take us downtown to visit a few discos, drinking holes, girlie bars and a sauna after we were given 10 minutes to change. You can imagine we were already in a bit of a state of inebriation, but once out, we could drink at our own pace and not for the enjoyment of senior officers.

Taxis could carry five people, three in the back, two in the front, hence the need to divide us into groups. We went to places like the Dickens Bar in the Excelsior Hotel and the Girlie bars in Wan Chai, where the girls danced topless and swung around poles. We were well impressed with the Cantonese ability of the intake guys senior to us, who gave the taxi driver the address and directions perfectly in a confident manner.

We were taught that if we got lost, we could jump in a taxi and say Ging Chak Hok Hau, which meant Police Training School in Romanized Cantonese, which we all quickly memorized. We were told the pitfalls of the Girlie bars and in some of the discos, such as the Front Page, we got to meet the so-called spoilt 6th Form girls who would usually ignore probationary inspectors. Finally, we went for a sauna and learnt more about the training school staff and who to avoid as well as what the training entailed. We got back to the Police

Training School (PTS) at about 08:00hrs, well ready to hit the sack as we had been awake for about 48 hours! Prior to sleep, we stated we would get up at 12:00hrs and do some exploring as well as get some lunch from the mess before going out again in the evening.

After lunch, we went to explore the infamous brick hill we had heard so much about and discovered it consisted of an uphill road after turning right out of the East Gate main entrance to PTS and heading uphill. About 300 meters up the road, there was a small pathway that led to steps under the cable car going to Ocean Park. Eventually, we levelled out after about 300 zig-zag steps, some of which had rails on either side, with some only having one rail on one side, while other sections had no handrails. Once reaching the top, the concrete path undulated along the ridge, with another path leading further uphill halfway along and the rest of the path going to the headland part of Ocean Park, which we reached.

We then returned the same way we had come, noting that if we ran this route, it would take quite a bit of energy and technique. On arrival at the PTS East Gate main gate, we jumped a taxi to Repulse Bay Beach, after which we went to Deepwater Bay Beach for a swim and then returned to PTS for Dinner.

In the evening, we went to the Bull and Bear Pub and after a few pints, we tried out the Old China Hand and Joe Bananas, ending up in a couple of girlie bars. By 02:00hrs, we called it a night and headed back to PTS. Noting that the Aberdeen Tunnel wasn't open, we had to go over Wong Nai Chung Gap Rd before dropping downhill to the East Gate to the PTS camp.

At about 10:00hrs on Sunday, the 2nd of January 1983, I went to the Excelsior Hotel to meet some relatives that were in town and had a long lunch and later dinner. At about 21:00hrs, we all travelled by taxi back to PTS, so they could see where it was and what it looked like, after which my relatives left and I returned to my dormitory. I got things ready that I would need the next morning, as by 08:00hrs, I had to have all the ex-pats assembled by the transport shed, with all already having had breakfast, showered, shaved and turned out smartly with their shirts, ties and jackets worn. The next day would be the first day of training with our local counterparts and the 13th ex-pat, who was already in Hong Kong. I went to bed and fell asleep immediately as it had certainly been a long four-day weekend, so to speak, action-packed with travel halfway around the world thrown in.

Part Two

1983

Chapter 7

Introductory Stage Day 1 and Week 1 Police Training School

At 06:00hrs Monday morning, I was already awake and quickly went for a shave and a shower before getting dressed and making sure everybody else was awake. We had all decided to get breakfast by 07:15hrs as the Officers Mess was only a five-minute walk from the Transport Shed. At precisely 07:58hrs, we arrived ready for our 08:00hrs fall in, with the Course Instructors already waiting. On exchanging good mornings, a police bus arrived and the remaining 16 local force and direct-entry Chinese officers got off the bus, plus the remaining ex-pat called [GRm]. Almost immediately, the ex-pats were asked to form three squads, having been informed the previous Friday which squad they would be in. A roll call was then made of the Chinese officers, which when the name of one of the Force entry officers was called, they sprang to attention with a crisp smack of their right foot hitting the ground with an answer of Sir? On being informed what squad to fall into, they crisply marched with arms swinging as high as their shoulders before crisply halting, after which they fell in.

I was shocked at the jumping to attention and crisp marching, but while waiting had noted senior intakes all marching in squads or running in step to where ever they were going next. I remembered reading that the Royal Hong Kong Police was a paramilitary force, but on seeing the reality, I was a little perturbed.

Soon everyone had fallen in and we were directed to follow the Course Instructors to the classroom block with a Force entry officer being told to keep the squad in step and march. At the classroom block, we were given a timetable for the day. This consisted of returning to the barrack block, which for the males was J Block so that the local Chinese officers could collect their suitcases and quickly unpack. There were two local officers and two ex-pat officers sharing each of the three sections on each floor, making a total of 28 males and two females who had gone to the women's block.

The next activity was a visit to the stores to collect all our uniforms and other kit items, including PE shorts, T-shirts, socks and Chinese white-soled plimsolls, all of which were placed in a large brown kit bag. Once all kit was collected, we marched back to J Block and were shown how to pack away every item in a precise manner so that the room boy could collect later, wash and launder as well as mark every piece of kit with our Unique Identifiable (UI) number and bed number. Once all kit was stored away, we changed into our PE kits so that we could run to the stationery store to collect our training manuals, Police General Orders and other items. All of these items were put into our brown kit bag and taken back to J Block via the barbershop, where we all had a very short and close-cut haircut. Later on, we were all shown around camp so that we knew where everything was situated, after which we returned to J Block to change back into smart trousers, shirts, jackets and ties to go for lunch in the officer's mess.

After lunch, we all went to our classrooms with all our stationery to be allocated a desk and marked our stationery with our names and UI number. We were shown how to update our Police General Orders and mark down the update number in the file index with the date it was updated. Later, we were all taken to see the Police Training School Commandant to be officially sworn in, paying allegiance to Her Majesty the Queen and promising to uphold the Laws of Hong Kong without fear or favour. Once this was done, we went to the photographic section to be photographed for the Police Training School Pass. Finally, at the end of the day, we were all given a timetable for the rest of the week, which we would have to follow religiously. Immediately after this, we went back to J Block to get all our kits ready that we would need the next day and adjust as needed. Once this was all done, we went to the Officers' Mess for dinner, checking out the bar, the TV room and the PTS phone.

During the evening, I gave much thought to what we had been told by the Course Instructors and other Probationary Inspectors senior to us. It was noted that there would be four stages, namely (i) Introductory Stage which for the ex-pats meant learning Cantonese for two months while the local officers undertook adventure and leadership training. The ex-pats would have to pass an Elementary Cantonese Exam at the end of two months which would be taken just before the next intake arrived. The next three stages would be progressively more difficult with (ii) the Junior Stage followed by (iii) the Intermediate Stage and (iv) the Senior Stage. Both the Junior and Intermediate Stages would have fortnightly exams followed by the end of stage main exam. The Intermediate Stage would also have the Leadership Week, which also had to be passed. Any failure of exams and or leadership tasks could see re-sits taking place, warnings for dismissal or back squadding to an intake below, or if extremely serious, expulsion from the Police Training School. The Senior Stage would also have fortnightly exams followed by the end of stage Professional Standard One Examinations consisting of four papers. Drill and Musketry exams would also be taken as well as stage physical fitness tests, all of which had to show an improvement on the one taken previously.

The rest of the week continued with half the day devoted to morning roll calls, drills and inspections, where we had drill Inspectors [SHm] kindly renamed Basil Faulty because of his resemblance to John Cleese and [TPm] or PTU TANG for short as that had been his previous posting. Physical training would also take place and the afternoon sessions would be devoted to visits to each Police Region and a Police Headquarter Unit, so we were more familiar with what the Hong Kong Police Force meant in terms of coverage. Morning roll calls were the highlight of the day as the intake above us, PI233 to PI235, had seven female inspectors who were in the squad position in front of our squads PI236 to PI238. As such, the PE kit left little to the imagination in terms of curves and bumps, causing a few male inspectors to get hot under the collar.

During the trips out to other formations, we had lunch at a Chinese restaurant on occasion and we soon learnt how to use chopsticks. Otherwise, you would end up not getting your fair share of the food.

Also, during the first week, we had our first fitness test, which consisted of five activities, namely (i) the 100m shuttle run, which meant over five back and forths of a 10m course. Faster recorded times scored more highly than slower ones. (ii) Pull-ups with the maximum number being 19, (iii) press-ups with the maximum number being 55, (iv) sit-ups with the maximum number being 250, and lastly, a 2.4km run with faster times scoring more highly.

The sit-ups were performed on a wooden floor with no mat and by the end of the 250 sit-ups for those officers that did that many, most, if not all, had blood stains on their shorts just above where the coccyx was situated. This was raised to the Physical Training Instructors, who just shrugged their shoulders and stated that was the way they had always been done while refusing the request to perform that exercise on mats, which the gym had in abundance.

Brick Hill was shown to us in its entirety, so we knew the whole course, which we had to run after. The 300 steps were hard work and in those sections that had handrails on either side, we could use both our hands to pull up as well as our legs. In those sections that had just one handrail on one side, we had to favour that side to use a hand to help pull us up. In the other sections that had no handrails, we just used our hands to push down on our knees as we climbed the steps. The whole run took between 17 to 20 minutes and was certainly a short, sharp shock to the system if run normally, let alone after a night out.

During the first week, I had extra inspections on three occasions for a member of the intake not having whitened his plimsolls enough, shaving having missed some bristles and socks and garters not being worn to the proper length. This meant I marched to the East Gate security house twice in the evening in camp kit at 18:00hrs and 21:00hrs to be inspected by the Duty Officer, who was from the Senior Intake. The task wasn't that demanding. However, it tied you up, meaning you couldn't get changed or go out of camp and certainly couldn't let your camp kit get creased.

Saturday soon arrived and in a short five days, we felt like veterans fully familiar with every part of PTS. The week had certainly been action-packed and informative. The only thing left to do was the Saturday morning drill and parade work on the drill square, which would take the whole morning. The session was taken by all the intakes and their drill instructors, overseen by Chief Drill and Musketry Instructor called [FBm] (CDMI), who had just joined PTS, having retired as the Regimental Sergeant Major of the Scots Guards (RSM). He demanded effort and unless he saw sweat, he would think you weren't trying hard enough. The drill sessions were physical, skill demanding and hard work, and once finished, you certainly knew you had expanded physical effort. The CDMI was a sound individual who let you know where you stood and he wasn't the sought of bloke who would go behind your back. What you saw is what you got. Once the drill was finished and everyone had showered and changed into smart civilian dress, the Officers Mess served drinks and cheese with biscuits between 12:00hrs to 13:00hrs with no signing required except for alcoholic beverages. Everyone was expected to attend and much was learnt while everyone unwound and talked.

That weekend, the ex-pats, as a group, had decided to visit Aberdeen to pick up some pirated music tapes and see the wet market where animals would be killed alive in front of you. Chickens had their necks broken and then were put in a barrel that spun around at a very fast rate to take their feathers off. Other things for sale were a lot different from the UK, with frogs, snakes and other animals, plus parts of animals that would be thrown away in the UK. Wong Chuk Hang Estate was visited to pick up stationery and the Jumbo floating restaurant was visited for afternoon yum cha and dim sum.

In the evening, we hit Wan Chai followed by Kowloon, where we visited the Blacksmith Arms followed by Rick's Café, which played all the best disco music with the then DJ [JSm], now being a RTHK regular. Much was drunk that evening, and by the time we got back to PTS, it was 02:00hrs with everyone ready for a good sleep and a lazy breakfast in the Officers Mess. The rest of Sunday was spent visiting Stanley Market and having a couple of drinks in the Smugglers Arms before returning to PTS to get ready for the start of Cantonese the next week. All our local counterparts had gone home, including the force entry officer, who had the bed opposite me called [WCCm]. He had promised to teach me some Cantonese if I taught him some English, which he already spoke to a good standard but just wanted to improve.

Chapter 8

Cantonese, Two Admin Officers & the Introductory Stage

During the next two weeks, each day was the same, with the start of the day being morning roll call which was good because of the eye candy even if half asleep. This was followed by morning ablutions which basically meant shit, shower and shave. This was followed by getting into our uniforms, having breakfast and then drill, although some mornings we had PE. The only uniform we put on were shorts, belts, socks, garters, shoes, hats and wrist indicators of rank, basically a black leather diamond shape with one pip in the centre and a white backing, indicating we were in the Introductory Stage of training. The two women officers also wore a uniform top. By 10:00hrs, we were in the Cantonese classrooms for two hours, basically singing the six tones of Cantonese, which we would have to know before we learnt any vocabulary or grammar. Mid-morning, we had a 30-minute coffee break with biscuits and by 12:30hrs, we had lunch. At 13:30hrs, we were back to the Cantonese classrooms for another two hours, after which we had weapons handling and range courses, followed by PE if drill had been in the morning or vice versa.

The Cantonese tone singing for two weeks was tortuous even if I had been a choir boy when much younger. The six tones consisted of (i) High Level, (ii) Mid-rising, (iii) Mid-level, (iv) Mid-falling, (v) low-rising and (vi) low level, all of which we had to sing. This was because Cantonese words could have six meanings, depending on the tone used and the context of the conversation. At the end of the two weeks, we were brain dead, if not brainwashed and were ready to learn some vocabulary, albeit some of our local counterparts had taught us the odd word or two.

At the start of week three, all the ex-pats were split into two groups, which were joined by two Administrative Officers from the Civil Service Bureau, namely [KTm] and [RCm]. The former being a part-time member of the Hong Kong Regiment and the latter a part-time member of the Royal Navy Reserve in Hong Kong.

Cantonese kicked off with each ex-pat being given their Civil Service created Chinese name of three syllables, which were supposed to represent the sound of our English names in a complimentary manner. These would be the names we would use during conversation and language training, although some of us had already made up some Chinese names such as Well Hung Chuk and Hu Flung Dung as a bit of a joke. Each day we were supposed to learn ten words which we had to remember so that by the end of the course, we would have a vocabulary of 400 words we could use at our fingertips. This obviously meant some work had to be done in the evening, but with numbers and place names, things were fairly straightforward as we could practice these when we went out.

Drill and PE continued daily, as did range and weapon handling. I remember on one run in which I finished first by some distance, the Physical Training Instructor (PTI) gave me a piece of paper to mark down the names of officers in the order they finished in together with their time while the PTI went to chase up the intake. The guy I sat next to on the plane out, who by now had become a good friend [SEPm], came in third, not happy that he had been beaten as he was very competitive. When he noted I was making a list, he screwed it up. I quickly gathered the paper and continued to take down the names and timings, noting how competitive [SEPm] was when it came to being beaten by smaller and less well-built guys in the intake. Luckily the scrunched-up state of the paper I gave to the PTI wasn't noticed, so I avoided extra inspection, something I regularly got at least twice a week, even if there was nothing wrong with my shaving, uniform, application or effort.

Coffee break time mid-morning was always welcomed as it was a good rest and also coincided with the arrival of post being given out, which always lifted spirits. One of the intakes [MPm] got a letter on a daily basis from his girlfriend in the UK on which she wrote on both sides of the paper. These letters soon became intake letters because as [MPm] read his letter, the reverse side was read by people being sat opposite who hadn't received a letter. After about three weeks, the intake asked [MPm] who Henry was, as his girlfriend always referred to him, as she missed him. This took [MPm] by great surprise as he wanted to know how we knew about Henry, so we told him we had been reading the reverse side of the page he was reading. He started to laugh with embarrassment and said that Henry was the name his girlfriend gave to his "John Thomas", his "little friend" or "middle wicket", which caused the whole of the intake to break out in fits of laughter.

By the end of the fourth week, I had also received two Saturday gatings. However, I didn't let this get me down as I made full use of the time writing my own letters back to the UK and also keeping fit, not to mention doing extra work in respect of my Cantonese. Despite the gatings and extra inspections, I had established a routine of playing water polo twice a week, either at the Jubilee Sports Centre in Shatin, Wong Chuk Hang swimming pool or when the venue changed, at the pool in HMS Tamar in Central. On asking about water polo and swimming, the course instructors stated that the Police only had rugby, hockey, cricket and football available. However, one of the PTIs mentioned an ex-pat water polo team appropriately called the wrecks, who were all civilians and good guys. Other nights, we went to the South Side Hash House Harrier Club once a week and when in PTS, I went jogging with [GPm] around camp as he needed the extra training being a bit older than most of us, having qualified as a SGT in the UK police in Wales.

Over the next two weeks, things continued as normal but at a quicker pace as Chinese New Year was fast approaching which would fall on Sunday the 13th of February. This meant that there would be 3 days off from the following Monday to Wednesday. It was soon learnt that our local officers would have the whole holiday off, but the ex-pats would go on a camp with the course instructors and a PTI.

The end of January arrived and our pay packets not only had our salary for the month but a 25% advance of salary because of Chinese New Year. We were paid on Monday the 31st of January and planned to have a good night out on the 5th of February after hitting the pirated music tape shops in Aberdeen to stock up on even more tapes, such as was the music scene at the time. We had been paid almost 1000 UK pounds even after deductions for our messing, room boy fees and one-third of the advance of salary I had taken prior to flying out to Hong Kong.

Some of us went across to Kowloon to a steak house near the Blacksmith Arms. We had a three-course meal with garlic bread and a huge steak, which was followed by a lump of vanilla ice cream, served in a metal dish more like a small dog bowl, which finished off the meal just nicely. We then retired to the Blacksmith Arms for a couple of pints, after which we went to Rick's Café for more drinks and a good dance, which was as far removed from the paramilitary setting of PTS as one could get and more akin to a student's disco with all sorts of local girls, school teachers, ex-pat girls, British Military Nurses as well as Cathay Pacific Flight stewardesses. Everyone was young and out to have a good time in a fast-moving city where things seemed temporary.

I remember getting back to PTS at around 04:00hrs, much the worse for wear with a few of the lads, including [SEPm], who on getting out of the taxi, proceeded to vomit, which was quite spectacular. [SEPm] was about 6 foot 2 inches; however, when he vomited, he did not bend over but just stood there with a waterfall of vomit coming out of his mouth continuously to the ground. It was unbelievable, however, when he finished and wiped his lips, noticing that all his mates had created distance between them and him so they wouldn't get splashed, the first thing he said was, "sorry lads, I thought I had asphyxiated myself there" then stumbled off to his pit in J Block.

Later that morning at about 10:00hrs, I was woken up by a commotion caused by [HNm], who was getting everyone up to tell all that we needed to have a whip-round for [WFLJm] as he had been robbed of all his salary. When everyone had gathered around, we heard that [WFLJm] had been to Wan Chai the night before and after a few drinks went to a girlie bar where he spent the whole night drinking, accompanied by the girls in the bar. He had bought them drinks but on being presented with his drinks bill, he was also presented with the girl's drinks bill. This was three times more than his, both of which amounted to nearly $9000HK, which is worth about $45000HK in today's money, taking present one pip inspectors' salary into account!

Much discussion took place and as [WFLJm] still had about $1000HK left, he would have to put it down to experience and have a quiet month until the next payday. [HNm] eventually accepted this and the rest of the ex-pats noted the dangers of drinking in the Wan Chai girlie bars, vowing to stay clear of them and went back to bed only getting up for lunch.

The following week went quite quickly as all the local officers were getting themselves ready for Chinese New Year. They were still working hard but there was an excitement that they would have four days off while the ex-pats had a camp to go on. I was given extra inspections twice during the week, both for reasons that didn't add up and were more for the sake of being given them. The drill instructors were the people who cited me for not having shaved properly but the rest of the intake stated there was nothing wrong with my shaving, even saying other ex-pats should also have been cited. The Emperor showed up during a self-defence lesson given by the PTIs and stood watching me while I was striking a pad that was supposed to be the chest of an attacker. He also paid attention to [SEPm], which the day before, didn't let [MCm] a PTI put a hold on him as he wasn't strong enough only to have [BGm], the Chief Physical Training Instructor (CPTI) be his personal PTI for the lesson. The CPTI was known for being tough, strong and possessing a very high standard of self-defence, which SEPm found out to his cost. I got to thinking that the Emperor was behind my extra inspections and gatings just for the sake of imposing them to see how I would react, so I got on with whatever was given as they were to be expected.

Chinese New Year's Eve arrived and after the morning drill session and parade, which was followed by the Officer's Mess cheese and biscuits, I found the whole camp was extremely quiet for the first time since I arrived. Some of the guys, including [HNm] and [GPm] decided to go downtown, despite the fact that we had been advised by MCm the PTI that our 2–3-day camp would be very tough, and we should get a decent night's sleep in preparation for a hard day. I spent the afternoon getting my newly issued field patrol kit ready together with a very thin shower-proof poncho and jungle boots, as well as my backpack with a sleeping bag and mat. I had a quiet night after dinner in the TV room and got an early night.

Sunday morning arrived and I got showered, shaved and dressed and then went for breakfast, taking my backpack with me. I saw most of the ex-pats from the intake but [HNm] and [GPm] weren't present, only arriving very late, looking the worse for wear. At 08:30hrs, we got our picnic boxes and went to gather at the transport shed, waiting for the 08:45hrs bus that would pick us up and take us to where ever we were going and pick up the course instructors on the way. Just before [MCm], the PTI arrived, both [HNm] and [GPm] threw up their breakfast together with a fair amount of the drink they had the night before, with both stating that they felt much better afterwards. The bus arrived and we boarded, going via Causeway Bay to pick up the Slug and then onto Kowloon to pick up the Emperor in Ho Man Tin Hill Road, followed by [CJm] from a place called Los Pinadas in Clearwater Bay Road. Apparently, this development had the nickname 'Lost Pyjamas' due to nocturnal things that went on. We then moved on to the Sai Kung Country Park, where we got dropped off into three groups, with the Emperor staying with the bus just in case of emergencies. The ex-pats in my intake went with [MCm], the PTI and got dropped off at a place called Pak Tam Au, while the other two squads went with their course instructors to commence their walks from different locations. The weather was overcast with rain and was cold as I remember putting the electric bar fire on when I got out of bed in the morning.

We commenced our walk with a steep climb, followed by a patch of flat land, followed by a steep descent, only to be followed by another steep ascent. The route we took, which I now know as Stage 3 on the Maclehose Trail, meant we made slow but steady progress. On our descent to Sai Sha Road, we were ahead of time for our meeting at the picnic area near the road, where we would stop for lunch. This is where we would be met by the other two squads. We all met up for lunch and managed to eat before it started to rain even harder than it had done before. The Slug and [CJm] went off on the bus to our night stop at the Tates Cairn Police Post, leaving strict instructions for [MCm] to let everyone have a go at map reading and arrive before nightfall.

All the ex-pats left together and we all had a go at map reading. During the uphill section to Ma On Shan, the rain came down in buckets and the ground became very wet, slippery and muddy. This meant that the downhill sections were treacherous and made for slow progress. After about two hours into the walk, [MCm], the PTI put me in charge of the map reading and told me to get everyone to Tates Cairn as quickly as possible as at the time, he certainly didn't look like he was enjoying himself. He stated that he didn't mind which route we took as long as it was the fastest. Eventually, we reached Gilwell Camp and had about another 30 minutes to go to the Tates Cairn Police Post, arriving just before nightfall. All three course instructors greeted us and asked why it had taken so long? [MCm] gave an explanation and it was half accepted. Upon going into the Tates Cairn Police Post, it felt really cold and we were shown where we would sleep during the night, laying out our floor mats and sleeping bags.

After we had a quick wash, we were given tasks to do, to prepare BBQ food and make salads which all got done fairly quickly. By 20:30hrs, we were eating our BBQ dinner and drinking beers, which the PTS Officers Mess had laid on. Some games were played as well as beer races with the course instructors treating the occasion like a royal court, where they were the royalty and we were the people to keep them amused. By 22:30hrs, we had all washed up all the pots used and tidied things away. A few more games were then played and as things got quiet, it was almost time for bed. This was after being told that we could go to sleep whenever we felt like it. A guy from my squad [LCAm] and I went to the sleeping area to get our beds ready, at which point [MCm], the PTI arrived and stated that the course instructors were asking where we had gone and wanted to see us. On seeing the Course instructors, the Slug asked where we had been, to which I answered, "getting our beds ready for the night as they had earlier stated we could go to bed when we wanted". The Slug jumped on this and berated the pair of us for not excusing ourselves and saying good night, so we had better join in some more games. I wasn't too happy but if he wanted a party, I would give him one. About two hours later, after many more drinks, we were told to go to bed while also being informed we had to be up at 08:00hrs. I went to bed having left the Slug absolutely shit faced and the Emperor wasn't much better as he had a face that was completely red as though he was having a high blood pressure problem. This condition, I now know, is called the Asian Flush.

In the morning, we were up at about 06:30hrs walking around the outside of the post to check the weather and see what we could see from our lofty vantage point. We were told that we should be able to see Kai Tak Airport, but the clouds had settled at a low height giving us only glimpses of the runway. At about 07:00hrs, we were informed by [MCm] that the Emperor and [CJm] had got the flu and we would be going back to the Police Training School (PTS) at 08:00hrs, so we had better get all our kit packed up quickly and be ready to go at 07:45hrs. The course instructors left by private car at about 07:50hrs, and we were on our way back to PTS by 08:00hrs. On the way back, [MCm] informed us in confidence that the original plan for the day had been an even more gruelling walk than the first day, but the Slug and the Emperor were both hungover and in no fit state. He stated that he didn't like the way he and we had been treated and reminded us to be careful of the Slug, who was only an acting CIP, out to get promoted and was, therefore, a dangerous person to cross. I noted this advice and then looked forward to having the next two days off to write letters, buy some more pirated tapes and maybe see a film.

We had another three weeks of Cantonese to go, which was very hectic with a lot of preparation for the Civil Service Elementary Cantonese Exam taking place. The exam would be held in the form of a conversation, asking us where we came from, what our English and Cantonese names were, how many people were in our family and where we liked to visit in Hong Kong, with the conversation lasting for about 15 minutes. Extra points would be awarded for the right tones and grammar, with it being known that Northern accents had more difficulty with tones than Southern accents.

I was given extra inspections on no less than eight occasions over the next three weeks and had two weekends of gating for a whole host of excuses that just didn't add up to me or the rest of the intake. One morning after being told I would be gated for the weekend, I stated what I thought of the Emperor to the Cantonese class before the teachers arrived. Unbeknown to me, [RCm] the AO, who was a member of the Naval Reserve, arranged to have me attend the HMS Tamar Officers Mess for lunch the Saturday after we had finished the Cantonese exam. This was something I could look forward to as it would be away from PTS, and all the bullshit that existed there, practised by a few little people who thought they had power. This had certainly gone to their heads as they treated Probationary Inspectors, the "Captive Audience", how they wanted.

On one of the nights that I didn't have extra inspections, I went for a drink with [SEPm] in Wan Chai, visiting all the known bars and discos such as Crossroads and Neptunes. We both got very drunk, and when getting a taxi to go back to PTS at about 02:00hrs, I heard a woman shouting, "you want girls, come to my disco!". I asked [SEPm] whether he wanted to go as we may have missed a new disco, but he was already legless so he left and I followed the woman to a staircase next to Neptunes. I followed her upstairs and on entering a room, I saw four males, one of which was being given a blow job, but the woman performing the act was obviously saying to the Mamasan that he was too limp. The second male was being masturbated by another female, and there were two males waiting, all of whom were ex-pats. I then noted that the first male with the limp dick was grabbed by the Mamasan, who had pulled her dress apart and pulled the male on top of her onto a bed, making sure she had put his dick into her, at which point he pumped back and forth quite a few times before he ejaculated and lay motionless. The Mamasan pulled the male off her and told him to go and, within the same breath, chastised the woman who had been performing fellatio earlier, who already had another male's penis in her mouth. Just as I was sobering up, very quickly, I felt someone grabbing the zip on my trousers and I immediately did a U-turn and legged it down the staircase to the street, feeling mightily relieved when I flagged down a taxi. In the taxi on the way back to PTS, I was still trying to comprehend what I had just seen but couldn't and I felt lucky I had escaped. On arrival back at PTS, I went straight to bed.

In the morning, I was one of the last to join the intake for morning roll call fall in and when I did, all the local male officers started to ask what had I been doing the night before and which woman did I follow in Wan Chai, who had shouted she could show me some women. I immediately looked at [SEPm], and no matter what I said about nothing happening, no one believed me.

During the last week of Cantonese, the male instructor taught us some Cantonese swear words and phrases that might be useful to us when dealing with unsavoury characters after much asking. What we were told echoed what my Chinese dorm squad member [WCCm] had taught us and more, with the instructor stating that swearing in Cantonese was much more flowery than English, which was more direct. In exchange for the Cantonese that [WCCm] had taught me, I had taught him some English and had even explained the meaning of the Meat Loaf songs 'Paradise by the dashboard lights' and 'On a Hot Summers Night'. He enjoyed these songs very much as I often played them on my ghetto blaster before going to fall in for drill in the mornings.

By the time of the Cantonese exam, we were told we would have to get ourselves to the address and arrive well before our designated time, as there was a tendency for exams to start early. We were informed to go directly there and come directly back. However, as [SEPm] and I had bought a Triumph Spitfire together, we had to get it insured, which [SEPm] stated he would do after his Cantonese exam. Travelling out during the day from PTS alone was unheard of, and I thoroughly enjoyed the freedom of the day, taking full advantage of the opportunity to soak in fully the side of Hong Kong I hadn't seen to date. Central, with all its hustle and bustle, was a completely new experience and added to the excitement of my understanding of Hong Kong, being totally full of life and much busier than anything I had experienced in the UK.

The results of the Cantonese exam came back the same day, and all 13 ex-pats had passed, with some even getting credit and great credit. I got a pass which I was more than satisfied with, as it was the first barrier passed in a series of many to successfully passing out of PTS.

On the Saturday Lunch at the Officers Mess of HMS Tamar, I was treated to a great spread and [RCm] advised me not to let the bastards grind me down and he could be contacted any time for a drink and a chat if needed. He stated his wife did a good Sunday lunch, and I would be most welcome to join them one weekend. The next week was devoted to drill, PE and range work, as well as a couple of visits to Police formations. This was before the arrival of the new intake and the passing out of the Senior Intake on Saturday, as they had already had their dining out on the night of the Cantonese exam.

Chapter 9

Arrival of the New Intake & the Junior Stage

On Friday, the last week of the Introductory Stage arrived and we had been told to gather in the Officers Mess by 16:00hrs to welcome the ex-pats of intake PI 239 to PI 240. On arrival, we were surprised to see only five ex-pats consisting of two nineteen-year-olds who were the kids of military families called [DAm] from Wales and [JBm] from Cornwall. The other ex-pats from the UK consisted of 23-year-old [SDm], who came from East Lancashire, with the other ex-pat [FMm] coming from London, who had been in the Merchant Navy. The fifth ex-pat [FDm] came from New Zealand. All were rugby players, apart from [JBm] and [FMm], and it must be said, they all looked like they had been travelling for 24 hours. The usual new intake mess games kicked off with beer races, mop handle shuttles, and bottle walking. It was noted that as there were only five ex-pats, they soon got drunk competing against the 52 ex-pats from the four senior intakes.

Soon it was time to take the five ex-pats on the town and we decided to take one ex-pat each and do a pub crawl ending up at the Old China Hand in Wan Chai. Two other ex-pats and I from my intake ended up with the New Zealander who, after getting even drunker in the first three bars we went to, introduced us to a new drink called a Depth Charge. He drank this drink like it was going out of fashion, making sure all in the group got very drunk. Soon it was time to meet up in the Old China Hand as we had already done the usual discos and girlie bars. On meeting up, it was very apparent all five ex-pats were well and truly pissed, so after two more drinks, we decided to return to PTS apart from the new ex-pat from Wales [Dam], who said he wanted to get a massage.

On arrival back at PTS, the ex-Merchant Seaman vomited everywhere, after which he swore blind that he never ever vomited after drinking, and the New Zealander was thanked for introducing the Depth Charge. We all turned in at about 02:00hrs and were up by 07:00hrs to get ready to watch the Senior intake Passing Out Parade. Upon going to the Officers Mess for breakfast, the new ex-pat from Wales [Dam] was seen entering still drunk, and on being advised he better get showered and changed into a suit, he said he had woken up all alone in a massage parlour. He found himself naked in a room of four massage beds with a huge tent pole, not knowing what had caused it. On leaving the massage parlour, he didn't know where he was. Even worse, he had no cash on him. He managed to jump in a taxi and somehow got the driver to understand he wanted to go to the Police Training School, with the men manning the East Gate guard post paying the taxi fare, which he would pay back after the Passing Out Parade. After a gallon of coffee, he went for a shower and seeing him later watching the Passing Out Parade, he looked much better but reeked of alcohol.

The rest of Saturday was spent buying more music tapes and having a relatively quiet night that included a visit to Rick's Café, which was fast becoming one of my favourite spots. Sunday was spent getting ready for the first day of the Junior Stage, which meant we progressed from white backing to our wrist pip band to a blue backing.

Monday arrived and after morning roll call, breakfast, drill and inspection, all three squads went to their respective classrooms. This stage had the ex-pats and Chinese officers being lectured together in their own squads. In my squad, 236, there was [WCCm], a force entry officer who had the bed opposite me in J Block, [LKKm], another force officer, [KHTm], a direct entry, and [Gm], who was another direct entry. We would start the eight-week stage learning all sorts of criminal offences and were all given a booklet containing the definition of all criminal offences, of which there were about 100 offences covered. We were expected to learn the definitions by heart as they would have to be recalled fortnightly, in stage and in the Standard One Professional exams. This I knew would take some time as I had some friends from polytechnic who had done law as a degree, and all they ever seemed to do was memorize cases and definitions.

The two weeks leading to the first exam went very quickly, and the three nights before the fortnightly test were spent on full out revision. Soon, the Friday of the exam arrived, and we had ten questions to answer within three hours. The exam results came back on the following Monday and all had passed, some better than others, with me getting a mark of 59%.

Usually, the weekend after a fortnightly was the time to go and have a good night out on Saturdays, staying out to the early hours of Sunday morning and only surfacing for lunch. This routine was like clockwork, with all activities carried out surrounding the fortnightly exam. Normally [GKLm], the Emperor, would be present during the exam and he would have one of the intake PIs hand out the examination papers while he watched on in an aloof manner.

During the course of the eight weeks, activities such as Hash House Harrier running were still undertaken as well as water polo for me when not on extra inspection or being gated. Most of the intake had also, at the start of the Junior Stage, moved up to Heath House to have their own rooms, which were vacated when the senior intake passed out. About three others, another ex-pat, two locals and I, including [WCCm], stayed in J Block for another two months. A decision we didn't have a choice in as the Emperor had decided that fate. The rooms in Heath House were for a single officer each, which meant you could close the door and revise or write a letter without being disturbed, unlike J Block, which was an open plan. I didn't mind in the end and just got on with things.

Socially, at a hash run, we had met three Peking British Embassy secretaries, all of which had names beginning with the letter A who we called the Three A's. They were on a bag run to Hong Kong carrying papers on the negotiations being carried out on the Handover of Hong Kong to be delivered to Government House. We got to know one better than the others as we took them to all the best discos and bars, and she was called [LAf] with another one being called [Kaf] and the last one whose name I can't recall.

In terms of reading, the ex-pats of the intake had all purchased a book called Legionnaire written by a guy called Simon Murray, who had joined the French Foreign Legion at the age of 18, straight from public school. He had served for five years and had been deployed to North Africa to deal with the troubles the French had in places like Algeria. Many of the ex-pats found his sense of adventure was similar to their own, and we all decided we would like to invite him to our dining out night at the end of the senior intake, as he was working in Hong Kong.

Easter was fast approaching and fell on Sunday, the 13th of April. However, I had been rostered by the Emperor to perform Assistant Duty Officer (ADO) duties in PTS, and that day fell in the middle of the holidays. Easter meant a four-day break and some of the intake had been given permission to take a short holiday, with some opting to go to Pattaya [LCAm], [CJm], [HNm] and [GPm], while another [PSm] went to Singapore to stay at the Raffles Hotel joining the family of his girlfriend he had met at the Smugglers Arms in Stanley. The group who went to Pattaya spoke of women they had met who needed to be paid taxi fares home in the mornings after their lustful trysts.

[SEPm] and I had met a couple of local female teachers at the Blacksmith Arms and had arranged to go for a drive around the whole of Hong Kong with them showing us the way in our Triumph Spitfire. The car had seen better days and was a bit of an old banger which survived the trip around the whole of the New Territories on Easter Friday. Soon after we had dropped the girls off and headed back to PTS, the engine of the car blew up on the approach road to the Cross Harbour Tunnel in Kowloon, so we pushed it onto a grass verge and had it towed away to the abandoned car centre.

The week after Easter, I went to see Swan Lake leaving PTS immediately after cheese and biscuits on that Saturday. The weather was beginning to warm up and drill in the morning and parade were exhausting. The show was in Central and I arrived promptly but had no time for lunch. None of the other ex-pats had gone as ballet wasn't really their scene. At the end of the show, I headed back to PTS, arriving at about 18:00hrs, thinking I would have dinner and a quiet night. I ran into the ex-pats from my squad, who were just leaving, having already eaten prior to going for a few beers. I got talked into going with them and what a night it would be.

[HNm], [CJm] and [LCAm] were present and [HNm] had a reputation for drinking many beers, which we did in Wan Chai and then we moved to Kowloon, continuing to drink. I got drunk very quickly and then on moving to the disco, Hollywood East, in Tsim Sha Tsui East, I mentioned the bouncers weren't very big when entering. The guys from my squad went dancing while I propped up the bar, just wanting to sleep. Eventually, I found a bar stool on which I could sit on that had a footrest. However, every time I nodded off, I fell off and woke up. The final time I got on the barstool, I had the great idea of putting my feet behind the footrest. I fell off again but landed flat on my face as my feet were behind the footrest and knocked myself out, bursting my nose, which ejected copious amounts of blood. My ex-pat squadmates were alerted and found me unconscious and carried me out to go back to PTS. I only became conscious going passed the bouncers I had berated on the way in, which they found amusing.

On the way back in the taxi, the guys were asking me if I had been jumped, but I was still not my normal self. Apparently, on being put on my bed, I shouted, "I hoped you got the bastards who had got me". I woke up in the morning with my neck feeling a bit stiff and noticing the blood on my clothes. I had a shower and then went for breakfast, and on having my first taste of grapefruit juice, I just managed not to spit out the juice as some of my teeth were chipped. The nerves in the chipped teeth didn't react too well to the cold grapefruit juice. Later on, the guys I went out with arrived and told me how they found me lying unconscious on the floor by the bar. I told them what I had done with my feet, which I admitted was stupid, and they stated that there hadn't been any fight.

The next day the course instructors gave my squadmates and I a Spanish Inquisition about whether we had been fighting as that was a sacking offence. In the end, they believed what I had said. They arranged for me to see the PTS dentist, and as I had been knocked unconscious, sent me for an x-ray. So much for Swan Lake being a quiet weekend for gentlemen! About two years later, I discovered that I had actually done more damage to myself than I thought I had at that time.

The fortnightly exams continued and I was constantly being reminded by the Emperor that I should be getting higher marks than the 55% I was averaging and so was [SEPm]. Soon the end of the Junior Stage exam was approaching and I was quietly confident I would do OK, having by now learnt all the definitions of criminal offences. The Emperor had been "kind enough" to ensure that I had a few extra inspections as well as a few weekends of gatings and Easter ADO duty, so my preparation had been thorough. I got through the Junior Stage exam with a mark of 60% and the Emperor had reminded me to maintain that mark.

Chapter 10

Intermediate Stage & The Emperor's "Interview"

The Intermediate stage commenced, and we changed the colour of the backing of our wrist pip again to yellow to indicate what stage we had reached. This stage would see a lot of leadership and team training. Near the end of the stage, we would have a leadership week that we would have to pass, not to mention the end of stage exam. Fortnightly exams continued, and as we were doing traffic and police procedures, new definitions and procedures had to be memorized.

In my first two fortnightly's, I had passed with a mark of 53%. After the third fortnightly, having obtained a pass mark of only 50%, I was given a Written Warning for Dismissal (WD General), having skipped the Verbal Warning. [SEPm] at the same time, was given a Verbal Warning for Dismissal, which was later changed to a Written Warning after his exam results didn't improve immediately. I took note of the warning and made sure I studied harder for the fortnightly exams.

We were still being given squad prefect duties, and strangely enough, being prefect in charge of the intake or a squad added to one's experience of commanding a unit. This involved getting our unit from one place to another, even when marching, without falling foul of senior officers. This gave us a sense of achievement. This was good grounding for the Intermediate Stage, which, as already mentioned, had lessons on leadership training and beat incidents. Ultimately, during leadership week, when each Probationary Inspector would be given tasks to complete, how they did it was down to them. Probationary inspectors could use the rest of the intake, either as observation teams, ambush teams, cordon duties, or undercover roles. The tasks had to be completed satisfactorily. Otherwise, there was the chance of being cut or back-squadded to the Junior intake. This was likewise true for the fortnightly exams.

The leadership week was always looming on the horizon. However, activities had been scheduled, such as team exercises getting from one side of an assault course to the other, either carrying equipment or persons with the dreaded danger that the ground was a shark-infested sea. There were also days out to Tai Tam Reservoir, going cross country by map reading and then returning to the Police Training School (PTS) carrying designated injured officers on stretchers. Everyone had to take their turn to undertake carrying duties even if they weren't that enthusiastic. There were several days like this, all of which were designed to instil teamwork before leadership week. This worked to some extent, although some recruits readily volunteered ahead of those who wanted to keep a low profile. Briefing formats were introduced and had to be learnt so that officers could be briefed about their roles, as well as positions and timings in a structured format such as GSMEAC (Ground/Map, Situation, Mission, Execution, Administration and Command/Communications).

The Emperor's Interview

Midway through the Intermediate Stage, I was informed that The Emperor wanted to see me in his office. However, I didn't know what it was about, although I had just been gated for the previous weekend as a result of an inspection. The course instructor's offices were on the first floor of the Administration block, and this was known as bomb alley in respect of PIs being called up for a bollocking. I marched up to The Emperor's Office and knocked at the door, and was informed by The Emperor through the closed door to stay in the corridor until he instructed me to enter. I stood at ease, but whenever another course instructor walked passed, I came to attention and saluted. I must have done this on about 10 occasions while also hearing the pages of a newspaper being turned from The Emperor's office.

Eventually, I was instructed to enter by The Emperor, so I marched in, did a left turn to face him and saluted. The Emperor continued to read his newspaper for about five minutes, after which he turned his head towards me and said that I not only looked stupid, but I was stupid. I didn't say anything but just thought back to his lectures about assaults as his head was just level with my fist. There was no one else in the office, so if I had started to shout "stop hitting me" and banged my head on the door handle to injure myself while I smashed his head in, it would be my word against his. I could say I was just defending myself. The urge for violence subsided as quickly as it had risen, and eventually, he instructed me to leave, so I threw a salute and left, later thinking he had been trying to provoke me.

The leadership training continued, and after a particularly hot day out with most of the day not wearing a top, I had sun-induced water blisters on my back, which were uncomfortable. On the way back to PTS, a local force entry officer from another squad was put in charge. He was known as the Warbler. He was called this as he incessantly called out left, left right, left, left, left right, left. On arrival at PTS, we were returning stores and equipment, and when almost finished, the Warbler was trying to get the ex-pats' attention when he snapped his fingers and shouted for us to listen. The ex-pats, to a man, all gave him dagger stares, which, if real, would have killed him. Later, he was educated on how rude the snapping of fingers was in the UK.

One morning a couple of weeks before Leadership camp, we were scheduled to have PE, and the fall in point was the cricket pitch. On arrival, we were informed by the PTI that we would be playing murderball on the cricket wicket, which had been soaked with water overnight. He added that the cricket club had asked for a new pitch to be laid but were informed it was still good to play on. Apparently, our job was to damage the cricket wicket as much as possible, and so the game of murderball commenced. Initially, everyone was reticent to get their clean white PE kit dirty, but as time went on and the wicket became a mud bath, those PIs still looking relatively clean were passed the ball, and when they caught it, they were pounced on. At the end of the game, not one blade of grass could be seen on the wicket area, and likewise, not one spot of mud-free skin could be seen on any PI. It was announced that we had achieved our mission, after which we were allowed to go and get a drink before showering. We later heard the Police Cricket Club were very happy with our assistance!

The week following the game of murderball, several of the intakes came down with infections of scrapes and abrasions suffered during the game. It was learnt that the cricket ground had once been a pig breeding area, hence the infections. Several other PIs came down with "Jock Rot" because of the rising temperatures and resulting sweat rashes around the groin area. On seeing the doctor, the magic medicine suggested was the use of talcum powder in copious amounts, which solved the problem.

Just prior to Leadership camp, we asked PIs from the senior intake if there was there anything to look out for or any tricks to be played. The main thing they mentioned was that near the end of camp, the course instructors and exercise director would go to the nearest town from the campsite, which was Sai Kung and get a meal, after which they would come back and attack camp. This was something we would remember and bear in mind.

Chapter 11

Leadership Camp

Leadership week kicked off with the whole intake being flown by helicopter to various locations in the New Territories near Tai Mo Shan, where exercises were undertaken by an allocated team leader. After the exercise had finished, the three-squad intakes would then navigate to another location where more exercises would be held. The whole day vanished very quickly, and after nightfall, a team leader was assigned to lead his squad to the designated whole intake campsite at Ko Tong in Sai Kung Country Park. I was appointed team leader of my squad for the night, and this involved my squad and me being shipped across Tolo Harbour from the old Tai Po Kau Marine Police North Base to Lai Chi Chong. We had been instructed to skirt around villages, not to wake the dogs and arrive no later than 06:00hrs, with much earlier arrivals being subject to punishment.

On arrival at the main campsite, one squad was taken by vehicle 10km away to run back to camp for having taken public transport. Another squad had another unpleasant task to do as their squad hadn't all arrived together. My squad got a rocket despite arriving before 06:00hrs as ordered, as we had a meal break before undertaking our night march. This was done so that the first village we went through had already gone to sleep and wouldn't be disturbed by our presence. The day saw all three squads, when eventually all together, set up the camp and do other chores and tasks purely for the sake of doing them. This, at the same time, made all the squads more tired, having had no sleep the night before. Later at about 01:00hrs, we were all driven blindfolded by Ford transit police vehicles to a location reached by multiple U-turns and other ploys so that we couldn't just do the route in reverse when we had to hike back to camp. We were dropped off at what I now know is the Sai Wan Beach pagoda, and after the leadership camp staff had left, we had to somehow find out where we were and plan a route back to camp that took us less than four hours. After locating two points on the map, we found where we were and then realized we still had three hours over the hills to get back to camp by the assigned time, which we did, albeit the last 30 minutes involved a brisk run. After finding out where we were, one of the local officers confirmed our position as he had been there before, but the ex-pats had wondered why he didn't say something in the first place. Little did we know, all the locals had been warned of being too helpful when position finding.

All the intake had one hour to sleep before the leadership tasks for the day were assigned, and this was after two days and nights without sleep. It was known that this day would be problematic for those who were assigned tasks due to the lack of sleep, so I wasn't particularly surprised when I heard my name called, followed by that of my tent partner, who would have the second assigned task.

My task involved the placement of a cordon, an observation post, and close ambush teams. Even if the area was not known to me, I could make my plan by using the map and marked footpaths. The end result was that the bad guys were caught, and I stood by my decisions when asked to explain them by the Slug and the Exercise Director [DPm]. At the end of the debrief, another course instructor [CJm] stated that whatever the instructors said, I would say the opposite. However, I didn't care as I had successfully undertaken my task.

During the second assigned task, I stood up for my tent companion [HCCm] when he came in for some criticism from another ex-pat trainee, named [TRJm], which wasn't really appropriate. This ex-pat eventually moved to the junior intake after he became ill and missed some training which wasn't a great loss.

The camp continued with trail walks and exercises near Hoi Ha involving illegal immigrants and staff acting as people smugglers. In one ambush, [SEPm] scraped his hip bone on a rock when diving in the sea, going after the smugglers in a rowing boat. I almost caught up with the rowing boat by swimming after it. However, I just missed catching it as the DMI [PTm], in his panic, rowed faster than I could swim, despite having no technique. The Slug lived up to his name that day when trying to examine [SEPm's] graze in an insipid manner.

On the fourth day of camp, I managed to wash myself down in the stream at Ko Tong and, on washing my private parts, noticed white paste, which I later knew as smegma. This was due to not having showered for five days, which was a first for me. So much for camp being hygienic!

On the day before the last night of camp, the course instructors went to Sai Kung to have dinner, and after they left, we had a war council amongst the ex-pat PIs about how we would defend camp if attacked. Many ideas were thrashed about, but in the end, we decided on their return that we would cover them with sleeping bags and give them a good kicking, which meant they would not see who had done it. Ambush and lookouts were set, which by 02:00hrs stood down with the course instructors only coming back at 04:00hrs.

The last day was set aside for cleaning the camp up and packing away gear that was no longer needed. In the evening, there would be a BBQ and plenty of beers. The day went quite quickly, all jobs were accomplished, and the BBQ went well. I had a few beers but was still wary of keeping my guard up. In the morning, I was up bright and early to find several ex-pats who had overindulged themselves asleep on sleeping bags in the middle of fields. An old lady from the village was collecting beer cans, much in the same way as is done nowadays.

The trip back to PTS went quickly, and all enjoyed a nice hot shower followed by some decent food in the Mess. Sunday, I was down to Aberdeen to buy some more pirated music tapes and spend the day revising as the end of the Intermediate Stage exam was in two weeks.

On Wednesday of the following week, I was taken down to Deepwater Bay by the PTI [MCm] and a Force swimmer called [PJm] and put through my paces, for some reason. This was never made known to me, but the PTS swimming Gala was coming up. On Friday of the same week, while playing water polo at the Wong Chuk Hang swimming pool, I had my eardrum burst, and this was the same one that I had perforated when I was in the UK. I knew immediately what had happened as someone had, after a shot, let his finger go into my ear when trying to block him, which caused all the water to be pushed through the eardrum. We were not wearing water-polo hats with ear protectors at the time.

The following Monday, I was sent to see an ENT specialist in Sai Ying Poon, who advised me to keep the ear dry. He also gave me some drops so the ear wouldn't get infected, advising me to stay out of the water for three weeks and wear ear protectors when playing water polo. Otherwise, I could go deaf if it happened again in the same ear. Prior to being treated, I had seen the ENT specialist take a small toy out of the ear of a small child, which obviously caused great pain, so I was thankful I didn't get the same treatment.

I had the Duty Officer duty on Friday night, and the Senior Intake were having a disco. The CDMI informed me if it got too loud, then he would ring the guardhouse and get me to turn the music down. All went well until the end of the disco, which was set for 23:30hrs. On arrival at the mess in uniform 10 minutes earlier than 23:30hrs, I went to the DJ to ask him to turn the music down a little and gave a ten-minute warning to all the PIs. This didn't go down too well, and one or two PIs that obviously had too much to drink raised their voices. A certain PI called [MNm], a son of a senior officer, was the loudest and probably youngest person to object and was objecting even after everyone had left the mess. A few lads from the senior intake had to run Brick Hill the next day, which included drinking a can of beer every 500 metres for their rowdy behaviour at the disco.

The ADO that night was another ex-pat called [TBm], and he thought I took too much on and worked too hard. He came across as a bit too full of himself, and when he smiled, you could see the gap between his top two front teeth. I took his words on advisement and would have to do the same again after passing out.

The whole intake passed the Intermediate Stage Exams, which brought to an end a stage that had its many ups and downs, not to mention its challenges posed by Leadership week. Letter writing continued, as did the odd IDD phone calls from the Central or the Kowloon Hermes House IDD call centres to my mother and friends in Glasgow. It was always good, especially hearing from friends and relatives that cared.

During this stage, my J Block companion [WCCm] and I moved up to the single male inspectors' rooms in Heath House just after the stage had commenced, which meant I had my own room and more privacy. Studying was much easier as the room had a large desk, a bed as well as a fan, in addition to a wardrobe. Showers and toilets were still communal, but that didn't matter, although on occasion, finding flip flop marks on the toilet seat took a bit of getting used to. Apparently, all the locals have squat toilets in their homes. Hence when they used a toilet you could sit down on which had a toilet seat, they would still squat on the seat. This went hand in hand with finding the odd pubic hair in the urinal, again down to the locals pruning themselves while urinating, as I had seen nothing like this in the UK when using urinals. On occasion, we would find four to six locals in one of the local PI rooms all sat down or lying on the bed, which was initially a bit off-putting until you realized how big a space they lived in at home.

Chapter 12

Social Life as It Existed & Life After Studies at PTS

Socially, things had gone well, and by now, most ex-pats had realised their newfound ability in Cantonese was a good aid to have when chatting to the local girls at the discos. Normally, you would come across the local girls who just wanted a dance and a little bit of chat and the local girls who were looking for a husband. The talks being held about the Handover of Hong Kong in 1997 had made some of the local girls want to find a love match with a foreigner. This was a bonus for the ex-pats, not to mention it was aided by the film, "An Officer and A Gentlemen", which was on at the local cinemas, making some girls think of a match made in heaven. Other local girls were like cash registers, and when you mentioned you were in the Royal Hong Kong Police, they knew exactly what increment on the Police Pay Scale you were on by your years of service and education standard. This wasn't helped when we informed them that we were still living at the Police Training School after they had asked which quarter we lived in. This was normally the last question they asked before excusing themselves. Ex-pat 6th Formers were occasionally good for a laugh, but they didn't know what they wanted other than to be at the same university as their fathers. Nurses based at the British Military Hospital were always good to be around, not to mention the Cathay Pacific Stewardesses I had met through a friend [NGm], who played water polo and the Malaysian Indian girl he knew [LCf] from Kuala Lumpur. One of her friends from Ipoh, [SDKSf], in particular, had taken my fancy as she looked like Whitney Houston's picture on the rear sleeve of her album with the same name. However, with her flying schedule and my training schedule, I didn't see her out and about too often or as much as I wanted. In conversation, she had let me know that she had a German boyfriend and was learning German. However, I was very taken and did not give up hope.

Life after studies at the Police Training School was mainly spent doing your own physical exercise with one guy [GRm] from the intake, often going for runs in black bin liners so he could get more of a sweat going. He also did sit-ups with his calves placed on the seat of a chair and his thighs facing upwards, which meant he did extreme stomach crunches. Often after dinner, if exams were not close, you played the "space invaders" arcade game or watched TV in the TV room. On one particular night, the TV room was full apart from one seat. When the guy [ADm] from the intake below us walked in, he looked at the channel the TV was on and changed the channel the whole room was watching. He was asked twice to turn the channel back, to which he answered "NO" and this caused 6-foot 2-inch [SEPm] to stand up and grab hold of him. Pretty soon, [ADm] found himself hanging by his ankles as [SEPm] went to eject him from the room, which resulted in [ADm] having his head used as a battering ram because the door only opened inwards. After the third bang of [ADm's] head against the door, someone opened it and he was thrown into a pile on the corridor outside, and the door was closed. A short time later, he entered and sat in the only remaining seat and watched the channel everyone else was watching without making a sound, much to the amusement of the other lads in the TV room.

Also, during the Intermediate Stage, a few of the ex-pats from the intake had been invited to a Vicars and Tarts party at a local pub, which eventually saw us going to several discos with many of the

"Tarts" being ex-pat Special Branch (SB) secretaries. Towards the end of the evening, I was in Kowloon, having just left one disco with several of the intakes, other more senior ex-pat PIs who had passed out of the Police Training School already, and one SB secretary who was up for having a full-on night. While we were all chatting, the SB secretary shouted that the party should continue at the Ho Man Tin Hill Road Inspectorate Service Quarters, which she followed up by saying, "come on, let's go back to the rabbit hutch and fornicate". On hearing this, I was one of the first to leave as she wasn't really my cup of tea, although several other "Vicars" shouted, "Tally Ho, let's Go". The next morning at the Police Training School, we were all given a lecture by the "Slug", who said we had not only embarrassed the Police Training School but the whole Force. This was after he had seen some things going on from his police quarters, overlooking the disco called Rumours in Causeway Bay. Luckily, I hadn't been to Rumours, so I avoided getting a gating, unlike others in the intake.

Chapter 13

Senior Stage, PTS Passing Out & The Emperor's Sinister Trick

The Senior Stage had arrived and we placed a black backing to our wrist pip. This would be the same colour we would use on passing out of PTS. The Professional Standard One and Drill and Musketry Training Examinations were fast approaching. However, there were still several fortnightly exams to pass, having just finished the Intermediary Stage Exam. Apart from pressure to get higher marks, these exams should be fine. Lectures would be on more police procedures and discipline, amongst other topics. There were also a couple of run-ins with the PTS Commandant and one particularly nasty trick played by The Emperor that, if not spotted, would have seen me on the big bird home.

Socially, a few of us spent six Sunday mornings down at Stanley Beach learning how to windsurf, initially on static boards on the sand and then on the water. We also had a visit from the three A's on another bag run from Peking, and we took them on our tourist tour. This consisted of a drink in the Red Lion Pub in TST, followed by a drink and poetry in Red Lips, followed by Bottoms Up, the Pink Giraffe Cocktail Bar on the top floor of the Sheraton Hotel, the piano room in the Peninsula Hotel and finally Rick's Café for a full night out.

As I could not swim for three weeks, I took to playing two-handed touch rugby, which happened once a week at PTS on the drill square. During one session, I was playing opposite the PTS Commandant [FJm] and was getting the better of him on occasion. He became a little frustrated and on one tackle, bearing in mind we were playing two-handed touch, he gave me a solid face handoff with one hand, which got called as a catch. I protested as it had only been one-handed, and the Commandant was shocked when I questioned him on the solid full-face contact as we were playing touch. He said all touches counted, even if it was one-handed touch.

The Emperor's Sinister Exam Trick

On the second fortnightly exam, The Emperor was in the examination hall, and unlike him, he handed out the examination papers. We had three hours and when I had finished question eight, I thought it was a bit odd that there were no more questions, as normally there were ten questions. On leaving the examination hall, we were all chatting about what answers had been given and when I was asked about questions nine and ten, I stated I had only eight questions. The Staff Officer Basic Training Wing (SOBTW) [WPm] was in camp, and I saw him and informed him that I only had eight questions which he said should not be the case. As he had been given the exam papers, he acted very surprisedly when he found my eight-question exam paper. Now I knew why The Emperor had handed out the exam papers, especially my special paper. The SOBTW asked me the missed questions, and on giving him the answers, he gave me five marks each for the questions, which was a pass mark.

Before the end of the Senior Stage, PTS would hold its swimming gala, and as I had been back swimming for a number of weeks, I entered three individual events and the intake relays. I won two of my individual events, but when it came to the 100-meter freestyle, I didn't hear the announcers call. However, I got down to the poolside and announced I had arrived for the event. The timekeeper said there was no space, but I pointed out to the timekeeper that only five out of eight lanes in the programme were full, including the one I was in. Now, we had eight swimmers present with no room for me when three of the swimmers had not even registered for the event. I protested and he said he would consult the referee.

The referee turned out to be the Commandant [FJm], who came to see what was going on, so I explained. I noted he was dressed in shorts, covered in suntan lotion, was wearing sunglasses and really didn't have a clue about how to run a swimming gala. He stated that he had reached a decision and as I was technically late, I couldn't take part in the race. He then added that I could swim for PTS at the Force Swimming Gala, to which I immediately answered that I would certainly not be doing that and left. PI 236-238 won the PTS Swimming Gala. However, I missed out on being awarded the Victor Ludorum.

Also, during this stage, The Emperor announced one morning that the whole intake would fall in at the small drill square at the end of the day dressed in PE kit but didn't state the reason why. Soon, the end of the day arrived, and we fell in at the small drill square in PE kit to find PTIs and The Emperor already there waiting for us with another intake at the opposite end of the small drill square. The Emperor told the intake that he had arranged for us to have a football match against another intake. However, psychologically we weren't ready. We were in Force issue PT kits, unlike the other intake, who had their own gear. The Emperor insisted on picking the teams. This, to most of us, seemed like a disaster waiting to happen and something the other intake had prepared for all-day, even taking the last lecture to warm up.

The football game started and within twenty minutes, we were three-nil down, and it stayed that way to halftime. During the halftime period, The Emperor looked imperious, but all the ex-pats as a whole informed him that they would pick the team, and several changes were made with those playing passengers being substituted, including the goalie. The second half kicked off, and it was apparent the other intake were sitting back thinking they had won, and at any sign of an attack being made, they just committed fouls. This

Senior Stage, PTS Passing Out & The Emperor's Sinister Trick 103

incensed our intake, and as I was on the right-wing, I had the ball passed to me and popped it by one of their midfielders, who stuck his leg out to trip me. I hurdled his leg and flew down the wing like Mike Summerbee and struck a pinpoint cross that was met by the head of [PSm], who scored, making it three-one. After this, my intake was in charge and the other intake was rattled. Pretty soon, the score was three-two. While I was on the right-wing, a female probationary inspector from the other intake was shouting like a banshee every time I went past her. At one point, I shouted at her that if she liked the game so much, she should play. Otherwise, she should shut up. Her squad Chief Inspector, a big and tall Rhodesian, told me to move on, to which I countered that he should get her on the pitch as his team might play better. He went a very deep colour of red due to this. In the last ten minutes, we had levelled the score at three-all and while walking back to the kick-off spot, we all agreed we would keep the score at that as The Emperor had been the architect of the game. No doubt, as a result of him bragging, his intake was better than any other, and he didn't deserve to win. The game finished and nothing more was said as the other intake was in tatters!

During this stage, [GRm] took some of the intake ex-pat PIs to the Chung Hom Kok Government Communications Club House. As there was a pool there, we made sure to take our swimming costumes. About an hour after lunch, after having several discussions, some members of the intake asked [CJm] and I who the better swimmer was as [CJm] had swum for Birmingham University, and I had swum for British Polys. This wasn't the first time this had been asked, and we both got talked into having a two-length race (50 meters) swimming freestyle. Both [CJm] and I took this very seriously, and at the end of the first length, we tumble-turned and were now neck and neck. With five meters to go, I pulled ahead of [CJm] and won by an arm's length, in good time of about 28 seconds. On leaving the pool and being congratulated for our efforts, an old crusty ex-pat member of Government Communications Hong Kong chipped into the conversation and stated that both [CJm] and I were too highly strung and we would later in life have difficulties. The group I was with thought the old crusty may have had too much to drink and misjudged our competitiveness. However, much later and well after leaving the Royal Hong Kong Police [CJm] died by his own hand. As for myself, I am still awaiting my fate, having had several near-death disasters!

On another day, during morning inspection, [WFLJm] was being inspected by Basil [SHm] and it was noted that he wasn't looking at Basil, but at some point, on the horizon. Basil mentioned this to [WFLJm] and asked what he was looking at, and [WFLFm] immediately answered that it was windy and he had been watching the Union Jack flag flying above Grantham Hospital fluttering in the wind. Basil immediately awarded [WFLJm] evening inspection and also a weekend gating for not paying attention during the inspection! This little hiccup soon paled into insignificance because when my intake was marched onto the main drill square, it soon became obvious that the CDMI [FBm] was not happy about something.

During the drill practice, he ran among the squads, shouting at them to apply more effort, and when standing at ease and given the order to stand at attention, this order was practised continuously for about 20 times. The CDMI complained he could not hear a crisp slapping of our boots hitting the ground together at the same time, and what we were doing wasn't loud enough and sounded like a machine gun. Eventually, all the DMIs were given a bollocking and urged to get their trainees in time and sound louder. Every trainee finally drove their foot into the ground so hard to make more noise. It was painful. This still wasn't good enough, so the CDMI gave the order to march in double time, which was more like a run. My intake was at the front as we were double marched around the drill square. The CDMI warned the DMIs that if any accoutrement fell off a trainee, the whole squad would run Brick Hill as they were dressed together with the DMI. On one circuit, the CDMI double marched us up an incline to the top and then about-turned us to the bottom, where another about-turn order was given. This went on for about ten times and was quite energy-sapping. On one of the laps, my hat began to slope at a precarious angle, and this caused

Basil, our DMI, to lurch forward to replace my hat to the proper position with a tug that glued my hat to my head because of the sweat. He obviously didn't want to run Brick Hill, and he himself was glistening with sweat. The hell session suddenly came to an end as quickly as it had started, and the CDMI thanked us for our efforts!

The week of the Standard One exam was fast approaching, and I had already done a great deal of revision and thought that during my breaks in revision, I needed something to do. So, I bought a simple air fix model aircraft kit. One evening, while having a break, a few of the lads had just got back from Wong Chuk Hang, and [LCAm] was one of them. Upon seeing me making the aeroplane model, he had a look of consternation on his face, as though he thought I had called it a day. Also, during this week, the very quiet direct entry officer [Gm] from Squad 236 was cut from training and left the course, but we never found out why!

The Standard One Professional exams were held, and on the Friday evening, we had all gathered in the Officers Mess to be told the results as instructed. While waiting, the course instructor [CJm] from another of our squads came in and saw me and said one person had failed an exam. All three course instructors thought it might be me, and I would be on the big plane home. However, it was someone else who, after remarking, had passed.

The whole intake had passed, and the CDMI, upon seeing my stripe-coloured T-shirt, thought it was sports-like. So, he asked me to change or leave. I left and told the lads I would be at the Bull and Bear and would have a drink while waiting for them. PI 236 ex-pats arrived, but [HNm] had brought The Emperor, who looked drunk. I wasn't very happy and said I would finish my drink and go elsewhere. While drinking up, I saw [HNm] vomit the Guinness he had been drinking. Later, just as I was leaving, I saw him being held off from attacking The Emperor by [LCAm] and [CJm]. I left immediately.

The next four weeks consisted of riot training week, followed by a week in North Point following various units, with the force entry girl from my intake called [WCf]. On one day during the week attachment, we had a half-day, so we went to see Flashdance, which had great music, not to mention the beautiful Jennifer Beals! During this week, I had seen arrested persons put in stress positions, which they had to maintain until they remembered what really had happened. These actions came under The Ways and Means Ordinance, as did very cold air conditioning, which also aided memory recall.

Chapter 14

Victoria Mortuary, Cocktail Night & Assault by The Emperor

The whole intake was scheduled to visit Victoria Public Mortuary together to attend a post mortem, so we would become used to it, should we have to, on passing out of PTS. We had all been warned by the senior intake that the smells would never be forgotten, let alone the sights.

We were all advised to take cigarettes to get rid of pungent smells that lingered in the nostrils and on one's own clothing.

On arrival, the pathologist had already had two bodies opened fully and, having a sense of humour, asked all of us which one of the corpses had been a smoker, directing us all to check the lungs, which were visible.

We all noticed that the lungs of both corpses looked identical, so no one gave an answer. The silence was soon broken by the pathologist pointing at one of the corpses stating he was the smoker, and then added that the non-smoker had black lungs also due to the pollution that existed in Hong Kong.

He then set about weighing various organs and then opened up the skull to weigh the brain, which caused some of the intake to take a step back as it was very graphic. On taking one of the brains out, he asked who was interested to see the empty inside of the skull, and [DBm] volunteered, even picking up a scalpel to poke around at something.

Not soon after he started to poke, he went a ghastly shade of white and looked like he was going to throw up. Most probably because he realized that the corpse had once been a living being. Soon after this, we were given a five-minute break in the open air outside the mortuary, during which everyone smoked, some more than others.

On returning to the mortuary, the pathologist was at another table with what looked like a several kilogram block of Danish Blue cheese. When we had all assembled, he asked everyone what we thought was on the table, and again no one had an answer. He then stated it was the body of a newly born baby girl that had been floating for many days in Aberdeen Harbour, and he was about to cut it open.

Almost in the same breath, he announced if anyone wanted to leave, they could do so. With the first slice of his scalpel, a most terrible smell was detected, and everyone left hastily! The visit then ended, and while returning to PTS by coach, I noted that everyone was very sombre.

The Friday of that week saw us have our Cocktail Night in the Officers Mess, and I chose to spend most of the evening drinking with the CDMI [FBm] and his wife. They were solid people and, unlike the course instructors, would not stab you in the back. This was especially so, as a few PIs from my intake and I had taken the CDMIs son out for a drink as he was home from university.

The CDMI judged the mission a success when his son came home unscathed and went to bed. Albeit, a short time later, he got up to vomit in the toilet, which indicated to the CDMI that he had enjoyed the night. Needless to say, I had a lot to drink and was one of the last left in the mess, along with the CDMI, the Commandant, the Commandants Deputy as well as some of my intake ex-pats.

Assault by The Emperor

Upon chatting to the ex-pats, I was talking and The Emperor came across drunk, but I continued to talk. Usually, when a senior officer comes across, the PI talking should give way. However, I was drunk and did not give way. The Emperor then asked me where I'd come from, and I said the UK. He then stated that he knew more about the UK than I did, so I asked him how could he, as he wasn't from the UK. The conversation went back and forth until The Emperor told me that he knew some police in the UK and would have me arrested if I went back. I immediately stated that I had friends in the UK who, if I asked, would mince him if he went to the UK. I had gotten very annoyed with his shit, and putting my hand on my mess kit breast pocket, I pulled out an imaginary UK passport and told him not to come knocking on my door in 1997. At that moment, his face went bright red, and he grabbed me with two hands by my mess jacket, pushing me backwards for five or six steps, screaming until I grabbed him and pushed him back passed the position we had started from. We soon got separated by the senior officers, after which I went to bed.

In the morning, I had a very sore head, and during breakfast, some of the ex-pats who had been present let me know what had happened, and I was flabbergasted, to say the least. Later, after morning inspection and drill, [GPm], [CJm] and I were called to see the course instructors for my incident with The Emperor and [GPm] and [CJm] for telling the Slug to piss off when he found them peeing in the bushes instead of using the toilet outside the mess.

I was marched in first and told by The Emperor to go immediately back to my room and separate my force issue kit from my personal kit and have it ready for inspection in an hour. I left and, upon getting back to my room, did only five minutes of work and thought, if I'm getting the big bird home, then I'll do my packing in my own time. One hour later, The Emperor arrived with the whole intake. Upon entering my room, he stated he thought I would have made more progress, as he wanted the intake to see how the room should be left after graduating from PTS. As The Emperor left and got near the end of the corridor, I shouted 'Foxtrot Oscar', but obviously he didn't know what I meant.

The following Friday was our mess dining-out night. [PSm] had been awarded the Slevin trophy, and as such, he would give his speech in response to the course instructors. The evening went well, and by the time [PSm] got up to speak, he stated that he had based his speech on our three course instructors and titled it 'The Three Wise Men', but as he couldn't think of them coming bearing gifts, he decided to call it 'The Three Little Pigs'! Much laughter was had in respect of the jokes in the speech, and then it came to the Course Director's favourite three scream phrases, with the last one being "Mr. Allen", to which all the course intake ex-pats sounded a loud round of applause, and cheers. Sadly, we did not invite the Legionnaire, Simon Murray, as a guest of honour. Mainly because every ex-pat in the intake to a man believed a real-life hero should not be exposed to the same amount of bullshit we had to put up with during our nine months of training.

The following week we had a walk around Lamma Island, and the course instructors exercised too little discipline, most unusually and were overly friendly. During lunch, some of the ex-pats, including [HNm], [MBm] and [WFLJm], drank quite a bit of beer, as did [PSm], with some of the ex-pats sticking chopsticks up their noses and falling backwards off a pipe they were sat on. After lunch, we were instructed to get to the top of Mount Stenhouse, and by the time we got back, we could have some more beer while waiting for the Marine Police launch. It was very hot, and the beer had certainly gone to the heads of some of the intake. I didn't have any beer as I could smell a trap. While marching through camp, the OC Visual Aids [DJm] stopped us and instructed us not to talk. He was jeered by a few people and reminded he was the same rank as us and told to piss off back to his marital aids office and use one of his dildos. The next morning, a few people got a very serious warning and [PSm] almost lost out on being awarded the Brian Slevin Trophy.

That next day, I saw the Commandant about my end of training report and my posting to Kwun Tong Police District. He noted that I hadn't particularly liked PTS and asked me why. So, I explained the treatment given to me by the Course Director and other matters. He listened intently and stated that he hadn't really been made aware of my treatment by The Emperor. He then raised the subject of the Force Swimming Gala and swimming for PTS. He stated he was aware that I wasn't too happy at the PTS Swimming Gala and that I had adamantly stated that I wouldn't swim for PTS at the Force Swimming Gala, and he understood. He noted my written Warning for Dismissal and stated that if I swam for PTS, he could have the warning removed from my record of service. I asked whether he could do that and he said he could do anything. This confirmed that he was the God of probationary inspectors while they were at the Police Training School. I mulled over the offer as it would be a huge climb down from my previous stance and would be yet another compromise. The silence ended, and we had reached an agreement that if the warning was removed, I would swim for PTS, which would be in four weeks after I passed out. The interview ended and to put it mildly, I was astonished at the outcome. On leaving his office, I wondered why he wanted me to swim so much for PTS and was sure time would tell.

This same week I saw a car called an MGC for sale in the South China Morning Post and went to see it. The owner was an engineer for the Hong Kong Electric Company who had just got a new wife, hence the sale. I bought it immediately and had it for many years.

The week of the passing out parade, Hong Kong was hit by Typhoon Ellen on the 8th of September, which hit Hong Kong directly with gale-force winds being classified under the Typhoon 10 Signal. This resulted in a sleepless night, as the winds blowing were like the sound of an express train. On emerging the next morning, the Police Training School Campus was a mess of felled trees, trees with broken branches and park bench seats overlooking the main drill square tossed about like match sticks. A major cleanup operation was launched by the CDMI. The cleanup took all day and resulted in the campus looking like there had been no typhoon, which was quite a contrast to the Wong Chuk Hang Estate just outside the West Gate. Stories were heard of the new intake who had just arrived trying to sleep and stay safe in J Block, with one new recruit [NMm] even sleeping with his boots on just in case he was turned out in an emergency. This didn't happen, and I'm sure he got a decent sleep despite the boots.

Eventually, our Passing Out Parade Day arrived on the 10th of September, and the passing out parade Reviewing Officer was the Commander British Forces, who went to the same school as [LCAm]. The parade passed off without anything untoward happening, and [LCAm's] brother took great photos of the day. I was in the lead squad together with [CJm], which was led by the Brian Slevin Award winner [PSm]. During the after-parade drinks and small bites, the CDMI informed me that I would come back to PTS for an afternoon per week for the next three weeks for further practice of giving instructions to marching squads on the direct instruction of the C PTS. This was something not mentioned to me in my final interview, but it would keep me attached to PTS right up to the Force Swimming Gala. Hence, my umbilical cord hadn't been completely severed. I was also informed that the District Commander (DC) of my new District had been informed and had no objections. It was also mentioned that The Emperor would have nothing to do with the drill sessions, which I took for face value and thought that would be the last I would see of The Emperor. However, with time, this didn't quite turn out to be the case.

In the afternoon, I was about to drive to Ho Man Tin Hill Road Inspectorate Quarters to move some of my belongings to my new digs when [HWm] asked for a lift as he was going to play rugby at the Police Sports and Recreation Club in Kowloon. I somehow

Victoria Mortuary, Cocktail Night & Assault by The Emperor

managed to squeeze him into the back seat, and after getting lost in Wong Tai Sin, during which we were jeered by some local youths, obviously a sign of things to come, we found our way to the Boundary Street sports ground. I dropped [HWm] off and then went to see my digs on the 5th floor of Ho Man Tin Inspectorate Quarters, 19 Ho Man Tin Road, Kowloon. A building that had been described as a rabbit warren and a suitable place for fornication as one SB secretary had christened it.

I was in flat 507A in A Block. The flat was four times the size of my room at PTS. It consisted of a small kitchen, a living room with a window overlooking Princess Margaret Road and Ho Man Tin Police Station, a bedroom with aircon, and a separate bathroom with a shower, bathtub and toilet. The building was U shaped, overlooking a courtyard and on the ground floor was a restaurant and bar. Below ground level was an underground car park, where I quickly claimed a spot for the MGC.

As it was Saturday, I got ready and went to catch a taxi to the Blacksmiths Arms, where I had dinner at the steak place round the corner from the bar. Afterwards, I had a couple of drinks at the Blacksmith Arms before going to Rick's Café, where many of the ex-pats from the intake had said they would spend their first night of freedom from PTS.

The DJ, who had just started full-time, was [JSm]. He played great music from Toto to Tears for Fear and Dexy's Midnight Runners. The place was certainly rocking with many ex-pats from other intakes and ex-pats who had long since passed out of PTS. The girls present were a great melting pot of all sorts of local girls, from nurses, school teachers and Cathay flight stewardesses. By the end of the evening, I was dancing with a small local girl who spoke good English who I had danced with over several weeks. The last two songs were slow ones, and after the songs had finished, I was asked if I wanted to continue the night, which I heartily agreed I did. We left Rick's Café and jumped in a taxi with the girl giving an address I didn't recognize. However, we ended up in Happy Valley at a motel that rented rooms by the hour. I paid for two hours, after which we went to the room for a lustful tryst. At the end of two hours, we parted company, promising to see each other the next weekend at Rick's Café. I returned to my Ho Man Tin Hill Road quarters satisfied and, upon turning into bed, slept the sleep of the dead, made more comfortable by the air conditioning.

Royal Hong Kong Police
Oath/Declaration of Office
皇家香港警務處
就職宣誓書/宣言

"You, (Alan CROWTHER) took the Oath or Declaration of office to well and faithfully serve Her Majesty Queen Elizabeth II, Her Heirs and Successors, according to law as a Police Officer, to obey, uphold and maintain the law of the Colony of Hong Kong, to execute the Powers and Duties of office honestly, faithfully and diligently, without fear or favour to any person and with malice or ill will toward none, and to obey without question all lawful orders of those set in authority over you."

『閣下　　　於　　　年　　月　　日宣誓就職，以警務人員身份，願依法竭誠效忠英女皇陛下伊利沙伯二世，其儲君及繼任人，並願遵守香港法律，維護法綱，執行法紀，勵行職守，秉公行事，不枉不徇，並絕對服從上級一切合法命令。』

(J.A. Finch)
Commandant,
Police Training School
警察訓練學校
校長

Date: 30th December 1982

An example of Oath of Office taken on 30-12-1982

On Parade

March Past

Formed Up

PI 236 Squad Passing Out Parade (POP)

Mess Dining Out

PTS Officers Mess

End Result of a Game of Murder Ball

Philippines Trip

Special Duty Squad SDS 1 KT DIST Dinner at Inspectorate Quarters

Dinner at Gaylords

Drinks at the Weinstube in TST

Trip to the UK in 1986

Jumbo Restaurant Choosing Dinner After Attending Beating Retreat Ceremony at PTS

Completion of Special Duties Unit Selection 1985

Police Training School Swimming Gala 1983

Police Training School PI 236 and The Emperor [GKLm]

PTU G COY 4/85 Officers and NCOs

Trip to Peking in 1984

[LAf] of the 3 A's in Peking in 1984

Diving in Thailand, 1986

Trekking in Nepal, 1986

The Last Two Female Flatmates Newcastle Upon Tyne 1982

Lamma Island Walk with Drinks for Some, 1983

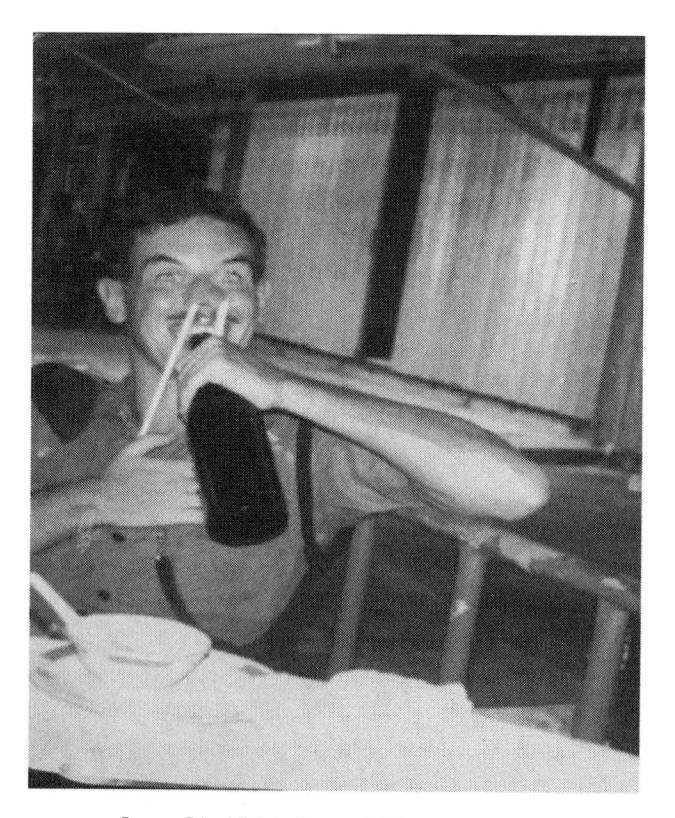

Lamma Island Drinks Party and Ambush Lunacy, 1983

Inspector not looking impressed with drunken behaviour of some intake members at Mount Stenhouse, Lamma Island as there will be "Trouble at Mill" because of drinks consumed causing some to throw caution to the wind.

PTU Golf COY 4/85 Platoon 4 1985

Manager at Rick's Café on a Night Out

Ricks Cafe

CDMI, PTS Mess night

Ex-pats PI 236 - 238

SDS 1 KT DIST

Chapter 15

First Posting to Kwun Tong Police District, Ngau Tau Kok Police Division

It can be said that the nine months of leadership and command training, no matter how small or large the task was, saw that we had been instilled with confidence. We also had a robustness, as well as self-belief to tackle any task expected of us when posted to our first postings outside PTS.

Upon leaving PTS, being posted to a real Police District was like a breath of fresh air. The contrast of seeing Hong Kong by day as opposed to by night at weekends when socializing in clubs such as Rick's Café, Hot Gossip, Hollywood East, Rumors, Front Page, or the Smugglers Arms in Stanley was inspiring. My liking for Hong Kong and all the issues that citizens of Hong Kong had to face, especially what was to become our bread and butter, illegal and criminal acts were a challenge to look forward to handling. It was good to know that we made a difference by carrying out our duties without fear or favour. Hong Kong always felt exciting, with everyone always wanting to better themselves either legally or illegally, no matter what the cost, be it hard work or running the risk of being imprisoned.

First Posting to Kwun Tong Police District, Ngau Tau Kok Police ...   131

On arrival at Ngau Tau Kok Police Division which was in Kwun Tong Police District, Kowloon Region, I was assigned to a patrol subunit, which had three inspectors, including me. This meant that I was the third I/C. I underwent familiarization training for each unit in the Division as well as visits to court and the Regional Command and Control Centre Kowloon (RCCC K). At RCCC K, I was introduced to the shift Controller, who was a superintendent and the two inspectorate supervisors covering Kowloon East and Kowloon West Districts, even though Kowloon was one Region at that time. One of the supervisors was a huge ex-pat and apparently a martial arts practitioner known as Desperate Dan. He had been posted to RCCC K because of a disciplinary problem, and the inspector leading the visit added that Districts would nominate officers for RCCC K duties who they didn't want to keep.

The shift system I would be working was an eight-and-a-half-hour day and six-day week (51hrs), which followed the shift system of night, afternoon and morning (CBA shifts). Each shift required a short change on a shift changeover unless you were lucky to have a day off. This point was driven home when during my familiarisation, the Assistant Divisional Commander Administration (ADVC ADM) Ngau Tau Kok had me understudy the Station Duty Officer who ran the report room. This was for three days, undertaking one C shift, followed by one B shift, followed by one A shift which required two short changes in as many days, making me think he had a sense of humour. The Divisional Commander was a local superintendent [KCCm] who had risen from the ranks and was a very personable and friendly person. He only wanted everyone who worked for him to work and pull their weight while maintaining discipline. At the end of the week, I was seen by the District Commander [WBm], who was a chief superintendent who welcomed both new inspectors to the District as my leadership tent occupant [HCCm] had also been posted to Kwun Tong Division, Kwun Tong District. After having our transfer in interviews, which in my case confirmed there was no mention made of a written warning for dismissal, we were asked if there was anything else in the District we wanted to see, and we both said the Rennies Mill Sub Division. This police station overlooked Junk Bay, or Tiu Keng Leng in Cantonese as it is called. This area was famous as it housed mainly Pro-Taiwan Chinese residents who made a living from scrapping large ships. The journey to the small police station took about 30 minutes via Anderson Road Quarry and Ma Yau Tong Village, but it was worth it as on arrival, we were struck that most huts had the Taiwan National Flag flying above their rooftops. While I was in Kwun Tong, I ran into [RJm], aka Jim Jam. He was an inspector from the intake above me at PTS who told me we were on the same shifts, so we should go for a drink sometime. I later took up this offer as [RJm] also lived in Ho Man Tin Hill Road Inspector Service Quarters, and we soon became a team and got in a few scrapes together while out on the town.

At the end of the familiarization week, I began work in my assigned patrol subunit, where I got to know the divisional boundary and all the beats, not to mention crime blackspots and other areas. Ngau Tau Kok had many different areas, with the Kowloon Bay Temporary Housing Area and rough unused land bordering the Kai Tak Airport. Next to this was the private housing estate known as Richland Gardens facing San Po Kong and Ping Shek Estate. Between these two areas was the open Vietnamese Camp called Kai Tak, as it occupied old military buildings once connected to the airport. Near this camp were the Discipline Services Club and the Detective Training School, which could be called the West of the Division. This led on to Clear Water Bay Road, which ran along the bottom of Kowloon Peak up to Shun Lee Estate in the North that had a Neighbourhood Police Office headed by a Station Sergeant (SSGT). The divisional boundary between NTK and KT Divisions ran down Hong Ning Road in the East and passed the United Christian Hospital to Kwun Tong Road, just past Yue Man Square in the South. At Kwun Tong Road, the divisional boundary returned towards the West along Ngau Tau Kok Road, passing Garden Estate, then going on to Ngau Tau Kok lower and Upper Estates (Resettlement Estates), Amoy Gardens, Jordan Valley Estate, as well

First Posting to Kwun Tong Police District, Ngau Tau Kok Police ... 133

as Lok Wah Estate North of Kwun Tong Road. South of Kwun Tong Road was the NTK part of the sprawling industrial area along Wai Yip Street and Tai Yip Street, which had many sweatshops and godowns. Lastly, Telford Gardens situated above the Kowloon Bay MTR Station and workshops.

In the subunit I was assigned to, mini operations which I had to plan, such as illegal parking as well as, in those days, illegal hawking operations. I was also shown the dangerous drug blackspots and soon got to know the name and identities of local drug traffickers, such as Fei Pa Tung (Fat Wife Tung with Tung being the surname), who lived and trafficked heroin in Jordan Valley Estate. The planning of operations, despite them being considered small, were tiny steps in the leadership and command functions of my inspectorate rank and taking command of my Junior Police Officers (JPOs).

Operational Experience

The mini operations were good as they gave me a chance to plan while using intelligence and the knowledge of my sub unit Police Constables (PC) and Non-Commissioned Officers (NCO either SGT or SSGT). This involved using the same terminology and also getting to know what experience the patrol sub unit possessed. These mini operations were building blocks to other more difficult operations. Especially when, in the near future, we would transfer to units which tackled particular problems such as District Crime and District Vice.

Ngau Tau Kok Division had its fair share of ex-pat inspectors, such as [MCm] in CID and [MDm] in the uniformed branch (UB), who was in a different subunit than me. [MDm] was about to transfer to CID in Kwun Tong Division mainly because he had previous police experience when he served in the Merseyside Police before coming to Hong Kong. He himself thought that he was being moved as he had just had a complaint against police (CAPO) made against him. This was after checking the license of the Telford Garden Sports

Centre, where a Eurasian female [SDf], who was the daughter of the owner, worked. During the license check, [SDf] had accused [MDm] of being too familiar and, at the end of the check, said he had asked her for her contact number, which didn't go down too well. Word soon spread that when carrying out future such checks, it was dangerous to mix work with pleasure. On one such check that I later conducted with [SDf] being present, I did note that she was very attractive and I later learnt that she had been a noted Hong Kong swimmer in her time.

I soon got used to being in Divisions and felt quite at home. English was widely used, especially by "red tabs" (police officers with a red tab backing behind their numbers indicating that they could speak English, and this ability was reflected in pay scales). Also in the Division were a number of interpreters who translated Chinese statements into English so that ex-pat inspectors could process crime, complaints and other files. One such interpreter was [Mf], who, upon meeting me, took the piss stating that I was very skinny, after which we got on like a house on fire. I later took ballroom dancing lessons with her at the YMCA in TST for about eight weeks but was always cognizant that she was the girlfriend of [SMm], who was away on his end of tour leave at that time. We stayed friendly all the time I was in NTK Division and KT District.

I soon settled into a system depending on what shift I was on, maintaining fitness by running, playing rugby, swimming and playing water polo. On A shift (Morning shift), I used to go to the Disciplined Services Recreation Club on the way home, running six laps of its 800-meter running track, alternating between doing 2 minutes 30 seconds for one lap and then 3 minutes for the next lap. On C shift (night), I would wake up in the late afternoon and, after fully waking up, would run three laps around Ho Man Tin Hill Road, with each lap being about 1700 meters long. I would attend water polo training on Tuesday and Thursday except when I was on B Shift (Afternoon), and undertake one mid-week session of rugby training at the Police Sports and Recreation Club on Boundary Street in Mong Kok with a rugby game on Saturday afternoon for the Police Casuals (3rd or 4th team). I also did runs up and down Beacon Hill after parking my car at the middle of the hill layby. On driving home, I would stop at a drinks store on the G/F of Carpenter Road in Kowloon City, which I later learnt was situated at the entrance to the Kowloon Walled City!

Chapter 16

The Force Swimming Gala at Tai Wan Shan Pool, Hung Hom

During my first three weeks after passing out from PTS, I had one afternoon back at the training establishment per week to practice giving orders to a squad of police constables marching on the drill square. The idea was to get the squad marching around the drill square by shouting different orders and then try to get them back to the exact position they had started from for a perfect score.

I didn't know why the C PTS had given this instruction, but I figured it still connected me to PTS so I could swim for them at the Force Swimming Gala, despite now being in Kwun Tong Police District, which was in Kowloon Region. I knew I was as good as everyone else in my intake in giving orders. Hence, the only purpose of these weekly visits was to document my attachment to PTS if someone should ask. No one else from my intake had been asked to do the same, so there could be no other reason.

The day of the Force Swimming Gala finally arrived on the Friday after my last drill session on Wednesday of the same week. It was being held at Tai Wan Shan Swimming Pool in Hung Hom. I had entered a number of individual events, which took place in the morning, with the team relay events taking place in the afternoon. I was given the whole day off to attend the Force sporting event. I finished in the top three in the individual events and then spent some time in the warm-up pool to stay lively and not stiffen up. While warming up, I got talking to a Cathay Pacific stewardess who was swim training in the warm-up pool and discovered she was from Malaysia and on a day off. Unfortunately, I had to concentrate on the swimming gala. Otherwise, I would have asked her out for dinner, but I was sure I might meet her again as she said she was a regular at Rick's Cafe.

The afternoon arrived and the PTS 4 X 50-meter freestyle squad assembled and comprised of three inspectors, including one police constable (PC) and me. The other two inspectors were down to swim the first two legs while the PC would swim the third leg, and I would anchor the relay on the fourth leg. We all practised in the warm-up pool, especially the takeovers, to ensure no one went too early and did some gentle swimming to ensure our arms did not get too cold.

The event was announced, and we took our positions with the PTS squad being in the lane to the right of the Force Champions, who were the Marine Police Region team. I looked into the stands and found the C PTS [FJm] sat next to the RC Marine [MJm], and they were engaged in conversation. I then checked out the 2nd and 4th leg swimmers of the Marine Police Region Team and noticed the 4th leg swimmer had skin the colour of mahogany and a very distinctive tide mark where his swimming trunks met his skin. He was about 15 years my senior but did not have an ounce of fat on him and was quite wiry with strong muscles. It was obvious he did nothing else every day but swim, and he would be the person I would be swimming against on the anchor leg.

The race was called, and after two legs, we were about four to five meters behind the Marine team. The PTS PC set off on the third leg, and I spat in my goggles and washed them out while at the same time taking a hand full of pool water to wash through my mouth and spit it out. At the halfway mark on the third leg, I could see that the PC had dropped another two meters behind and I noticed the mahogany skinned Marine anchor leg get on the starting blocks, ready to take over and swim the fourth leg. I stood on my starting block, put on my swimming goggles and then the Marine anchor leg swimmer leapt off the starting block, surfaced and started to swim quite fast. I also noted we were ten meters down. Then I looked to where the C PTS [FJm] was sitting and saw he had a look of utter dismay on his face while the RC Marine [MJm] was sat there with a smug grin, not worried at all. I then checked on our PC swimming our third leg and willed him to touch the end of the pool.

The PC touched the wall, and I executed a great takeover and swam the first 25 meters without taking a breath. Noticing that I had halved the gap between the Marine anchor leg man and me, I took a breath and hammered on, reducing the gap to a body length with about 15 meters to go. At about the eight-meter mark before the finish, I drew level with the Marine Police Team anchor leg swimmer. However, he sped up and, despite my body knowing it had swum hard, I picked up my pace to match. Upon checking, I found that we were level and swimming in perfect synchronicity, arm by arm and heartbeat for heartbeat. My heart was beating so fast that it was trying to explode out of my chest. I could hear the strokes match each other and thought I heard perfect resonant frequency, and then slowly but surely, I began to pull ahead, eventually touching the wall by half a body length ahead of the Marine Police Team anchor leg. On touching the wall, I gulped down several breaths of air and immediately after the Marine Police Team anchor had touched, I looked to where [FJm] the C PTS was sat. He was smiling from ear to ear like a Cheshire Cat, while the RC Marine [MJm] had a look of dismay on his face like he was being hounded. I realized that the C PTS [FJm] must have won quite a substantial wager hence my worth to him by remaining at PTS, which also explained the swimming audition I had undertaken. I then turned my gaze to the Marine Police Team anchor and he looked totally dejected, so I congratulated him on a race well swum and wished him all the best.

Chapter 17

Beat Incidents

Telford Gardens Roundabout

One day on morning shift, I had been patrolling Amoy Gardens and Jordan Valley by myself. I did this most of the time, knowing that if I needed assistance, I could call for it on the beat radio. I then decided to go back to NTK Police Station for lunch. On the way back, I heard several times on the radio that the roundabout at Telford Gardens was heavily congested. So, as I was on my way back to the station, I decided to check the report out. On arrival, I told the Regional Command and Control Centre Kowloon (RCCC K) that I was there and confirmed that the roundabout was indeed gridlocked mainly by cars waiting for space to be freed up in the Telford Gardens open-air car park. One person, in particular, was causing the blockage by not allowing a gap between his car and the car in front, stopping all traffic. I asked the driver to move forward when space became available and leave a gap. However, he refused to do so, which caused more traffic congestion. I approached him again when more space became available and told him to move forward but leave a gap. This time, he did move forward but didn't leave a gap. I then instructed him that if he didn't follow my instruction, I would give him a ticket! Again, he didn't respond and, in my opinion, he was being very selfish. I then told him to pull over and when he had stopped, I gave him a ticket and explained why he had been given one. It was obvious from his body language that he wasn't very happy, and he seriously disputed the ticket in a raised voice, but I stood firm and explained again. Eventually, I left and on arrival at NTK Police station, I spent half my lunch hour filling in my notebook, making a comprehensive entry fully covering all my actions. I also noted that he had stated that he was a teacher and that he had totally objected the ticket and fully expected him to make a complaint. Hong Kong at that time didn't have many vehicles on the roads, and even the police station car park was sparsely used. Telford gardens, however, was known for its traffic and was a noted black spot.

Sure enough, a few weeks later, I was notified that I had a CAPO complaint made against me. I had to go to the CAPO offices in Tsuen Wan to give a statement explaining my actions, but nothing came of it. A short time later, I learnt that the driver had contested the ticket and that I had to go to San Po Kong Magistrates Court to give evidence.

The day of the court hearing arrived and during the court proceedings, I noted that the driver, who was a teacher, represented himself in front of the magistrate, who was an ex-pat. Sure enough, I was called to give evidence which I did, after which I was cross-examined by the teacher who accused me, on no less than three occasions, of being a liar and fabricating my version of why the ticket had been given. I was far from happy and after the third occasion of being abused, I looked at the magistrate for him to intervene and have the teacher challenge the facts as opposed to make accusations. The magistrate eventually intervened and advised the teacher about his line of questioning, which then finished. The magistrate then asked why I, as an inspector, had issued the ticket, to which I replied that the rest of my subunit were dealing with other reports, and as I was passing, I actioned the traffic congestion case being in possession of both static and moving offence tickets. The magistrate accepted my account and duly convicted the teacher of the offence for which he would have to pay a fine and court costs.

On my way out to leave the court building, I noted the school teacher was standing still on the staircase looking for the shroff office so he could pay his fine. I then took the opportunity to approach him and asked him if he was looking for the shroff's office, to which he stated he was, and then using my best Cantonese, wished him and his mother well, which allowed me to get rid of my pent-up anger. There were no witnesses and if the teacher made a complaint against me, I could honestly say he was being informed where the shroff office could be located in a succinct manner!

Factory building Noise at Night Case

One night on C shift, I was on patrol in the mobile patrol car when RCCC K directed us to check out a noise at night complaint in one of the industrial buildings in the NTK factory area. On arrival, we found three men speaking at the top of their voices and almost shouting at each other while they packed boxes of metal. Some of the metal being packed was being hammered and hence the 03:00hrs noise at night complaint.

As usual, we introduced ourselves even though we were in uniform and asked for their identity cards (ID) so we could check with RCCC K whether they were wanted or not. During this process, one of the men was extremely rude to the police constable doing the ID checks, so I admonished him very strongly in the same language he had used when addressing my officer. Things got quite heated, and after a period of time, things quietened down after they had locked up their factory unit and left. Albeit, the man I had addressed, was far from happy. A few weeks later, I was informed that I had another CAPO complaint, and so the whole mobile patrol crew I had been on duty with that night had to give statements. The complaint was not substantiated, although it was noted that I had two CAPOs made against me.

Theft of Fuel from a Private Car

During one week on C Shift, I was asked to do morning prayers with the ADVC OPS NTK [HAm], who held the rank of Chief Inspector. (CIP) The prayers started at 08:00hrs, about 25 minutes after I was supposed to go off duty. The extra 25 minutes made a big difference as I felt much more tired on reaching home and starting work for the next night. During the meeting, I was informed that I would have a new inspector during the next shift who was doing his familiarization. I was asked to show him around the Division and point out the black spots. On arrival for duty the next night, I had planned a route to take to show the new inspector, and I thought I would check out a theft from vehicle black spot location during the middle of the night.

On arrival for duty, the new inspector sat in on the subunit briefing and then we set off on a mobile patrol showing all the main parts of the Division, even going to the Kai Tak Vietnamese Camp police post. The entrance to the camp was often the scene of crimes, such as street robbery and taxi robbery. At about 03:00hrs, we proceeded to the Ngau Kok Road Market building, where we got off to check the nearby theft from vehicle black spot in On Wah Street. We all turned our beat radios to low noise and then hugged the vehicles parked at the side of the roads in a bent-over position. About halfway down the road, I smelt strong petrol fumes and told everyone to be still, after which we edged forward, eventually seeing one Chinese male bent over a jerry can syphoning petrol from a car. We quickly moved forward, grabbed him and stopped the petrol flow. After being arrested, he pointed out his car, which we then searched. We seized two long club-like sticks and cautioned him again for possession of an offensive weapon. We all then went back to the police station, and after giving statements, the male was handed over to CID.

At morning prayers that morning, the ADVC OPS congratulated me as he had also noted a number of thefts from vehicle cases in that same area. I was quite pleased, and the new inspector was happy for the experience. A few months later, when the case went to court, the defence lawyer asked if the possession of offensive weapon charges could be dropped. However, I objected. Eventually, after trial, the man was convicted of theft from vehicle but was acquitted of the possession of offensive weapon charges, much to his astonishment but relief!

Armed Robbery at a Chinese Restaurant in Hong Kong Island

One Sunday morning, I was on A Shift (morning shift) and in the report room speaking to the SSGT Duty Officer. The morning had been very quiet. However, by about 10:00hrs, the patrol subunit SSGT reported that the Duty Officer had received a phone call stating that a hut in the Kowloon Bay Temporary Housing Area (THA) had stolen property inside it from a robbery. The Chinese phrase used meant that we should get there as quickly as possible as the occupants might leave soon.

On being informed and sensing the excitement in the SSGT's tone of voice, I instructed that we set off immediately so we would not miss out on verifying the allegation. On arrival at the Kowloon Bay THA, we parked our police marked vehicle well away from the stated hut and proceeded on foot, moving stealthily by hugging the lines of huts for cover, as we were all in uniform. On reaching the line of huts that the stated premise was in, we split up with the SGT and a couple of PCs going to cover the left of the stated hut while I, the SSGT and two more PCs approached the front of the hut from the right. There was no back door as THA huts were single decked, consisting of a living cum sleeping area, a toilet with shower and a small kitchen. They were also built back-to-back.

On arrival, we listened from outside and there were several male voices talking. Discussion on how they would split up the rest of the money could be heard from outside. We immediately knocked on the front door and stated we were the police and to open the door. All conversation inside the hut ceased and some furniture could be heard being moved about. Eventually, the door was opened and the whole of the police party went inside, where we found four males. Some of which had tattoos, all of which looked furtive in their demeanour. Hong Kong identity cards were demanded as well as who was the resident in charge of the hut. All four males were informed of the reason for our visit, after which they were searched, with three out of the four males having a large amount of cash on them, amounting to nearly $20000 HK each. None of which could give an explanation for having the money other than winning on the horses. The SSGT directed a PC to search the hut, and a number of crowbars and melon knives were found together with a large red tablecloth dumped in the corner of the hut. On checking the tablecloth, another $20000 HK cash was found inside when it was opened up, with the fourth male stating it was his again from winning on the horse races. The PC who was searching also stated that the tablecloth had a dry-cleaning company label on it and the name and address of a Chinese restaurant on Hong Kong Island. The SSGT asked another PC to be the exhibits officer and another PC to draw up a sketch of the hut marking where the exhibits were found as well as where each male was stood. Once this was all done, each male was cautioned by an officer for the offence of robbery and another two police vehicles were asked to come to the scene to take the males and exhibits back to the police station.

On arrival at Ngau Tau Kok Police Station, all the four males were presented to the report room Duty Officer (DO). Then they were placed in the temporary holding area cell once the DO was satisfied with the caution and arrest. When all four males were in the cell and out of hearing distance, a phone call was made to Wan Chai Police Station, and they confirmed that the Chinese restaurant named on the seized tablecloth had been robbed by armed robbers. Further, a large amount of cash had been taken from what was believed to be an illegal casino run from inside the restaurant after it had closed for the night by six males. The DO informed the Wan Chai DO that four males had been arrested and exhibits, including a large amount of cash, a table cloth, together with breaking tools and melon knives, had been seized from a hut situated in the

Kowloon Bay THA after a tip-off phone call to the police station. Later on, a Regional Crime Unit arrived at Ngau Tau Kok Police Station from Hong Kong Island. After satisfying themselves that the four males were involved in the robbery from their tattoos, they took over the case and took statements from the Ngau Tau Kok Police Officers involved in the case, including myself.

About six months later, in about April 1984, I was informed that I would give evidence in respect of our raid at the High Court, despite my part in the whole proceedings being minimal by leading the arrest and seizure party of police officers. Up to that date, I had never given evidence in any court, so I was a bit nervous as the Judge had to be called your Lordship as opposed to your Worship, together with other customs that were only used in the High Court. On the day of the High Court hearing, I went unarmed in my best police uniform. While waiting in the small canteen to give evidence, I noticed a well-dressed Chinese male, aged about 26, accompanied by two very tall and well-built bouncers, come into the canteen to order a tea. One of my officers informed me that he was Dennis CHIU, the Managing Director of Asia Television (ATV).

On hearing this, I instantly knew who he was as when still at the Police Training School in July 1983, his case had appeared in detail in the South China Morning Post. The article stated that he had been drinking at a TST East night club and while on the way back to Kowloon Tong, together with some young starlet, he had run into a young Police Tactical Unit (PTU) police constable Cheng Man-fai who was dismantling a police roadblock. The Volvo CHIU was in, knocked over the PC and dragged him under the car for about 100 meters, with the officer sustaining life-threatening injuries. The article noted that at least two rounds of ammunition had gone off in the chamber of the officer's revolver while it was still in its holster. As when being dragged, the leather had worn through, and the bare metal of the revolver had been heated up by the friction with the ground. It was also noted that the ex-pat PTU Platoon Commander had instructed his platoon to unload before they ran to the car that had, by that time, crashed and come to a stop before arresting the driver. The article inferred that Dennis CHIU was in some compromising position with the starlet. Hence, he took time to stop his vehicle as well as being under the influence of drink. At that time, there was no drink driving law in Hong Kong, and one only came into effect in December 1995. About two weeks after dragging the young police constable under CHIU's car, he died of his injuries. Dennis CHIU had been charged with manslaughter as a result. On checking the cases that were being heard in the High Court that day, CHIU's name was on the list in a different court.

Returning to my case of armed robbery, in which I gave evidence that day in an assured manner, I later learnt that all six males had been sentenced to more than ten years in prison. This experience stood me in good stead for the many other court cases in which I would be a police witness, including traffic prosecution complaints.

Third Alarm Fire, Ngau Tau Kok Road

In November 1983, while on a night shift (C Shift), I was on patrol in a police mobile transit vehicle when we spotted a rooftop fire on Ngau Tau Kok Road near the junction of Ting On Street at about 03:00hrs. We immediately went to the scene and cordoned off the road so that when the Fire Services Department (FSD) vehicles arrived, they could choose where they wanted to park their vehicles. Soon after this, several fire appliances arrived, and as it was a fire, they took charge. We played a secondary role of traffic and crowd control until the fire was put out. The fire was soon upgraded to Third Alarm, meaning it was more severe and the FSD turned out their Mobile Command Vehicle.

I was being pressured by the Police Regional Command and Control Centre Kowloon (RCCC K) for more information. Each time I went to the FSD command vehicle to ask for pertinent details, I was told nothing was known or was ignored.

After about two hours, RCCC K became very insistent and I was getting annoyed at being fobbed off, so I approached the FSD command vehicle and gained entry to find a couple of their senior officers having a cup of tea. I asked for an update, as it had been two hours since they had arrived, but heard them say in Cantonese that I was a virgin inspector, being a lowly one pip inspector. On hearing this, I went on the attack and said that FSD had told me nothing in two hours and RCCC K wanted updating! If I wasn't updated, I would withdraw all police manpower, and FSD could manage the fire as well as the crowd and traffic control themselves. Their attitude changed immediately, and I got all the information and more that I wanted. After which, I left and updated RCCC K. At the end of duty, I asked the on-coming police inspectors about what I had experienced, and they stated it was normal! When I heard this, I found it incredible that two government departments could not work better together, and this was something I was determined to try to improve.

Sick Person Case Jordan Valley Estate

By November 1983, my subunit police constables (PCs) and Non-Commissioned Officers (NCOs) had gotten used to me and knew that I pulled my weight when it came to work. They took it for granted that if I wanted someone to patrol with, I would ask. Most of the time, I would go out by myself and check the beats as well as the visiting books (VBs), applying my signature after checking how often they had been signed and by whom. They also knew that if I wanted to meet or needed assistance, I would call them out on my beat radio. This wasn't very often, as I had picked up enough Cantonese to undertake a simple stop, question and or search. I was also, by that time, proficient at issuing traffic fixed penalty tickets. If I did use the radio to call out an officer, it was to meet up and undertake a check of their police notebook and ask how they were doing.

On arrival at Ngau Tau Kok Police Division, I was tested to see how green I was by the Duty Officer SSGT SIT. He was a very likeable man, totally dependable and who also had a sense of humour. When I understudied him, he asked me for instruction on meal breaks, so I immediately asked him what did he normally do with the report room staff when I wasn't there. Upon being told, I directed that he should do the same and I would choose a time when it was quiet. I successfully passed this little test which reminded me of when I worked as a fitter's mate during the summer vacation at Polytechnic while in the UK. The fitter, for a joke unbeknown to me, sent me to get a long rest from the fitter's store. Ten minutes after I had asked for the long rest, the person manning the store let me know that I had sufficient rest, and I could go back to work, telling my fitter the mission had been accomplished! What a hoot and embarrassment, but I soon learnt!

On one morning shift, I had been patrolling the industrial area conducting an anti-crime patrol when I heard my name being called out by the NTK console at RCCC K. They were asking me to attend a sick person case at Block 1 of Jordan Valley on the first floor, end premise right-hand side near the nullah. I was approximately 15 minutes away but walked quickly, wondering whether the sick person had been assaulted as a purely sick person call didn't usually merit one of the subunit inspectors to attend the scene. I also checked my duty list, and the beat PC was on his meal break. It was also of note that I didn't see any other beat PCs, even though I passed through several other beats. On arrival at Block 1 Jordan Valley, I found it strange that no police mobile patrol car was in attendance. When I went up to the first floor, the end premise on the right, I smelt a terrible smell which got stronger the nearer I approached the end premise. The smell was overpowering and one I wouldn't ever forget, and on reaching the end premise, I knocked on the door but got no answer. The premises were about 200 square feet in size and had an open corridor outside, as did all the flats on that floor. The window was an iron-barred vent just above head height, and along the corridor, there was a concrete bannister wall that was as high as my waist.

I decided to step on the top of the concrete bannister wall so I could see through the barred window vent, and when I did, I saw the cause of the smell, which suddenly got a lot stronger. Lying on a sun lounger type bed face up was an elderly man fully dressed in his pyjamas. However, he was motionless, his eyes had started to putrefy, and there was a pool of body fluids on the floor under the sun lounger. I then stepped down and reported to RCCC K that the sick person was, in fact, a dead body. I then asked for the black morgue van to be sent as well as the fire services so we could break open the door.

After I made this report, RCCC K informed me that arrangements had been made, and the police mobile patrol car (MP Car) was on the way together with the fire services. A short time later, the MP Car arrived quickly, followed by the fire services. The first fireman arrived at the front door of the address, so I informed him what I had seen and he jumped on the top of the concrete bannister wall to check on the door lock on the inside of the door. While he was doing this, he saw the dead body. He abruptly pulled himself back in shock from the window vent and was lucky not to fall to the ground floor.

The door was broken open, and on waiting for the morgue van to arrive, a newspaper reporter appeared with a camera who wanted to take a photograph. I told him that if he went in first without the camera, I would later allow him to take a photograph. However, as dead bodies are bad luck, he didn't accept my offer of having a look-see first without his camera to hide behind and soon left the location.

On arrival back at Ngau Tau Kok Police Station, I asked the subunit SSGT why I had been the first to arrive, having walked 15 minutes to get to the location. He stated that it was my first dead body case and I was allowed to have the experience personally, which I handled correctly, even certifying that the body was dead! I noticed while he was telling me this that he had a smile on his face, so I knew that my fellow colleagues had played a joke on me as they knew me that well. I then knew I had been fully accepted by my subunit and was reassured that all was well. They obviously knew I could take a joke and one I would never forget. I took this as a coming of age and acceptance by the subunit officers and endorsement of my work ethic and practices.

MP Car Patrol/Report Room Duties and the Lads and Girls

After about three months in Ngau Tau Kok Police Division (NTK DIV) Kwun Tong Police District (KT DIST), I had settled in and had been accepted by the police constables, both male and female. All the red tabs (police officers with red felt backings behind their number indicated an English speaker) didn't hesitate to speak conversational English. However, I insisted that I also improved my Cantonese. Indeed, when something was said in Cantonese that I didn't understand, I asked for it to be repeated and explained. This made for some interesting banter and was a good opportunity to learn.

In the report room, there was one officer who had the last three digits of his official number as 747, and quite rightly, he was known as "Jumbo", as in the type of aircraft. One female constable who was known to daydream or be away with the fairies on occasion was known as the flying saucer (Cheung Soh Gei). This was because she never remained on topic and lost track of events, much like a spinning alien device. Also in the report room were 'The Bibles', which were the Miscellaneous Reports Book (MRB) and the Crime Complaint Register (CCR), both of which recorded none crime reports (MRB) and crime reports (CCR). Rumour was that in some police stations, the CCR was kept in the Divisional Commanders Office and was only allowed in the report room for really serious crime as a way of controlling the actual crime rate! Thank goodness in NTK Division that didn't happen, and reported crime was accurately recorded and actioned accordingly. This was probably why Kwun Tong District was known as Red Indian Territory, as it had a high crime rate with many offences against the person, such as assault and robbery.

In undertaking mobile and anti-crime patrols, some police constables would laugh when asking a person what his age was, who was subject to a stop, question, and search. This was especially so when persons in their late teens were stopped and that had stated they were either seventeen or nineteen years of age. This was because the Cantonese pronunciation of the number 7 or 9 could also mean penis. Hence, the officer carrying out the stop, question and search would repeat the age but use the tone that meant penis, insinuating they were wankers! Indeed, the slang for the physical attributes of persons stopped would be used such as fat boy (Fei Jai) or someone with dyed hair being called golden-haired boy (Gam Mo Tau). If someone wasn't particularly attractive, they would be called ugly (Yuk Suen), and indeed females who were flat-chested would be called airport runways (Fei Gei Chueng) as aircraft runways are flat.

One day while driving down the main road in NTK DIV, the whole mobile patrol car fell into laughter when one of the officers saw a procession of wedding cars. He had said something I hadn't heard before, but obviously, whatever had been said was very funny. After the laughter had subsided, I asked the officer to repeat what he said and explain it. This turned into a long conversation as there was no "red tab" in the car, and English was limited. Eventually, I understood the phrase used meant, "the penis had found a new home" (Bun Jau Yap Foh) as the male getting married in moving out of his parents' house would be living with his wife, who had the gear to house his penis, which was a fiery place when used. Some police constables, when reporting on duty in the morning, would ask their colleagues whether they had been married that day (Gam Yat Yau Mo Git Faan Mei A?) as an alternative to saying good morning but usually only the young ones. This meant whether they had sex that day or not. It can be said, having some knowledge of Cantonese in order to conduct conversations was useful, but there was a whole new language when officers used slang! One final example is when a person is called someone who shoots down the aircraft (Da Fei Gei Yan), as this means he is a masturbator or wanker. The ultimate swear phrase used in Hong Kong is Diu Lei Lo Mo or, in English, "go and bonk your mother". This could be extended to Diu Lei Lo Mo Chow Lan Hai, which translates to "go and bonk your mother's effing smelly reproductive orifice". This, indeed, is much more flowery than English swear words and always sure to add oil to the fire of an argument. By the end of my first three months of operational duty, I could string together a Cantonese swear phrase consisting of between 12 and 14 syllables. It must be stated that terms such as Leng Lui (good looking Girl) and Leng Jai (Handsome Boy) were used more often than not. However, when someone invited or attracted more blunt talk, being a paramilitary force meant it would be used.

Car Theft and Theft from Vehicle Cases

NTK had a huge problem when it came to vehicle crime. Two cases spring to mind.

The first case involved a mobile anti-crime patrol conducted on night shift (C Shift) in the Kowloon Bay Area at about 03:00hrs in the morning while checking a black spot. The police vehicle went down a long line of parked cars, and when nearing the end, the driver, through his rear-view mirror, spotted several males running out from behind a car we had just passed. The driver immediately stopped and excitedly informed us of what he had seen. We debussed and ran after the 4-5 males, who by now were some 60 meters away from us and trying to get into a private car. We were closing quickly, so they started to run again, which allowed us to catch two male teenagers while the other three escaped. We handcuffed the two teenagers and then went back to the car they were trying to board to make good their getaway. The doors of the car were open, but no keys were in the ignition. I then opened the bonnet and on finding the rotary arm housing, I opened it and took out the rotary arm, so the vehicle couldn't be used if someone came back after we had left. We then went back to the car the 4-5 males ran off from, and on meeting our driver, he pointed out that the passenger door had been prized open and things in the vehicle had been disturbed, which was enough for an attempted theft from vehicle case. On taking down the particulars of both vehicles, we went back to NTK Police Station to hand over the case to the Criminal Investigations Department (CID) and prepare our own statements. After being back at the station for about an hour, the Duty Officer (DO) got a telephone call from a male who told him that we could keep the getaway car, to which the DO asked the male to come to the station to surrender.

In respect of the second case, I, as the 2I/C of the patrol subunit, would go out with the Auxiliary anti-crime patrol plain-clothed officers who used their own private cars to patrol. The officers would come on for about 4 hours on night shift (C Shift), which started at about 23:00hrs and finished at 03:00hrs before they went home to sleep before their day/office jobs.

The usual routine was to go get a bit of a night snack (Siu Yea) immediately after briefing at the cooked food store at the junction of Ngau Tau Kok Road and How Ming Street. I normally had an egg sandwich and a cup of coffee while the 3 to 4 auxiliary officers had a simple Chinese dish which used up about 30 minutes of the shift. On this particular night, we decided to visit the Shun Tin Estate car park as it had been hit badly by vehicle crime. The car park was open to all traffic, and there were no security guards, so the safety of vehicles parked could not be guaranteed. After going up to the first level, nothing was found. However, on approaching the back of the ground floor level, a car was found with its engine running. On seeing us drive up to the car, two males went to board the car. However, only one was successful, while the second male hurdled the wall and went like a bat out of hell towards the extremely steep incline heading towards the United Christian Hospital. I decided not to follow as it was pitch black and then got back on the auxiliary officer's private car and shot off after the getaway vehicle, which was a Suzuki Jeep. We chased the car up Shun Lee Tsuen Road, reaching speeds of 90 Km per hour and the Jeep turned left onto Clear Water Bay Road before turning right onto Fei Ngo Shan Road. On taking this very tight right turn, the Jeep flipped onto its left-hand side. The vehicle I was in stopped, and we got out and apprehended the two males in the car as well as seized many vehicle breaking tools such as screwdrivers and crowbars.

Upon debriefing, the two males both admitted to theft from vehicle in Shun lee Estate car park, and the driver stated that the Jeep belonged to his father. While waiting for the CID to turn up, the tow truck arrived. When trying to get the Jeep upright, it had to drag it about ten feet backwards, so there was enough room to pull it upright. The scraping of the metal bodywork of the Jeep on the road certainly wasn't appreciated by the car driver, who would have to face his dad on return to NTK Police Station and explain the damage. All in all, it was a good night's work, and the auxiliary officers all got complimented but worked well passed their 03:00hrs off-duty time.

Theft by Finding Case in Kowloon Bay

On one afternoon shift, I was down to undertake a range course at Smugglers Ridge near the Kowloon Reservoir. The range course went well, and we went through the Chinese instruction of "don't move or I will open fire" (Mo Yuk fau jak ngoh hui cheung) before shooting at the bad guy silhouette that did move to use his revolver. Little did I know, while undertaking this course, that what I learnt and practised would come in useful later on in the shift.

On return to the station, I had dinner and then went out on foot patrol with an anti-crime team in uniform. One of the areas we covered was Kowloon Bay, which had some construction sites that had reported several thefts during the course of the last 3 to 4 weeks. After checking several sites, we decided to check one last site, and on entering the site, we saw some figures in the shadows. We shouted we were the police and they should stop where they were. This was ignored, and three males ran towards Kai Tak nullah. I was pretty fast at running, and when getting close to them, I shouted for them not to move. However, they carried on running. I got annoyed with the whole situation and shouted one more time in Cantonese that if they did not stop, I would open fire. This had an immediate effect, and all three males stopped immediately. This allowed all the police officers to catch up and apprehend the three males who were found in possession of tools from the construction site. On arrival back at NTK Police Station, my sergeant later told me the three males stopped because they could tell from the accent it was a foreigner who had shouted that he would open fire, and they thought I meant it. I assured the sergeant that I would not have opened fire but said I was trying my luck! This obviously worked, and I was happy to have attended the range course earlier in the day.

Hawking Without a License

When I joined the Royal Hong Kong Police and on being posted to NTK Police Station, I found out that the police also undertook anti-hawking operations. At that time, there were many hawkers, some selling rice boxes from trucks in the NTK and KT industrial area, as well as those that sold fruit, vegetables, cooked foods and clothing from carts that they pushed or set up on the street.

I once heard a story about a Chief Inspector in Kwun Tong that went on patrol with a one pip Inspector to Yue Man Square to tackle the hawking problem. On reaching a hawker selling glasses laid out on a blanket on the pavement, the Chief Inspector instructed the hawker to move, but he didn't. The Chief Inspector then instructed the one pip Inspector to march across the blanket and about-turn and march some more before again about-turning. In no time at all, the glasses on the ground were all broken. I personally thought this was being too extreme and could result in trouble as I heard quite a crowd gathered to watch.

I myself, upon leaving NTK Police Station, would walk along Tai Yip Street once a week during lunchtime and ask the food trucks to move on. The trucks wouldn't move on because they had up to 200 people queuing up to buy rice boxes, all of which worked in the sweatshops and had limited time for lunch. It took me all of 20 minutes to issue each truck a fixed penalty ticket for illegal parking before I finished my book of ten tickets. The operators of the food trucks took it as an operating cost, one that they could easily bear and pass on the costs to their customers.

During other operations, I noticed that the police constables would confiscate only part of the hawker's goods and then the hawker would be summoned to go to court. Immediately upon leaving to go elsewhere, the hawkers who had only lost part of their wares would start hawking again, knowing the police would probably not return.

During one operation, we stopped one hawker selling watermelons, and as we summoned him, he picked out five watermelons, which we could take as exhibits. I got very annoyed at this, and when one of my PCs asked me how many watermelons we should take, I told him to take the whole cart, which had about 50 whole watermelons on it. On explaining to the hawker what was happening, the smart PC moved the chopper away from the hawker, which he used to cut the watermelons. This was a precautionary measure, just in case he was tempted to use it against us as he had nothing else to lose. On returning to NTK Police Station, I explained to the team why I had taken all the watermelons and they accepted my explanation. The seized watermelons being perishable, were sent to the Old Aged Home on Clear Water Bay Road opposite Ping Shek Estate.

I was obviously still learning as I found out on the next anti-hawking operation I went out on, all the hawkers must have heard that I had taken all the watermelons from the hawker on the last operation. Upon seeing me, all of them sped off at top speed. This, most of the time wasn't a problem, but for those hawkers using hot oil, they became dangerous. In other parts of Hong Kong, such as Mong Kok, members of the public had been seriously burnt during anti-hawking operations.

Case of Wounding at Daai Paai Dong NTK Upper Estate

Nearly all residents of public housing estates in Hong Kong in 1983 only had a fan to keep themselves cool at night. This meant it was hard to sleep, and many chose to sleep only a few hours because, without air conditioning, which was expensive, they couldn't sleep longer. It would be fair to say that while waiting to go to sleep, many residents went to have a night snack (Siu Yea) to pass the time.

On one night shift, at about 01:00hrs, reports of a disturbance at the Daai Paai Dong at Ngau Tau Kok Upper Estate came in thick and fast into the station report room. I immediately got into the mobile patrol transit van, together with about six other officers and sped to the scene. The Motorola radio was going crazy with reports of weapons being used and people being chopped by meat cleavers. On arrival at the Daai Paai Dong, things were quiet apart from one overturned table and scattered stools and crockery. We asked the few people present what had happened, and they stated that the people involved in the fight had all run towards On Tak Road and On Shin Road. We all headed off in that direction, and while progressing along the route, we found discarded flip flops. They had hastily been left behind by people fleeing. At the top of the hill, we saw one young male in what we thought was a red T-Shirt. When we approached him, we soon noticed that he wasn't wearing a red T-shirt but was covered in blood that covered the whole of his naked upper torso.

On reaching his location, it became obvious that he had been the slowest person escaping and had been chopped several times with 3 or 4 chop wounds on his head that had split the skin down to the bone. The peeled back scalp looked just like a thick elastic band held tightly. While calling for an ambulance, he said that he and six of his friends went to the Daai Paai Dong and beat another group of about ten people to a table, and as a result, the other group were far from happy and upon leaving, they said they would be back. When the other group came back, they were armed with melon knives, meat cleavers and water pipes. They then chased the group he was in, and, being the slowest, he got chopped. All his other friends had escaped and he thought they were safe. As he finished explaining what had happened, I flagged down a taxi and got two of my officers to escort him to the United Christian Hospital, much to the disgust of the taxi driver, who was far from happy. I then set about searching all the adjacent roads but to no avail. I was thankful I was carrying a firearm!

Chapter 18

Social Life at Work & off duty from Sept 1983 to Jan 1984

Sports Events.

Kowloon Region Annual Sports Day 1983

During the autumn of 1983, Kwun Tong District took part in the Kowloon Sports Day and the DC KT DIST WBm had arranged [RJm], better known as Jim Jam, and I to take part. The only problem was that we were both on night shift. However, we were scheduled to do half a shift and sleep the second half so that we would be ready to run for 10:00hrs. We gave it our best attempt, but other Districts had arranged their runners to be off the whole night.

Telford Gardens Community Run

Telford Gardens was a residential estate on top of the Kowloon Bay MTR Station. Once a year, they organized factories and shops in the area to take part in a run around the gardens in teams of four, with each member running one lap of 800 meters. This was good fun as the MTR, Fire Services, shops such as Pizza Hut, and other community groups took part, all for charity. It was of note that the Pizza Hut situated in Telford Gardens was the biggest store they had in the world at that time. It had opened up two years earlier, with it being unknown whether cheese would be liked by the Hong Kong locals, but it was a roaring success.

Senior Officers Versus Junior Officers KT DIST Football Match.

This football match took place at the Tsui Ping Road football pitch and I, being a junior inspector, played for the junior officers. This was made up of a number of PCs and NCOs, all of whom played football for KT DIST. The senior officer's team had the DC KT DIST [WBm], the ADC Crime KT DIST [CSMm] and the DVC KT DIV [NIm], all of whom had been good sportsmen in their day.

The football game kicked off, and after about 15 minutes, it became obvious that the junior officers were holding back from full-on tackling the very senior officers. This meant by halftime, the junior officers were losing by 3 to 1. During the halftime break, I asked my team what was going on as we should be winning and that I fully expected to see an improvement in the second half.

On the resumption of the game, things continued as they had done in the first half, with halfhearted tackles on very senior officers. After one such tackle, I shouted to the players on my team that if the senior officers all put paper bags over their heads, would there be any more halfhearted tackles. Things improved a bit however, by the final whistle, the senior officers had prevailed by 4 goals to 2.

About a month after this football match, the DC KT DIST [WBm] saw me for my annual report. Upon going through my District Report File (DRF or Record of Service), he noted that my Course Director at PTS [GKLm], The Emperor, had described me as being introverted. However, after the senior versus junior football match, he believed I was outgoing and gregarious! He then informed me that as I had been earmarked to go to Special Duty Squad later on in 1984, I would undertake a three-month attachment to the District Intelligence Section KT DIST from the middle of January to the middle of April 1984. He also stated that the DVC NTK [KCCm] would be transferring out in early December 1983, and the new DVC NTK would be [RKm].

Chapter 19

Shift Duties in NTK Division

It goes without saying that the busiest shifts were B shift (Afternoon) and C Shift (Night), and the beat incidents attended described earlier cover these busy shifts comprehensively. Normally on a night shift, there would be a couple of roadblock duties to undertake, which were set up on roads leading to crime hit areas or residential sites where it was known that some of the residents were likely to be involved in crime. Vehicles approaching the roadblocks would be stopped, and the people in the vehicles would all have their Hong Kong Identity cards checked to see if they were wanted or if the card was false or not. Codes words such as 'Oscar' would be used if a person was wanted. This was done so that the person being checked didn't understand what was being said on the Motorola radio. Persons being checked who had a conviction but were not wanted would be indicated by the Chinese phrase "Yau Daai Mo Min", which literally meant "has record and no face". Vehicles would also be searched for contraband, such as drugs and offensive weapons. My favourite roadblock location was near the Kowloon Bay Temporary Housing area near Richland Gardens, which was normally held near dawn. Most of the time, the roadblock was quiet, but occasionally we would get a result. By the time the roadblock was being dismantled, dawn had broken and the sun would be high above Kowloon Peak in all its glory, indicating that the night shift was almost finished.

The A Shift (morning) was always the quietest, and you had time to yourself to catch up on checks such as notebooks and also undertake full inspections. File work could be undertaken and beat patrols could be taken leisurely. If things were quiet, I would leave the station at about 09:30hrs and patrol to Ting Yip Street, where there was a small café where I would get a coffee and a "Daan Tak" (egg/custard tart) for 15 minutes making sure to enter in my notebook that I was on my tea break and also advise RCCC K. I would then go to the Belgium Bank on Ngau Tau Kok Road near Garden Estate and sign their visiting book (VB Book), making sure to check who else had signed it, especially the beat PC and supervisory NCO. I would then go to the town area of NTK Division and patrol and, if necessary, undertake some stop and questions. I would also visit the general store situated on Yee On Street opposite the amusement games centre as the owner had two daughters who my patrol subunits PC had taken a liking or so I heard. On my first visit, both daughters were present, and after talking to their father to ask him how business was (Good for community relations), I was engaged in English conversation with his daughters called, Yvonne and Winnie. They told me they would like to practise their English and gave me their phone number to let them know when I would patrol the area as I could have 10 minutes of conversation. I agreed, and I noted that the younger sister, who was about 17 years old, was very attractive, albeit her smaller older sister spoke better English. I now realized why the beat PCs liked being assigned that beat, and it is of note that, on occasion, off duty, I would ring them to see how their English was going and give them a chance to practice. The younger daughter, about two years after I met her, came third in the Miss Hong Kong competition and started to work in the film industry. Normally after the town centre patrol, I would go to the industrial area and return to the police station, later undertaking mobile patrols or license checks. Everything I did was documented in my police notebook, which was referred to as a police officer's best friend. The more comprehensive it became, the better the friend it was. A Shift, being a 3rd or 2I/C of the patrol subunit, allowed me to get the cobwebs out of my head. Especially if I had a late night when a brisk patrol would work wonders in ensuring you were fully alert. I believe on one morning shift, I patrolled the entire boundary of NTK Division, which took me four hours and involved walking 12 kilometres as I had only had two hours of sleep. I had a break halfway around at the Sun Lee Neighbourhood Police Office (NPO), which was commanded by an officer who held the rank of Station Sergeant (SSGT) and was very experienced.

The shift system consisted of C, B, and A shifts in that order. Doing a six-day, 51-hour week meant that doing short shift changeovers from Saturday to Sunday shift was best, despite being tiring. This was because when you had your day off, you could take advantage of more time off duty. For example, if I finished B Shift (afternoon) on Saturday, I would finish at 22:45hrs and be back in at 06:45hrs on Sunday, only having had about 5 to 6 hours of sleep. The best shift to have a leave day would be at the end of A Shift as you could have a night on the town on both Friday and Saturday before reporting for night shift on Sunday. On some occasions, I would work 12 days, so I could have two days leave together, meaning I had the best part of three days off, but this was only occasionally. In such circumstances, using the example above, I would also have Sunday night off as well, but as stated, only exceptionally as old officers and family men were given priority to take a leave day at weekends.

My conditions of service saw me earn one day of casual leave per month as well as being given all 17 days of public holidays per year. Annual leave amounted to 36 days per year, but this could only be taken at the end of the tour contract as vacation leave unless there were compassionate reasons to ask for an advance of annual leave, such as illness or death in the family. Overtime work went on your time off card, but it had to be fully documented. Otherwise, it could be written off, especially when transferring posts.

Chapter 20

Activities Off Duty

Moving into Ho Man Tin Inspectorate Service Quarters saw me quickly obtain a car park space for my MGC and also make some improvements to the single inspectorate quarters I had been allocated. The first thing I did was purchase plates and cutlery from the SOGO Department store on Nathan Road in Yau Ma Tei, as there weren't any in the flat. The second thing I did was change the government bed for a king-size rattan bed that I found for sale on the quarters notice board. This was not a straightforward activity, as it was being sold by an ex-pat in the private building next door. He lived on the 8th floor however, he had already said it wouldn't fit in his building's lift or mine. I, therefore, borrowed some long rope from the emergency store from work and enlisted the help of [RJm] (aka Jim Jam) to lower it down eight floors from the balcony and then carry it to my building and haul it up five floors to the corridor just outside my flat. Other than that, it was a piece of cake. Bedding and a quilt were also obtained from SOGO and the Chinese Products store. I also bought towels, a lamp from Henry's Lampshades in Tsim Sha Tsui as well as some posters that I framed and hung on the walls. I also got my own telephone line which had International Direct Dialing (IDD), so there was no need to go to either Hermes House on Hong Kong Island or the one in Middle Road TST. I must admit that on occasion, after a late night out with plenty of beer, after I had satisfied my hunger with a tube of cheese crisps, I would make calls to my mother, who was very understanding, to say the least, knowing what state I was in. The length of these calls would be fully reflected in my bill, which on occasion raised my eyebrow!

Each floor at 19 Ho Man Tin Inspectorate Service Quarters (HISQ) had a Chinese amah that would tidy each flat on her floor on a daily basis as well as do all washing. This resulted in the clothes that I had bought at the Police Training School suddenly having two numbers permanently inked on the inside of the back of the collar or shirt, namely that of the number of my room at PTS and the flat number at HISQ.

As [RJm] worked on the same shift as me, but in Kwun Tong Division in the same Police District as Ngau Tau Kok Division, we often went out for drinks together as drinking in twos was more social, and the odds of meeting girls out on the town increased dramatically.

Chapter 21

House Warming and Meetings with SDKSf

I had a mini flat warming party to which [RJm] was invited. I also invited [SDKSf], the Cathay stewardess and her flatmate, a Chinese girl also from Malaysia. On the day of the flat warming party, I made some spaghetti bolognese with plenty of garlic just like my student days and made up a big jug of bloody Mary, also stashing plenty of beer in the fridge. Late afternoon, [SDKSf] rang me saying she might not come, but I persuaded her, saying I had already made the food, so she said she would make it but might have to leave early at about 20:00hrs. The house warming meal went well, and [RJm] brought some good music we listened to while chatting about everything and nothing. [SDKSf] let me know that she had been busy flying and was lucky she could make the meal, which she enjoyed very much, as she had a long-standing appointment with her colleague she had forgotten about when accepting my invitation. Indeed, I only saw her twice again over the next two months due to her flying schedule and my shift work. One time was in Rick's Café when she was at a gathering organized by my water polo-playing friend [NGm], who had an ongoing thing with [SDKSf's] Malaysian colleague [LCf]. The evening went well, however, after a few hours, [SDKSf] decided to leave as her friend

[LCf] wanted to stay, despite agreeing to go back with [SDKSf] that night. I noted she was quite upset and offered to give her a lift back to her flat at Chong Chien Court in To Kwa Wan. During the drive back, she was far from happy. However, she did agree to stay in touch, so as far as I was concerned, it was a successful night. On the second occasion that we met up, [RJm], a few others, and I ended up going swimming at the Police Sports and Recreation Club situated on Boundary Street. The day went really well and I was happy we were becoming closer. My lasting memory from that day was seeing her walk on the poolside looking exactly like Whitney Houston, in the picture on the rear of the album by the same name, only wearing a red one-piece swimsuit and not a white one like Whitney.

On our adventures on nights out, both [RJm] and I hooked up with the British Military nurses I had met as well as checked out all the nightspots, thoroughly enjoying ourselves, especially when meeting new females who we befriended.

During the autumn of 1983, [RSm] (aka Rob the dog), one of the medics (then a newly qualified doctor) I knew from water polo in Newcastle upon Tyne, informed me that his parents were coming out to Hong Kong. He, of course, gave them my contact details, and we met up for what was now the full tour of nightlife spots in Tsim Sha Tsui (TST) with the nurses from the British Military Hospital, as I knew his mother was also a doctor. The night went really well and ended in the early hours of the morning with his mother stating I had soon established a new group of friends in the short time I had been in Hong Kong. I stated that was what Hong Kong was all about; work hard and play hard.

Shortly after this, [RJm] and I met two Chinese girls in Rick's one night who also knew a few other police inspectors. One thing led to another as we all hooked up for about five weeks. This was totally unexpected, but initially, it was comfort and company that drew us all together. As time wore on, I felt a little trapped as shifts had to be changed to match their leave days, and I didn't see my other friends as much as I wanted. Things came to a head one Friday when I was contacted about going out on a Saturday night. I had arranged to do some sightseeing and sunbathing with my intake friend [MBm], his then-girlfriend also from our intake [YCWWf], as well as [RJm]. I was adamant that I would do my own thing Saturday night, as I didn't know what time I would finish and the phone call ended. About 30 minutes later, [RJm] rang me up and said we should meet the girls later on Saturday night. I asked him whether that was his idea, to which he said he had just received a phone call from the girl he was hooking up with, who made the suggestion. I then explained my phone call, and we both agreed it was like the song 'Making Plans for Nigel', only it was me who was being manipulated. I quickly made an executive decision and rang up the girl I knew to let her know that I knew what she had done and let her know that I would not be seeing her anymore. This was taken badly, but it was something that had to be done, as I didn't want to feel claustrophobic. In reviewing the last five weeks, it had been good fun while it lasted, but it was time to move on as it was obvious I was being set up as a marriage target. I had a life to live and wanted to do that under no misunderstanding. I did learn, however, at the time, the girl I knew was a bit tunnel-visioned, and despite having some comfort, company and lustful trysts, that wasn't everything. On one occasion, after an oral tryst, I had gone to the toilet only to return to bed, noting the girl had spit out what was in her mouth. After this was done, I was told that if 'it' was swallowed, she could get pregnant. I then had to explain the birds and the bees, such was the state of sex education in schools in Hong Kong at that time.

Letter Writing, Being Best Man, Trips and Nights Out

My letter writing continued after leaving PTS but not at the same rate as it had been while still a trainee. I often wrote to my last flatmate [ERf], my friends in Glasgow, [MIm] who had taken me sailing, as well as the Dilston Boys and [LIm's] girlfriend [RAf]. I remember in one of [RAf's] letters, [LIm], being a doctor, had suggested that she may have one ailment with her female orifice after symptoms appeared, but after she saw her doctor, she knew she had a cyst. This was operated on and removed, but she had to have a short back and side shave, which she informed me, was most embarrassing at the supermarket cash register waiting to pay, especially if she got an itch. This admission was typical of [RAf] as she was always down to earth and a good laugh to be around. In a later letter, she told me things had not worked out with [LIm], and she had moved to London, but we should stay in touch.

I had other letters off [MIm], he informed me he would be married in June 1984 to the girlfriend I had met before I left for Hong Kong, and he wanted me to be his best man. I, of course, agreed and thought going back to the UK 18 months after I had left for Hong Kong would be a good trip for all the right reasons. Just after leaving PTS, [WIm] the Navy submariner also asked me to be his best man with his wedding arranged for the summer of 1985, and again I agreed.

[LAf], one of the 3A girls doing the dispatch runs from Peking to Hong Kong that we had met at PTS also during the autumn of 1983, had invited [RJm], [SPm], and I to visit her in Peking during Easter, after which she would come back to Hong Kong with us on a bag run. We all agreed but knew we would have to jump a few hoops to go to the People's Republic of China as it was, at that time, a restricted country to travel to for obvious reasons.

Fitness-wise, I kept myself busy, and I noted at the RHKPF rugby club training I would be paired up with one of the first team players in joint training sessions just to ensure he did his press-ups and other exercises because of my high work ethic. In the sprints, I even made the speedster [SIm] run faster than he thought he had to, and he was a regular first-team and Colony player. At HISQs, I had also discovered the fitness trail that went up to Kings Park Rise to the Royal Observatory Weather Station. This fitness trail was good for uphill running, doing chins on pullup bars, and press-ups on parallel bars spread along the fitness trail. This was especially challenging during the summer months.

After leaving PTS, it took me a couple of weeks to get back to Rick's Café on the weekend, and when I did, I thoroughly enjoyed myself.

It was fast becoming a police watering hole, as was the bar Someplace Else in the Sheraton Hotel. During my visit back to Rick's Café, I was busy dancing with one female when I spotted the girl who had taken me to Happy Valley on the day I left PTS. It took a while before I could speak to her. However, not having met her the week before hadn't gone down well, and so I was ostracized a little bit by her and her friends. However, that didn't matter as Rick's Café was such a fun place.

During the autumn of 1983, Rick's Café was my number one watering hole where I would end up at the end of the night, if not the beginning. It had a great DJ [JSm], who is on RTHK Radio 3 today, and I also got to know all the staff and owners. I believe one of the inspectors who were at PTS the same time I was but was senior to me married one of the waiting on staff who was a beautiful girl. On some occasions, off-duty inspectors with their girlfriends were a good source of information, especially if you wanted to know how to say something in Cantonese. The music being played was very danceable, and it also had times when the ever-observant DJ played slow music very conveniently. One night when I was present, an announcement was made to clear the dance floor as a group of off-duty police were going to entertain the patrons to a well-rehearsed floorshow. In the group that all lived at the "Shang", a police quarter situated in a large house on Waterloo Road, Kowloon Tong, was [SMm], the ex-boyfriend of the interpreter [Mf] I had undertaken ballroom dancing classes with. The music started and the dance floor became populated with about six guys in dark suits and trilby hats. They were all strutting their stuff to the music dance scene from the film the "Blues Brothers", which was done very professionally, so much so that at the end of the dance, they got a rapturous round of applause. That night, the atmosphere in Rick's was electric, and I was glad I was present. A few weeks later, [HNm] did something similar but in the theme of a Viking Funeral, which went well until the person being carried, was hit by the overhead fan!

A few weeks after this, we all went to a party at the Shang, which had a reputation for being a wild place. In the lounge was a set of antlers on the wall from which girls who had stayed the night in one of the six inspector's rooms would be asked to hang their knickers up on the antlers. The amah who kept house by doing laundry and cooking was said to have seen every sight possible and was known to have warned her granddaughters never to go out with an ex-pat police inspector!

On arrival at the party, I noticed the music was good, but behaviour was very civil. Unfortunately, no one had told [HNm] from my intake this, as he turned up absolutely smashed out of his head, expecting an orgy was going to take place. During one dance to the music being played, [HNm] stripped off all his clothing, which initially was thought funny until he refused to put it back on. He was soon asked to leave and the group who were with him escorted him home to HISQs. [HNm] looked a bit like me, and I must admit that, on occasion, when entering bars in TST, I would get a few strange, if not hostile looks, only to find out [HNm] had been in the bar before me.

On a night out, the best place to go was a curry place at 11A in Chung King Mansions. The curry was very good, cheap and the beer was very cold. I remember one night being there when [SEPm] challenged me to a vindaloo eating competition after everyone else had opted out. The vindaloo curry went from very hot to volcanic, so much so that we both had tears running down our faces from the sweat on our foreheads. We agreed to call it a draw and then went on to the chapatti Frisbee challenge. This involved ordering many chapattis, and the winner was the one who could fling the chapatti frisbee across the whole width of Nathan Road through the restaurant window. This was thought extremely amusing, especially when the chapatti Frisbees hit people. How we never had a visit from the local police to investigate the chapattis falling from a height, I will never know!

Chapter 22

Scuttlebutt

Munich Bar Disturbance

Just before Christmas 1983, the Munich Bar Incident occurred. This bar was situated in Yau Yat Chuen, Kowloon and is more a local bar than an ex-pat bar. However, on this night, a group of mainly off-duty ex-pat inspectors made arrangements to meet at the bar, many of which worked nearby in Shek Kip Mei or Mong Kok.

A large number of beers were drunk, after which a mountain of a man [HWm], a huge rugby player, decided to try and dance with a group of local girls dancing by themselves on the small dance floor. Apparently, he was rejected at first but persisted with his efforts to have a dance when it became apparent that the girls had a large group of local males with them. Exception was made to the advances of [HWm], and a wrestling match started, which got out of hand, with tables being overturned and glasses being thrown.

The bar owners made a 999 call, at which time one of the police inspectors present [LBm] decided to return to his CID office in Shek Kip Mei Police Station as he was on duty. He did this so he could take over the case, which was being reported as Disorderly Conduct and Criminal Damage. The Kowloon West Emergency Unit turned up and escorted most of the males in the bar to Shek Kip Mei Police Station for enquiry and investigation. Eventually, the case was dropped, however, many of the off-duty inspectors had to compensate the bar owner for damage done and loss of business. Word of the incident got out, and those reported as being involved were hauled over the coals by their bosses. The CID Inspector who took over the case and had been present when the incident occurred did a good job of closing and curtailing the case without anyone finding out he had been present.

Berlin 1936 Inspection and Carnal Knowledge at Rick's Cafe

Another story doing the rounds in the Autumn of 1983 involved an Inspector working in Kwun Tong named [FSm] (Aka Steve Spanish) as he organized an inspection on a Sunday morning A shift duty as it was the time uniforms changed from summer greens to winter blacks. The inspection was more full-on than one held at PTS. However, as the subunit marched passed [FSm], who was on a raised platform, he gave a salute that would not have been out of place in Berlin in 1936. Apparently, on the same day when off-duty, he went to Rick's and met a more than willing girl who he is said to have had carnal knowledge of in the broom cupboard situated on the corridor leading to the toilets, which could be locked from the inside. I have lost count of the number of inspectors who checked this broom cupboard out on hearing this scuttlebutt!

Devoted Girlfriend Too Fussy

Just after Christmas, I had been in HISQs for about four months, and as previously stated, gossip soon spread. One piece of scuttlebutt involved an inspector [MNm], who had a beautiful local girlfriend. He often told his friends he wanted her taken off his hands as she was too demanding, especially when he drank too much. On

Christmas Eve, he went out with his best friend [FMm] together with his girlfriend, and upon returning to his quarters for more drinks, he passed out on his bed. Apparently, things turned very amorous with [FMm] and the girlfriend, and before he knew it, he had sex with his best friend's girlfriend. Nothing was said of this until about three weeks later when [MNm] again told the mates he was with that he wished someone would take his girlfriend off his hands. [FMm], having had too much to drink, told him what had happened on Christmas Eve, so [MNm] went to confront his girlfriend, who was in his quarters. His girlfriend obviously denied having had sex with [FMm] and, after further argument, grabbed a sharp knife to slash her wrists to prove her innocence which, after further argument, she did, resulting in her being hospitalized.

Coming and Going of Girlfriends from the UK

In fact, I lost count of the number of girlfriends who came out from the UK to visit their boyfriends at HISQs. Most visits went well, but one or two hit the rocks after a couple of weeks with the then ex-girlfriend asking for a couch to sleep on in another inspector's quarters, only to later shack up with the good-intentioned inspector.

File Tossing from Office and Raid on a Police Quarter.

Another story doing the rounds concerned a police inspector who had passed out from PTS a couple of years prior to my intake. This inspector [DPm] had his contract cut short when one day, in his office in Sham Shui Po Police Station, he threw all his files out of the office window. The last straw was that on one evening at the Kennedy Road Police Inspector Quarters, he went to visit an inspector who had just been successful in being posted to the Special Duties Unit (SDU Anti-Terrorist Unit). On arrival, he didn't ring the doorbell or knock at the door, but he tried to smash his way in, which was ultimately stopped and shushed up. Ultimately [DPm's] senior officers got to hear this, and his contract was cancelled.

Playing the Field and Its Consequences

Another story concerned an inspector living in the New World Apartments, which because of their proximity to nightspots in TST, plus their luxury setting, were always a big attraction when chatting up girls. This particular inspector [SCm] had met a young Chinese girl and soon developed a relationship with her, telling her she was the only one. This wasn't exactly the truth as [SCm] played the field, and on one occasion, his "only" girlfriend, who had spotted him with another girl, confronted him at his New World apartment. During the argument, the girl grabbed a knife and slashed him across his chest before she was disarmed. The relationship finished immediately, however, the girl's father was a serving SSGT who visited [SCm] and taught him a good lesson, which went unreported.

Sexual Experimentation and Deviance

Another piece of news that was doing the rounds concerned an inspector [GMm], who lived in a Police Station married quarters in Kowloon with one or two other inspectors. One night, he was successful in bringing a girl back to his quarters who was into all sorts of kinky stuff, which was what attracted [GMm] to the girl he had met in a club in Wan Chai. During the course of the evening, many strange things took place. However, what was doing the rounds was that [GMm] said he laid under the glass top coffee table while the kinky girl performed both of her body motions on top of the glass. I suppose that is what happens when you attend an all-boys public school and get to work in Hong Kong, which on occasions rivals Bangkok for strange happenings.

Playboy Police Inspector Who Looked Like George Michael

Another inspector [BTTm] who served in traffic was given the title "The Biz" due to his success with women. Mind you, he looked a little bit like George Michael and could speak excellent Cantonese. Having known him for about nine months, the last time I saw him, he looked pretty much washed up due to burning the candle at both ends or, as he would have you believe, he was all shagged out!

Sexual Gratification and Surprises.

Finally, the last piece of scuttlebutt concerns an inspector who lived at the Shang [SMEKm], who was at least two years senior to me. He became famous over the course of about two months, as he woke up all the Shang residents. This was because, during the course of doing doggy style with the girl he had brought back on Sunday morning after a Saturday night out, he slipped into the rear orifice unannounced, which resulted in a high pitch scream. Once the girls had left the Shang, he openly admitted what had happened had been more by design than error!

Part Three
1984

Chapter 23

Back to Police Work & the Events of January to April 1984

Dowman Road Race

The Dowman Road race, which is named after a long-retired officer, was held in early January 1984 on a Saturday. The course then went from High Island West Dam and ended up at the sports stadium next to Sai Kung Police station, covering a distance of 12 kilometres and close to 1500 to 2000 runners took part. That year, I managed a time of about 49 minutes together with [RJm], still had time for a full game of Rugby at the PSRC on Boundary Street for the Police Casuals as well as part of a game for the Police second team. The level of fitness for many inspectors was quite high. At the start of the Dowman, I saw a Chief Inspector [MCm] drink a can of beer, which apparently was a habit he had acquired when he served as an officer in the Black Watch.

Taxi Riots 1984

On Friday the 13th of January 1984, Hong Kong, Kowloon and New Territories taxis blocked Nathan Road as two days earlier, Alan Scott, the Government's Transport Secretary, increased taxi license fees from 4% to 90% of the cost of the taxi. Crowds of undesirable people descended on Yau Ma Tei and Mong Kok, leading to an atmosphere that indicated that trouble would break out.

That day was my day off, and I had met [SEPm] as arranged to go to Rick's Café, but on entering at about 22:00hrs, we noticed it was almost empty. The staff, upon seeing us, asked what we were doing out as all our mates had been called back to duty to their parent police station. We decided to leave and go back to our quarters so we could make a phone call to the police station to ascertain whether we needed to return to duty. On reaching the junction of Nathan Road and Mody Road, we saw masses of vehicles parked up either side of Nathan Road and dense crowds for as far as I could see looking back up to Austin Road. A litterbin was then thrown through a shop window near where we were, and an Emergency Unit Land Rover pulled up with the whole crew getting out, lashing out with their long batons to stop looting, after which they sped off. Immediately after this, more looting took place and [SEPm] asked whether we should take action. I stated we best not get involved in what would be another Custer's last stand and that we should leave and contact our own police stations. On arrival back at HISQs, we made our call back to our stations but were not required to return.

The next day when I started A Shift duty, the DVC NTK briefed me that we should monitor MTR stations in the division, as well as other transport interchanges, looking for people who had visible injuries. If we saw anyone fitting this description, we should arrest them and bring them back to the station for questioning as they may have been involved in the riot that occurred overnight. We eventually took a handful of people back to the station for questioning. During the course of the day, we heard that B and C shift duties on the day of the taxi riot had been doubled up for patrol. This allowed one of the officers to tune his Motorola beat radio to Kowloon West Division channels or the regional channel so they could monitor what was happening.

PTU HQ had been turned out, bringing with them their Saracen Armoured vehicles. The PTU COY Kowloon West had their platoons undertake sweeping of streets in Mong Kok, even using tear smoke to disperse the rioters. The Commissioner of Police, Ray Anning and his deputy, LI Kwan Ha, appeared on TV appealing for calmness, and if that didn't happen, full force would be used, advising everyone to stay at home. The Regional Commander Kowloon West [HGm] earned a new nickname of Chicken George, and his deputy, a giant of a man [RBm], took charge and was overheard on several occasions saying that he could smell fear when hard, harsh decisions had to be made.

The DO MK DIST and The Emperor CIP OPS MK DIST

The Duty Officer in Mong Kok Police Station on the night of the riot was [CJm] from my squad and intake at PTS. The Emperor, our squad instructor and course director, was the CIP in charge of Operations in Mong Kok, but on the night of the riot, he was the meet and greet person that arrested rioters saw when they first entered the station. He was very enthusiastic in this role, so much so that [CJm] had to instruct him not to be, as he had to make a note of the physical state the rioters were in when they were presented to him to make note of their arrest.

Chapter 24

Meetings with SDKSf January to May 1984

It is of note that the taxi riot trouble ended as quickly as it started, and Hong Kong returned to normal very quickly.

This is just as well as I had arranged to see [SDKSf] the following week after rugby training, and it would be the first time that we would go for a meal and a dance at Rick's Café. Unfortunately, during training, I ripped all the soft tissue in my left shoulder doing a training drill, which should have resulted in a roll forward rather than ploughing the rock-hard grass with my left shoulder. I was admitted to the Queen Elizabeth Hospital in Jordan, and I got [RJm] to ring [SDKSf] to inform her of what had happened. They both came to see me for about an hour as the hospital thought I had broken my collarbone and were detaining me overnight so that I could get an x-ray in the morning. Other than that, I felt pain every time I moved, and I was also not happy about not taking [SDKSf] on what would have been our first time out together.

During the next two months, Jim and I took [SDKSf] to see the movie Tootsie starring Dustin Hoffman, which had just been released. On another occasion, while shopping with [SDKSf], she grabbed hold of my hand to hold hands and walk together. I took this as a sign of getting closer and was more than shocked at the electric feeling I got when she held my hand. This would have been the first time in 18 months that I felt close to anyone I wanted to know better and felt relaxed as well as reassured.

Chapter 25

NTK Police Station after the Taxi Riots

On being released from hospital after my rugby training injury, I had my arm in a sling. However, the DVC NTK [RKm] insisted I report for duty, as I was right-handed. He even had me undertake traffic operations in plain clothes with my arm in a sling, which severely tested my sense of humour.

The other reason why he called me back to work was so that he could brief me to be his spy in KT DIST HQ when I undertook my three-month attachment to DIS KT DIST, which started in another two weeks. His main concern was that he believed that KT DIV was being given more PTU deployment than NTK. That was something he wanted to know about, despite the PTU tasking sheet for the month being sent to Divisional Commanders (DVC), who in turn passed it down to subunits to prepare deployment if it hadn't already been done by DIS KT.

Letter Writing and Arrangements.

I continued my letter writing to my friends in the UK and also Peking. This was done mainly to tell them that I was arranging a visit to Peking at Easter as well as being best man at a wedding in June in Yorkshire for an old flatmate.

My last flatmate in the UK [ERf] seemed very glad that I was coming back to the UK for a visit as we had been in constant contact. Indeed, I had arranged for a relative I had working in Dhahran, Saudi Arabia, to send 100 pirated cassette tapes as it was her 21st Birthday in January 1984, and she was over the moon with the present, bearing in mind the cost of tapes at that time in the UK.

In respect of [SDKSf], I kept in contact by phone as our schedules kept us apart. I did make arrangements for her to visit my relatives in Dhahran when she had a Bombay flight as on that flight, she also had to operate a Dhahran flight, which meant she had a one-night layover. I offered to put her in contact with my friend [KMf] in Heidelberg while she did a Frankfurt flight, but she was too busy to take up the offer.

Chapter 26

Standard Two Inspectorate Professional Exams

Standard Two Exams are held in January and July every year, and Standard Three Exams are held in April and October each year. Four papers had to be passed, and all Standard Two papers had to be passed before Standard Three papers could be taken. If you wanted to come back for a second tour, all Standard Two papers had to be passed before the end of the first tour.

I took one paper that January, which I ended up passing, but it was interesting to see during the exam how many people walked out because they hadn't revised enough due to not allocating enough time or being in busy postings.

I heard of one inspector [HWm] when answering what the correct procedure for dealing with mendicants (street sleepers) was. He put down that they should be picked up in the mobile patrol car, taken to the next division near the police station and given a rice box telling the mendicant that it had been bought by the report room staff who would buy him more. Thereafter, return to your own division and close the report as being actioned no one found! He scored no marks for this answer but got quite a few laughs.

Chapter 27

Attachment to DIS KT DIST January-April 1984

Exactly four months after I passed out of PTS, I undertook a three-month attachment to the District Intelligence Section Kwun Tong District. The attachment was plain-clothed duty, and it would give me experience in handling police intelligence, compiling monthly crime reports and undertaking crime casework. The work was extremely interesting because I got to know all the areas that triads in the district operated in, as well as some of the higher office bearers. Triads ran the local fish market, and the Assistant District Commander Crime [CSMm] had the legal power to command the head of the triad to attend for an interview, which he did.

While I was in the unit, there was an open fire case in Yue Man Square just outside the Hong Kong and Shanghai Bank that I had missed being in the same location by 10 minutes. I was heavily involved in the follow-up searches and raids by applying for search warrants and the likes from Kwun Tong Court, which were required like yesterday.

Illegal bookmaking and other intelligence were also actioned. These were normally done on Operation Levington, which was operations in that crime units actioned intelligence they had gathered or undertook license checks at premises frequented by criminals and triads.

Most of the illegal bookmaking operations, at one time or another, ended up in the Lam Tin hillside wooden hut squatter area. Here, the addresses were not neatly laid out but scattered, and illegal bookmakers would lay hundreds of yards of telephone extension wires from the actual, registered address for the use of bookmaking to the premise where the illegal bookmaking on horse racing days took place. At that time, as there were no mobile phones, the extension wires had to be found and then followed until the bookmaking premise was located. The OC [IDm], no matter what the weather was like, often gave me, being the youngest in DIS, the job of following the extension wire. The CIP in charge of the unit was [CVm], whose main hobby was lawn bowling, and he answered to the ADC Crime [CSMm].

My average day saw me go through all the district's crime messages and ascertain whether the descriptions of culprits fitted other offences or indeed whether the description of the culprit was unique by looks or by tattoos, etc. The beats which had the greatest number of crimes occur were noted as well as the timings so that at the end of the month, I could produce an intelligence report that could be digested by uniformed officers and also used to bid for Regional Police Tactical Unit resources.

Most days, during lunch hour, we would go to a nearby restaurant or the Disciplined Services Recreation Club at Kai Tak. In the afternoon, there was always a coffee break, and this was served with egg tarts. The hours of duty were 09:00hrs to about 18:00hrs, six days a week unless we were involved in an operation that covered the whole of B Shift and part of C Shift.

In terms of socializing, the hours of duty were better than being on A shift. I often ended up going out mid-week, getting home at about 02:00hrs, having 5 hours of sleep and then heading off to work. After one very late night, which saw me have a curry, I got into work with next to no sleep and about mid-morning dropped a silent but deadly fart, which I knew immediately I shouldn't have done because it had a ghastly smell. This resulted in the open office of about eight officers having to evacuate, and the OC DIS [IDm] made me later buy afternoon tea to quell an uprising!

Chapter 28

Inspectors Continuation Training Mid Way Through DIS KT Attachment

Inspectors Continuation Training had parts one and two and lasted for a week between 09:00hrs to 17:00hrs. During part one, each inspector had to compile a Complaint Against Police Report (CAPO), a death report, a record of service entry, an annual report, and a statement, so it was a full-on course. By the time the course came around, many officers had already compiled many of the tasks that had to be accomplished.

The hours meant that a lot of drinking could be undertaken, and the state some people were in when they came in at 09:00hrs usually indicated what time they had gone to bed, if at all! On my course, I met [RJm] one night to have a quick drink, but we both ended up in Rick's Café. We had a table to ourselves but halfway through the evening, the manager knowing us, asked if two girls could also sit at the table. The girls were from Australia, we soon got talking, and it turned out they were backpacking around Asia and staying at the YMCA on Salisbury Road. We had quite a few drinks, and the girls asked if we had tried Bundaberg Rum, which was made in Australia, and we both said we hadn't. They then said we should try some and that they had a bottle in their room at the YMCA. We left to go there at about 01:00hrs, but on arrival, all doors were closed as the YMCA had a curfew for quests in those days. We immediately offered them to come back to our quarters, and they could have the couch to sleep on.

On arrival at my flat, I made some tea, and while drinking it, the smaller of the two girls fell asleep on my couch. On finishing the tea, [RJm] said he was going to his flat, and the taller and slimmer girl went off to his place for the night after I said I would be up at 07:00hrs to get ready for a course I was attending. On locking my door and getting a blanket for the girl asleep on my couch, I put it over her, at which point she woke up and grabbed my hand and took me to the bedroom for a lustful tryst. In the morning, I was late getting up, so I quickly got dressed and took the girl who had spent the night with me to [RJm] flat, dropping her off as I rushed to get a taxi. Mid-morning, we had a tea break, but all I could smell was ammonia on my moustache, so I quickly went to the bathroom to wash my face, as I hadn't had time for a shower that morning. That night I got home and was well tired, so after a shower at about 21:00hrs, I pulled the sheets back to get into my bed and saw a brown skid mark on the side of the bed where the girl had woken up that same morning. I quickly changed the bedsheets and telephoned [RJm], who couldn't believe what I told him had happened. He did admit that the girl who went back to his place slept on his couch with no monkey business occurring.

The Saturday after the Inspectors Continuation Training Course had finished, I had arranged to see [RJm] for a drink and said I would call round at his flat before we went out. Jim let me into his flat and seemed a bit sheepish, at which point I detected a very strange smell similar to fish in the whole flat. Just then, a girl came out of [RJm's] bedroom, and as I asked [RJm] what that smell was, the girl immediately answered in perfect English that it was the smell of love. She kissed [RJm] and left. After she left, I started to gag, and we opened all the windows in the flat to get some fresh air. I told [RJm] that was the first time I had ever experienced halitosis of the female nether region, and [RJm] refused to tell me where he had met her but emphasized that he wouldn't be meeting her again. I took the piss out of him the whole night as he did me about the skid marks I had found on my sheets earlier in the week.

Chapter 29

Return To DIS KT DIST

One day after my return to DIS KT DIST, word went around the station that the Kowloon Regional Special Duty Squad had arrested a case of a drugs divan and had made about 16 arrests, including the operator. The Divan (Drugs smoking premise) was on the top floor of a building just off Yue Man Square, and rumour had spread out in the station that film cameras had been seized and that the operator had stated he could not be arrested as he worked for a law enforcement agency. Later on that day, the rumour had changed substantially as it was stated that the Divan had been set up by the Independent Commission Against Corruption (ICAC) to see if any officers attached to Kwun Tong Police District would approach it and demand protection money. Just prior to hearing this, I had been in the cells seeing to a prisoner arrested by DIS KT DIST when I took the time to walk slowly past the so-called "ICAC" enforcement officer in his cell who ran the drugs Divan to see what he looked like.

The ICAC officer was later released, but only after he had complained that an ex-pat (European) officer had slowly walked past his cell when he was being detained. I know this because another European officer working in CID KT Division [DMm] was on duty at the same time and had been blamed by someone for being that officer. He had told me about the accusation, as he knew I was also on duty at the time. I then saw my immediate commanding officer and explained what I had been told and said I had been in the cells seeing to one of my DIS KT prisoners.

This case showed that breaking the law by running a drugs divan was in those days a tactic adopted to try and arrest police officers by another law enforcement agency. I found this to be absolutely incredible!

The rest of the attachment to DIS KT DIST went on as normal. However, during my remaining five weeks, I applied for leave to go to Peking at Easter and also to the UK in June to be best man at [MIm's] wedding in Skipton, Yorkshire.

The application for leave to go to Peking took some time, as it needed special permission, as China was a communist country. The permission was granted eventually, as my address while in Peking would be the British Embassy Quarters, which obviously was very acceptable. Before long, my attachment came to an end, and I got a very good report. I was also told my next posting after my leave to Peking would be Patrol Subunit Commander 1 NTK Division, the subunit I had originally been posted to on leaving PTS.

Chapter 30

Trip To Peking (Beijing) Easter 1984

The trip to Peking by [RJm], [SEPm], and I was on mainly because of our official invitation and our residential address while staying there for a week. [LAf] one of the 3 A's we had met at a hash house harrier event while still at PTS. She would be our official host, and she stated that her flat could accommodate all three of us easily.

Our flight was on British Airways, leaving on Thursday the 19th of April 1984 and returning a week later on the 26th of April. This allowed us to make the most of the Easter weekend public holidays. Prior to catching the flight, [LAf] had given us a shopping list, which included one tyre for her car, lots and lots of cheese and other items she couldn't get in Peking. She stated that at that time, Peking was designated as a hardship posting mainly because of the inability to buy or purchase western goods in the country.

On arrival, [LAf] picked us up in her car at the airport and gladly took the receipt of the items she had asked us to bring with us. We immediately went to her quarters, which was nowhere near the British Embassy and quickly unpacked in her fourth-floor flat. The roads were empty, apart from a few private cars and military vehicles. Her building and those quarters of other embassies were in a building, the tallest of which was about eight stories tall and, at that time, were considered some of the tallest buildings in Peking.

After unpacking, we headed off to the pub situated in the British Embassy called the Bell Inn. The night was long, and the bar was very busy as the next day was Good Friday. The beer in the bar was European and British, and while speaking to other staff, they warned me off drinking the local Peking beer as it was green in colour and tasty ghastly, or so they said. It also gave a very nasty headache if hungover. At the end of the night, I do remember the toilets being full and, being a bit drunk, I helped myself to urinate on the wall of the British Embassy, hidden behind a bush.

The next morning, [LAf] woke us up early, despite us all having a hangover. She explained that we would have an action-packed week. This consisted of visits to the Great Wall with her friend who worked for the New Zealand Embassy, as well as setting a hash house harrier course on the grounds of the Fragrant Springs Hotel. We would also go to see the Forbidden Palace, the Summer Palace, as well as have meals at the Tsing Quo Hotel and afternoon tea at the Great Wall Hotel, where I found the very tall Shandong waitress, who spoke impeccable English, very attractive. On some trips, we would use her car, and we would take an embassy coaster vehicle to the Great Wall, which would include the Ming and Ching Tombs. While she was at work, we could cycle around Peking and see the official gift shops and Hutongs around Tiananmen Square.

Friday saw us sightseeing around Peking, and after parking the car, we all hired bicycles and went for a long ride to ensure we had our bearings, which I must say did wonders for the hangovers we all had. I believe we had lunch in the Peking Hotel, which was then on the corner of Tiananmen Square, later stopping to get coffee and cake at the French restaurant Maxims, which I think had just opened up. In the evening, we went for a traditional Peking dinner at the small Tsing Quo Hotel, which was washed down by plenty of the local Peking beer. The colour of the beer was indeed green, but after the first bottle went down, the taste didn't matter.

Saturday saw us go up to the Summer Palace for sightseeing which took a long time, as the site is huge. We also hired a rowing boat, and once in the middle of the lake, [SEPm] took his shirt off when it was his turn to row because the weather was quite hot. This caused all other rowing boats to head for our position just to see [SEPm's] hairy chest, which is a rarity in China. We tried to communicate with the other boats, but I don't know if they understood us telling them that [SEPm's] nickname was Daai Sing Sing or gorilla. [SEPm] eventually put his shirt back on, which ended the free show for the locals.

On Sunday, we went to the Frequent Springs Hotel and met the Hash House Harrier (HHH) route setter. He explained the course would be a long and hilly one, and we could help him set the course, which would take about one hour. In helping set up the course, we were astounded that the course setter didn't mark the end of the false trails because this was done in Hong Kong and ensured there were no arguments.

That afternoon, the people doing the HHH course arrived, and they were nearly all men. The course took much longer than normal, and when everyone had finished, there was much talk about the unmarked false trails. [RJm], [SEPm], and I seemed to get the blame and criticism, which we took well over the course of a few beers. Just as we stated we had to go to attend a dinner, the HHH runners informed us that we hadn't done the initiation ceremony. We stated we didn't have time and started to walk away with many of the runners stating we couldn't do that, but we insisted on leaving and said we would probably meet up later in the week.

On reaching [LAf's] car, we decided to get bottles of beer out of the boot, take the tops off and shake the bottles to run back to the runners and spray them. [LAf] would have the car ready for our escape and warmed up to being appointed the getaway driver! On rushing round to spray the runners, we noticed their wives had joined them, but we sprayed them nonetheless and legged it off to the getaway car to a hail of protest!

The next day, we gathered at the New Zealand Embassy as we were going on their coaster bus. We had to bring our passports as some of the sites we would visit were in restricted areas. The trip went well, but the mother of [LAf's] friend who worked at the New Zealand Embassy was a non-stop talker, and it was rumoured that she had a good chance of being a prime minister. On reaching the Great Wall, we walked a section, which was quite steep, and much to our amusement, one of us farted while the female politician was going on about something, which she didn't find amusing! At the end of the trip, there was another boozy dinner, and the next day, [LAf] went back to work. After waking up late, we went cycling around Peking and Tiananmen Square with me in my Union Jack running shorts, which attracted many looks. In the evening, arriving back at [LAf's] quarters, she informed us that her being quiet at work had been noticed, which she said was down to a headache rather than a hangover. She didn't need much persuasion on having the hair of the dog!

That night, we went out for drinks at the flat of one of the HHHs, so we had a few cocktails before we left. On arrival at the 8th floor flat, we were supplied with plenty of beer, and when we were nearly drunk, the HHH runners who were present informed us that we had to do the initiation ceremony we had missed after the hash run. Each of us was given a position, with [SEPm] being first, me second and [RJm] third. An actual bedpan was produced, which we were informed held two and half-pints of beer, and it was handed to [SEPm]. I tried to tell [SEPm] that the beer looked flat and may have been tampered with, but being competitive, he didn't listen but downed the whole lot with some difficulty. I was next and insisted on seeing the beer poured into the bedpan, after which I downed it. [RJm] was next, and he, like me, watched the beer being poured before drinking most of it and showering in the rest. About 10 minutes after this, [SEPm] didn't look well and headed for the balcony where he vomited over the railing onto the cars of the HHH runners present, which I thought, was poetic justice. After that, we proceeded home, and as the next day was the last in Peking before our flight on Thursday, we had a well-earned lie-in, after which we packed and went to get some last-minute gifts. It was early to bed that night as we had to be at the airport by midday.

At Peking Airport, [LAf], who knew the British Airways manager got us all upgraded to business class, which was great news. Also, in business class was a group of computer nerds who were quite loud when talking. We engaged in conversation, and soon, a rivalry developed, which during the serving of our meals resulted in bread rolls being thrown at each other, much to the disgust of the cabin staff, who couldn't do much to stop the missiles. On arrival in Hong Kong, [LAf] went to the Hong Kong Hotel, and we went to our quarters, agreeing to meet in Rick's Café at 22:00hrs. It was noted on the return trip back that we all needed two small bottles of gin and tonic as opposed to only one being needed on the trip up to Peking. On meeting [LAf] at Rick's, we saw the British Airways cabin crew, who recognized us calling and then shouted at us that "the animals are here!" when they saw us, much to our amusement.

Chapter 31

Peking Photograph Development

A couple of weeks after I got back from Peking, after [LAf] had left, I went to collect my photographs from a developer I normally used in Ocean Terminal TST. On arrival, the developer said he had bad news as not all the photographs had developed very well. Upon checking, I reckoned up to 90% of the developed photographs, as well as the negatives, had white blotches on them. I was far from happy, but there was little I could do, so I took possession of the photos and accepted a slight discount.

I decided to get a taxi from outside the Hong Kong Hotel, and as I arrived, a female with bags was getting out of a taxi, but the taxi driver was giving her grief in Cantonese for not having small change to pay the fare. I immediately stepped in and spoke to the taxi driver in Cantonese, advising him that it was he who was wrong, as he had no change, not the female. I then spoke to the female and explained the problem, and she said she had just arrived from Australia and only had $100 notes. I told her I needed the taxi and would get her bill and asked if she had nothing better to do, perhaps, I could buy her a drink some time during her stay in Hong Kong. She said that would be good and tore off one of her baggage labels, which had her name on it. I said I would give her a ring after she said she was staying at the Hong Kong Hotel, later adding she was in town for four days.

I took the taxi back to HISQs and, after arriving back at my flat, I waited an hour and gave her a ring. She was in her room and was up for a tour around the nightlife spots. I met her at 21:00hrs and gave her the normal visitor's tour, and we ended up in Rick's Café having something to eat and having a dance. When Rick's closed, she invited me back to her room for a nightcap, which later turned into a lustful tryst.

Upon leaving in the morning, I said I would meet her for dinner that night after I finished work. That evening, we had dinner, but the novelty had worn off, and at the end of dinner, I stated I had an early start and left to make my way home. I couldn't help but notice she had a bit of a bulbous bottom which explained why I had slipped out of the lustful tryst on a couple of occasions the night before.

Chapter 32

Patrol Sub Unit Commander NTK Division

On return to my division, I was made the Patrol Subunit Commander (PSUC), which I did for two months before going back to the UK for [MIm's] wedding on the 30th of June 1984, leaving Hong Kong on the 8th of June.

The DVC NTK [RKm] briefed me that he only expected me to travel directly to the UK and directly back, which I said I would do as far as possible. I said this as the cheapest airline I could find was Air Lanka, which had stops in Bangkok, Colombo, and then London. I, therefore, planned to have a week in Sri Lanka and, while in the UK, see my friends there and in Heidelberg in Germany. The trip would be action-packed, but I promised [MIm] I would be in Yorkshire the whole week before the wedding and leave the day after to fly back to Hong Kong.

Life as a PSUC meant I was in charge of everything for the subunit, and that involved a great deal of paperwork. This included annual reports, CAPO complaints and other file investigations, especially concerning noise, illegal parking and a whole host of other topics. The eight and a half hour shifts passed very quickly, and there was never a dull moment.

It was during this period that [RJm] and I gave much thought to leaving HISQ and finding another quarter we could share, away from all the gossip and unwanted knocks on the door.

Life still went on fitness-wise, and a few of us decided to learn how to scuba dive, initially with the Police Sub Aqua Club. This club was predominantly Chinese run, and normally ex-pats joined other private clubs. However, we persisted. The swimming test that was held at the Disciplined Services Recreation Club pool, even for me, being a good swimmer, was tough! It involved swimming half the whole length of the pool with head down. On reaching the halfway mark, you were allowed to take a breath of air, after which you dived down to the bottom of the pool, put your weight belt on, flippers and facemask, which you had to clear, and then surface to clear the snorkel. Putting on the weight belt and flippers meant that the body bent double, which caused some of the saved air to be blown out. I must admit I didn't see the locals do this, and when I achieved it, the instructors looked surprised. Another test was out in the open waters of Sai Kung, where you had to descend 30 feet down a rope to a diver sitting on the sea bottom. Going down the line, you had to clear your ears several times, and for the last 10 feet of line, there was practically almost zero vision. Eventually, we joined a private club. However, I only finished half the course as I was sent to SDS KT DIST in September 1984.

Chapter 33

Visit of SDKSf at my Workplace

The position of PSUC allowed me to task all the subunit personnel, and on one B Shift, this allowed me to have [SDKSf] visit me at work, where I showed her what my job entailed and also went on patrol, showing her a part of Hong Kong she hadn't seen before. By that time, we were getting along quite well, and everything seemed good, albeit I still knew she had a good friend in Germany.

Rick's Café was still visited with and without [RJm], and we had some really good nights. On one particular night, when I was on A Shift, I went to Rick's, and while being sat by myself, the manager asked if I minded if three other people sat at my table, to which I replied that I didn't mind. The three people were Chinese, and there was a boyfriend and girlfriend, and the girlfriend's friend, who was quite good looking. We talked some but danced more, and when Rick's closed, I asked if they wanted to come back to my place, as it was not far away, for a coffee or tea. They all came back, so I made drinks, after which the boyfriend and girlfriend left as the other girl wanted to stay longer. The boyfriend, upon leaving, asked me if I had protection, to which I said I did and then left. The girl then indicated she wanted to use the bathroom and I said, "go ahead", and I just lazed and almost fell asleep on the sofa. After a while, the girl came out of the toilet dressed in her nightie, looking like a Christmas present that needed to be unwrapped, so we retired to the bedroom for a lustful tryst. I was up at 05:30hrs and quickly got a shower, after which I woke the girl up and said I could drop her off as I was getting a taxi. I told her I was working but would be off the next day so she could ring me if she wanted, and I gave her my number.

Chapter 34

Unexpected Call and Visit by SDKSf

The day at work went well, but I was tired. In the evening, [SDKSf] rang me at home and asked if she could come round, and I, of course, said yes. I quickly made some dinner and we ate when she arrived. She was on standby the next morning and was in two minds to go home, but as things between us were going well, she decided to inform crew control to ring my number if she was called. As I said, we were getting on really well, but I still had not had the conversation with her about her German friend and us. We ended up in the bedroom, but it was only a platonic tryst as I was tired and thought we could speak in the morning as I had a day off, and I was feeling a little guilty about the night before.

The next morning the phone rang but I didn't hear it, [SDKSf] did, so she answered the call as she was on standby. She came back into the bedroom and told me the call was for me. I answered the call and noted it was the girl from the previous night who was asking me who the girl was. However, I didn't have an answer and she hung up. Eventually, [SDKSf] and I got up and I made breakfast, fully intending to speak to her, but my next-door neighbour knocked on the door, insisting on having a cup of tea. While he had his tea, he had the odd leer at [SDKSf], and after he left, it was only a short time later that [SDKSf] also left, and I still had not had that talk. They say things happen in threes, and they certainly did that night and morning, and I couldn't help but feel I had waited too long for that perfect opportunity to express how I felt or what I wanted. I had certainly played my cards wrong, and I didn't feel good. I wondered how I would put things right, if ever!

Chapter 35

Sighting of The Emperor, Ho Man Tin

One afternoon I was walking down Homantin Hill Road heading for the Waterloo MTR Station to go on B Shift duty. On the way downhill, I saw The Emperor coming uphill. When he saw me he had a smug look on his face knowing that I would have to acknowledge him and call him Sir! The nearer I got to him, the bigger the smug look on his face, so I walked past him as though he wasn't even there, which I knew would piss him off almost as much as it would make me feel better. That was the first sighting of The Emperor since leaving PTS other than what I had heard of him on the night of the taxi riots when he was in Mong Kok Police Station and had to be spoken to by the Duty Officer, who was [CJm].

Chapter 36

Visit of Son and Cousin of my Mother's Friend

One week while on C Shift (Night shift), I went to Kai Tak Airport to pick up [GLm] and his cousin as they were visiting me for five days to see Manchester United play against Bulova. On meeting them, I took them to Ngau Tau Kok Police Station, got changed into uniform, and showed them around the station.

On visiting the cells, which were empty, the cousin of [GLm] said it was the first time that he had been in a police station and hadn't been under arrest. The two of them were on their way back from Australia to the UK after having three weeks off work to visit a relative.

After the night shift briefing, I took them both on patrol for three hours to give them a feeling of being in the program 'The Hong Kong Beat', which they both had seen. One of the last places we visited before I drove them back to my flat in HISQs was the Kai Tak Vietnamese Refugee open camp at Kai Tak. They found it to be an amazing place and noted all the human turds scattered about the place, with one of them pointing out an exceptionally large one that if he had done it, he would've put a flag in it. On checking the camp's police post, I found the PC asleep. The cousin of [GLm] took [GLm] to one side while I issued a stiff bollocking to the PC as he understood the seriousness of the incident being in the British Army himself.

On arrival at HISQs, I gave both of them a key to the flat with the address in English and Chinese and said I would see them in the morning after I finished work. In seeing them later, I pointed out all the tourist spots and bar areas, especially the Wan Chai bars, as I would be working until I had my leave day for the Manchester United game.

The next day when I came home, I found them on my doorstep having just arrived themselves as they had lost the keys to the flat. That day I got new keys and put them on a piece of string they could hang around their neck. The following day when I got home, they told me they had got really drunk in Wan Chai and took asleep on the kerb until the US Navy shore patrol came along and woke them up to take them back to their ship until they explained they were British and not American.

The day of the match arrived, and we went for lots of pints before the game. I distinctly remember on the way to the game, in a taxi, I had to relieve myself in an empty beer bottle in the back of the taxi. This was easier said than done with five people in the car taking bets I couldn't piss straight. Manchester United won the match, after which we dashed to Kai Tak Airport and poured them onto the plane. It had been a tiring week but thank god I had a king-size bed and was on night shift.

Chapter 37

Three Weeks for Wedding in the UK June 1984

On leaving Hong Kong on Friday 8th of June, my DVC NTK [RKm] had been assured I would stick to the itinerary of Hong Kong-UK-Hong Kong as best as I could. However, I had decided to visit Sri Lanka for a week leaving for London on the 16th of June. I had told [RJm] my plans and asked him not to say anything and that I would send him a postcard or two.

On checking in at the Air Lanka counter at Kai Tak Airport, I was questioned about my ticket, but nevertheless, I was allowed to board the plane. The trip to Colombo was via Bangkok, and it was in Thailand that the flight was delayed for two to three hours. This meant that on arrival in Colombo, we were given accommodation in a colonial hotel by the docks, which I enjoyed immensely as it had a balcony, and the rooms had high ceilings with a fan and air conditioning.

In the morning, I got up and had tea on the balcony looking at the map of Sri Lanka I had taken from the airport and also my Lonely Planet reference book. The captain of the Air Lanka aircraft that flew us from Bangkok to Colombo named Capt. C.K.Pathy gave me a card for a beach resort he ran in Trincomalee called the Florina

Inn when he bid me well on leaving the aircraft. I decided to go there for a couple of days and get some sun as it was right on the beach. I had been warned off going to Jaffna because of the troubles between the LTTE (Liberation Tigers of Tamil Eelam, known as Tamil Tigers) and the mainly Sinhalese dominated Sri Lankan Government. I was told Trincomalee and south of there would be good, and that is what I believed until later in the trip.

The two days in Trincomalee were great as I got plenty of sun and managed to read a couple of books. It was very relaxing when compared to Hong Kong, and in fact, it was far too relaxing and far less hectic. In the morning, I used to walk the beach, watch the school kids walking to school, and watch the Asian Windsurfing Competition out in the bay. The food was great, not to mention it was a fraction of the cost of food in Hong Kong. I was backpacking and had got to Trincomalee from Colombo by bus.

Before leaving Sri Lanka, I decided I had time to see Sigiriya and do a mini safari. I got to Sigiriya in the evening and found somewhere to stay, intending to visit the rock fortress the next day. On getting to the fort, I was glad I had left my backpack at my hotel as the ladders and walkways up the 180 meters of rock were very rickety, and obviously, there was no health and safety in those days. Once on top, I latched on to a German couple, and we all followed a guide who explained the fortress to us. Suddenly on taking some water, two rough-looking middle-aged Sri Lankan men approached me and asked me where I had come from, so I said Hong Kong. They asked whether I was from Israel and I said no, after which they asked about my khaki shorts and my very short haircut, insinuating that I was in the military and training the Sri Lankan Police. This was starting to get nasty, and I could see myself being thrown off the rock. I luckily had my UK passport and Hong Kong Identity Card, even speaking some Cantonese. Eventually, I convinced them, but things were getting hairy for a while despite the help of the German couple and guide.

I later descended to ground level, well after the two guys had left and made a mental note to be more observant of my surroundings.

This I did and noted that any police patrols were heavily armed, and police stations and checkpoints were sandbagged.

The safari went well, and washing the elephants was great fun. Soon it was time to head for Colombo, and the airport and all went smooth when checking in. On taxiing down the runway, there was a terrible noise of metal scraping, and the aircraft returned to the terminal where we were allocated another aircraft. The delay lasted four hours. This was annoying as [RAf] would be picking me up from Gatwick and there was no way I could contact her. The flight went well and landed 3 hours late.

On reaching the arrivals, [RAf] was there with a friend to meet me and we hugged and said hello, as it had been some 18 months since I last met her. I had arranged to stay with her and her new boyfriend for two days, while I arranged transport. On the first night, they were having a party. I got very drunk and, after a shower, fell into a deep sleep, having to be carried to the bed allocated to me. The next day, I rented a CX 500 motorcycle for two weeks, and on the following day, I was off to Skipton, where I stayed for two days. I gave [MIm] my schedule, and he was okay as long as I was back for the week of the wedding. He understood I wanted to see some other friends and family as that was natural. I next went to Newcastle and stayed with [LIm], we all went out for a meal, and I asked [ERf] to join us, giving her a huge cuddle on first meeting, which she reciprocated. After the meal, we all went back to [LIm's] house, and at around midnight, I called [ERf] a taxi. After she left, the lads said she could have stayed as that was what they thought she wanted to do. Oh well, live and learn!

I then went to Glasgow cross country but got a puncture in my rear tyre near East Kilbride, so I had the bike towed to a repair garage and was picked up by my very close friends [WKf] and [WNm]. We had a great meal and a few drinks, and the next day, I was back off to get my bike. The repair shop said a nail had gone through the side of the wall of the tyre. Therefore, a new tyre was needed. I rang the London rental garage, and they said they would pay for it. I then went to Manchester to see my mother and my brother, and I also saw my aunt and uncle, who had just come back from South Africa after 16 years. I stayed in Manchester for three days, even having time to see an old girlfriend [SEPf], where I stayed for a night. She later wrote me a letter that I received on my return to Hong Kong. I then took the bike back to London before going to Heidelberg to see [KMf]. It was of note that the bike shop did pay me for the tyre, minus the VAT they wouldn't have paid being trade.

I enjoyed three days in Heidelberg, albeit [KMf] wasn't at her best because of the pressures of her course. We had a wonderful time nonetheless, and I picked up a poster of Heidelberg for my wall back in my quarters.

I then headed for Skipton and spent the entire last week going through service practice, speeches, and even getting myself decent clothing for the wedding, so to speak. The wedding went really well, and my best man's speech was taken quite well, especially when I informed the guests that they were a captive audience, much like my customers in Hong Kong, so they better listen.

The day after the wedding, I went to Gatwick by train and took a flight to Geneva to catch my Air Lanka flight. This had two stops, namely Colombo and Bangkok, before reaching Hong Kong on a Monday morning. I was back at work that afternoon on the same day.

On arrival at work, I was made the Officer in Charge of the Divisional Task Force, which was a new unit created after the Force expanded in 1984. I remained in this post for about three months, and for the first six weeks, I was by myself before they brought in a confirmed Inspector called [WMWm] as I would transfer out soon.

The post let me choose my own hours to suit the timings that crimes occurred, and the biggest crime prevention operation we did was in connection with a rape that occurred at the Shun Lee bus terminus. This saw my team and I lay in the bushes for three days to see if the rapist would strike again, which was very taxing but worth it.

Chapter 38

Visit to See SDKSf After UK Trip

Once back in Hong Kong, I contacted [SDKSf], to who I had sent postcards and met her at her flat. Strangely enough, I stayed the night on her sofa until she came out and led me by the hand to the bedroom. However, as we hadn't had that talk, it was a platonic tryst, yet again. There was no explanation for this, only that I wanted a relationship other than a one-night stand, and this needed a talk, especially with her German friend still being in the picture.

Chapter 39

The Long Letter from SEPf

One day on returning home from work, I found an airmail letter from the UK in my letterbox 507A. It was quite thick to the touch and was from [SEPf], who I had stayed a night with in Manchester on my recent leave to attend [MIm's] wedding.

The letter consisted of eight pages and was sent outlining her feelings for me and to rekindle a relationship we had while in the 6th Form and the first year at Newcastle Upon Tyne Polytechnic.

Page six was the last page of the letter before two other pages, which had the lyrics of two songs that stated how she felt.

Page six went on to say,

> "I want to tell you the truth about my feelings. I'm not trying to interfere with your life in any way, and I ask nothing of you other than your understanding.
>
> Maybe one day I'll get lucky again and will be able to show you how much I love you. You once said there's no going back. Well, I don't want to go back……I was different then. But, if you ever give me the chance to go forward with you one day, I'm sure you wouldn't regret it. I will be here if you should ever need me.

I would really love to come out to see you sometime if I wouldn't be in the way. It's a place I've always wanted to visit, and your company would be an added bonus. But I will want to be invited.....this letter is enough of an imposition on your time without you having to put up with me in person as well. But if you'd like me to come, I will.

I was going to send you a cassette of songs, which would have said better what I've been trying to say in this letter. But in the end, I just wrote down the words of the two most appropriate ones. Please don't laugh at me for this. Remember, it comes from the heart and has taken some courage to write and send it. But I just had to tell you how I feel, no matter how clumsy I've done it......I might never have the chance again.

I love you and I will love you always..... [SEPf] X

The two songs were by Lionel Richie singing the song "Still" and Olivia Newton-John singing the song "I Honestly Love You".

To say the letter was a surprise would be an understatement, so I wrote back as best as I could, saying how much I appreciated it, but that my life was in transition, many things were temporary, and that I wasn't ready for commitment as I once had been, six years previously in the 6th Form. I was a different person, and no matter how unfortunate it was for her to hear, I was discovering life in what was a transitory city and to do that, I had to be on my own. Two years later, when I saw her in Manchester in 1986, she had already been married for more than a year.

Chapter 40

Flat Hunting with RJm

RJm and I started to look for another flat we could share to get out of HISQ and by October we applied for a three-bedroom flat at Ming Court on Boundary Street, which we successfully got allocated to us. Before I get ahead of myself let's get back to TF SU NTK Division.

On the arrival of the confirmed inspector WMW to Task Force he told me he would do all the paper work and I could do the operations. This was good news especially as one night I was in Rick's Café late despite being on an early shift the next day. I had been attracted to a South American girl from Colombia who danced like there was no tomorrow. Anyway, when Rick's closed, I convinced her to drive with me to the top of Beacon Hill to see the lights of Hong Kong, which she did. While at the top of Beacon Hill we had a lustful tryst which meant I had to take the wing nut off the back of the passenger seat so it could lie flat on the back seat. We then went back to my quarter and showered to get rid of the smell of smoke from Ricks and again a lustful tryst. We turned into sleep but in the morning, things got heated and there was another lustful tryst after I had rung WMWm to get him to change my A shift to a B shift and advise the DVC NTK RKm I was doing a special operation on short notice information.

In the summer I went to a curry at Ho Man Tin Police Station being invited by MBm from my intake where I met a Chief Inspector BMm who asked where I worked and who was the DVC. I told him I worked in NTK DIV and the DVC was RKm. On hearing who the DVC was he said did I mean "Tits" and I said I had heard that name but the DVC was Sir to me. About one week later while urinating in the senior officers toilet in NTK Station the DVC walked in and while he urinated asked whether I had been for a curry the previous week and advised me to watch names I used. I told him exactly what had happened and made a mental note the next time I saw CIP BMm to advise him accordingly about dropping me in the shit!

Chapter 41

Special Duty Squad One Kwun Tong Police District

I became the Officer in Charge of Special Duty Squad 1 Kwun Tong (KT) Police District in August 1984 with the responsibility to tackle drug, gambling and prostitution in both Ngau Tau Kok and Kwun Tong Police Divisions. It was only a small team of myself, a sergeant and five police constables including one women officer who would mainly undertake administrative duties in addition to operational work while her male counterparts would be arresting and exhibits officers. Being from the UK and bearing in mind the long hours that we worked together my team soon became my family and we all supported each other as a very close-knit team.

I came under the command of the District Operations Officer (a CIP) and in turn answerable to the Deputy District Commander (DDC). The DDC KT DIST was WCSWm a man mountain in size and he held the rank of Senior Superintendent and was a Chinese gentleman in his late forties to early fifties.

There was no pressure for cases as long as I made arrests figures similar to previous OC's so any pressure came from myself especially if we had a few days without an arrest. We actioned files assigned to us as well as looking at information that we obtained from arrested persons, especially in relation to their source of drugs. We also had several known gambling black spots that we could action at any time if we felt we needed to raise our case figures. Dangerous drugs cases were the best because at that time the main drug was heroin. Anyone taking heroin for some time had similar looks such as being thin, unkempt and having older looking facial features than their real age and also normally looking very haggard. I could spot them a mile off and on occasion thought that my team were not being observant only to realize that local drug addicts were very common at that time and lived in the neighbourhoods they also lived in.

On arrival to SDS 1 KT DIST I noted that there were two teams one run by a female inspector much senior in service to me and she kept herself very much to KT Division especially when it came to distribution of intelligence files. She also concentrated on gambling daai dongs (Premises) unlicensed massage parlours. The female officer in her team was MMf and she was the sister of my team female officer JJf. I got drug files from all over KT DIST with a split of about 60% in NTK Division and 40% in KT Division but none of the information we got merged with any of the information that SDS 2 KT DIST got.

During my first week the team showed me around KT Division black spot areas and I remember going to both Tsui Ping Estate and Lam Tin Estates which were the biggest in KT Division both of which used H shaped six storey housing blocks with no lifts. These blocks had communal toilets and women and male showers outside the flats and cooking was undertaken on gas stoves outside each flat. I noted that they were similar to Jordan Valley Estate in NTK Division but different from newer estates in NTK Lower and Upper Estates as well as Sau Mau Ping and Shun Lee Estates. I did note that they were very much Chinese areas and Caucasians would be noticed immediately if they didn't proceed carefully. I do remember seeing a Caucasian female with a baby strapped to her back in Tsiu Ping Estate washing clothes by hand but she was the exception.

During the tour of Lam Tin, I noticed the football pitch, which had a tarmacked surface, had a football game being played and was being watched by quite a big crowd. I eventually managed to get a game which was very competitive so I guess my cover was blown however it would not affect the SDS Teams tactics of Observation Posts and close ambush teams

During the first six weeks we got a few cases and also undertook court cases achieved by my predecessor with me having to attend as officer in charge of the case. This meant that I ensured all officers needed for the court case turned up together with exhibits.

At the end of the second month, we were a bit down on cases so decided to get two gambling cases one in a wood yard opposite the KT Police Station and another street gambling cases mainly undertaken by taxi drivers at the back of a Chinese restaurant either before or after yam cha. During the first gambling case we entered the wood yard at speed in the unmarked police van and debussed chasing the startled gamblers who were slow to move. I had been warned about the low overhead wooden beams but in chasing a gambler hit a beam only to land flat on my arse. The gambler was caught and my team thought I was funny getting up from the ground and rubbing my head. The case went to court and was convicted, as was the one involving off duty taxi drivers.

On another occasion while passing Wo Lok Estate one of the team near off duty time spotted a light on in a flat that had been the target of a drug intelligence file and informed me it was the first time; he had seen the light on and we should check it out. On reaching the outside of the flat we heard noise inside the flat and decided to execute a Dangerous Drug General Authorization (DDGA) immediately after knocking at the door. When the door was kicked in, we sped into the flat only to find the mother injecting herself in her thigh in front of her two young kids both of which were under five years old. She was immediately arrested for possession of instrument fit for injecting a Dangerous drug and also possession of a small amount of heroin also found in the flat. We arranged a relative to pick up the women's two kids and took the women back to KT Police Station for processing and detained her to appear at Kwun Tong Magistrates Court the next morning.

I brought up the old file the next day which stated that the women we arrested was a drug trafficker and so ear marked her flat for a future observation and raid. The next time we raided her flat she was found inside just coming out of the toilet and her kids were also present. We searched the flat and I noticed a set of syringes at the bottom of the toilet bowl appearing as though it hadn't been used. I decided to seize it despite it being of no evidential proof but had one of my team translate to the women that we knew she was a trafficker and it would be good if she gave us information. She seemed reluctant to cooperate so I told one of my team to tell her that I had just stuck my hand into the filthy toilet water in her toilet that she had pissed in, shat in and menstruated in and the next time I came to visit she better cooperate otherwise who knows what I might find searching her flat. She understood I meant business and I warned her that if she was arrested again for drugs, I would apply to court to have her kids taken off her. A few weeks later we visited the flat again but she had moved out and we couldn't find a forwarding address.

One time in Tsui Ping Estate we executed a DDGA at one flat but found nothing other than a few teenagers one of which had very short hair and was wearing new clothes. It turned out he had just been released from prison and had been picked up by his trafficker boss given money and bought new clothes. The best-looking girl in the flat was also a gift for him to spend the night with and do what he wanted. My team informed me after the raid he would be trafficking again soon and would no doubt also get hooked to drugs.

During this time, I had quite a few court cases to attend in court and I think I worked for 21 days flat out. During one of the court cases I had to arrange transport for the European Magistrate to visit Jordan Valley Estate as the defense lawyer had claimed that the officer conducting observation could not possibly have seen drugs changed hands due to the waist height of the corridor wall. This proved to be correct and the trafficker was released and the drug addict was convicted of simple possession of a dangerous drug. (Poss. Of DD).

Having been in **SDS 1 KT DIST** for about six weeks I had arranged to go to the Legal Department to get legal advice on a number of cases so had to put on a shirt and tie and long trousers different from the T-shirt and shorts and trainers I normally wore to go to work. I took the MTR to Central and on exiting at Admiralty noticed the high fashion and good dressing of both male and female office workers. I felt out of place mainly because I had been working for three weeks solid in local housing estates mainly on B and early C shift duties and reached into my jacket pocket to see if I had brought my passport only realizing I was still in Hong Kong. The legal advice was obtained and I went back to Kwun Tong only after having a coffee at the coffee shop in the Mandarin.

Socially I had lost contact with all my mates due to my working hours and had also had to stop the scuba diving course which I had only completed half of the course. On occasion during the week after I finished work after midnight, I would dash to Rick's café to have a drink and see if there was anyone, I knew there but most of the time I didn't see anyone I knew. I eventually heard that the inspector from two squads below me at PTS TBm based in Ho Man Tin had said to people I knew I should not work as hard as I was doing. I found this quite interesting as I heard he was moonlighting as a strip tease artist normally dressed as a Chief Inspector or Traffic police officer. I also didn't have time to see SDKSf because of my working hours and her flying schedule.

Chapter 42

Visit of Mother and her Friend Mrs. T October 1984

It is of note that during October my mother visited me at HISQ for just over two weeks with the first four days being by herself and then after one of her friends arrived to spend time with her. The first day my mother arrived I went to pick her up at Kai Tak Airport and then brought her back to Kwun Tong Police Station being looked after by a female officer while I went to raid a flat for drugs. We got a case and after all the paper work was done I took her back to my quarter so she could shower and have a rest until I got back from work. I took her out for morning yam cha and showed her around Kowloon in the mornings before going to work in the afternoon. On the Sunday before her friend Mrs. T arrived, I took her for the buffet breakfast at the Hong Kong Hotel which had a number of women my mother's age and older who kept looking at us having breakfast as though I was her toy boy which was most funny.

Things improved when Mrs. T arrived as my mother had company and they could be pointed in the right direction if they wanted to see or do something. During the time Mrs. T was in Hong Kong I asked SDKSf to take them for a curry which she did with LCf and I would pay for them going to the Gaylord buffet.

During the next two weeks I went with them to Ocean Park, which was fun until I told them to sit on the back seat of the pirates galley ride. I have never heard women scream so much before but I could understand why. We had a couple of nights on the town and even went to see Beating the Retreat at PTS.

Sleeping arrangements meant my Mum and Mrs. T had my bedroom, which had the aircon, and I would have the cushions off my sofa albeit I worked quite late. RJm's father came out to see his Passing Out Parade at the Police Tactical Unit Headquarters (PTU HQ) and we all got together for drinks in TST and of course Ricks Café. As my mother and Mrs. T had been to a works BBQ, my team asked if they would cook for them one night despite my flat only having a baby belling cooker. They agreed. The night of the meal arrived so my work schedule that day was mainly office work with dinner being at my quarter. The food prepared was great and I got in a lot of beers and lost on playing the Chinese fingers game Open hands, Closed hands and 5, 10, 15 and 20. At the end of the evening I drove the team back to the station dropping off one or two officers in Kowloon City where I also skidded and hit three or four street railings but with no injuries albeit the hire van we had would have to be repaired. On arrival back to KT Police Station I parked the van behind the station and informed SDS 2 KT DIST that the van would be in repair for two days and then took a taxi home. In the morning I woke up thinking it had all been a dream but when I realized it wasn't I rushed back to KT Police Station and met one of my team who knew a good garage and the vehicle was repaired in two days with no one noticing but cost me a week's salary.

Eventually my Mum and Mrs. T left and I was once again left to my own devices mainly concentrating on work.

Physically I was still running and swimming and had even entered The Coast of China Marathon to be held in January 1985 in the Sai Kung Country Park between Man Yee and Wu Kai Sha and back. I made use of running trails from KT Police Station that went around Devils Peak and its Tofu Farms to Ma Yau Tong and back to the police station. Eventually I would up the training and run to Beacon Hill, down to Smugglers Ridge, Tai Po Road and back to the new quarter that RJm and I had been allocated at Ming Court on Boundary Street.

Chapter 43

New Quarter Ming Court Boundary Street

Just after my mother returned to the UK at the end of October 1984 RJm and I were informed by quartering that we had been allocated a quarter on the 1st floor of Ming Court Boundary Street. The flat would be available from the 20th December so I booked a station Bedford truck to assist us in our move and my boss the DOO KT DIST approved it.

I took the 19th of December 1985 off and while busy packing my things up I suddenly realized there was no traffic noise coming from Princess Margaret Road. On looking out to see what had happened I saw both sides of the road empty and then traffic motorcycles appeared leading the Governor's car towards the Cross Harbour Tunnel. About five minutes after this happened the road was back to normal and I later learnt from the news that Margaret Thatcher had arrived from Peking after signing the Memorandum of Understanding between Britain and the Peoples Republic of China on the return of Hong Kong on the 1st of July 1997.

The next at 12:00hrs both RJm and I had finished packing up all our belongings in our HISQ quarters just in time for police Bedford truck I had arranged to use for 4 hours moving arrived to move our stuff from Ho Man Tin Hill Road, which were mainly our sofa's and my large rattan double bed and mattress, to Ming Court Boundary Street. My telephone number was also transferred to Boundary Street and we had extensions put in the two double bedrooms we occupied. A main line was also put in the living room. The move went surprising easy and RJm got the topless picture of a blonde girl from the locker that used to belong to WWm in KT barrack that had just left KT Station. This picture was stuck on the glass panel in the door going to the kitchen which meant when the sun was shining or the light was on in the kitchen all you could see was the upper torso, head and of course the breasts. RJm had the double room with the bathroom attached while I had the bedroom on the front with the Daikin air conditioning unit, which I had installed. There was also a small bedroom that could be used for guests. From the living room window and balcony, we had a direct view to Beacon Hill and Lion Rock as well as aircraft landing at Kai Tak Airport over Kowloon Tong. It soon became a bachelor pad and was good for all forms of transport and runs. I had a car park spot for the MGC so everything was hunky dory.

Work continued with a vengeance and I was kept busy but the new quarter made for new energy. Again, on the odd night during the week finishing at around midnight I would still go to Ricks Café for a quick drink and see if any friends were in.

Chapter 44

Occurrences While Visiting Rick's Café

Triads in TST

One night going to Rick's café mid-week it was quite quiet but I had two beers and left calling in at the 7-11 to get some milk and bread. On grabbing the items, I was third in the queue to be served until some tattooed Gam Mo Tau walked in and picked something up and went to the front of the queue. I shouted at him that there was a queue in Cantonese and he better get behind me. At this moment he slammed his goods he wanted to buy and kicked open the door and stormed out.

I figured out correctly he was going for reinforcements so if he did come back looking for trouble, I would give him some. Surely enough he kicked open the doors of the 7-11 and he was with another male slightly older. He started to swear at me to which I answered in Cantonese while holding my police warrant card if he wanted a big problem and trouble, I could give him both. The second male looked at me wearing a jacket and long hair over my ears and must have thought I was CID and from my attitude armed.

They both left at which point I paid for my milk and bread and walked out of the 7-11 into the street and both of them were still having an intense conversation. I looked at the guy who shouted at me and shouted to him to give my respects to his mother with the smelly female orifice (Diu Lei Lo Mo Chow Laan Hai) and walked to my car in a confident manner and drove off with a huge sense of relief.

Hostess from Club Volvo

On another occasion I left Rick's Café at about 02:30 and drove my MGC with the soft top down along Nathan Road spotting a European female dressed smartly in a white dress standing on the steps of the Sheraton Hotel. I give a honk of my car horn and I waved. I then had to stop at the lights at the junction of Nathan Road and Salisbury Road and the female who I had just seen came up to the passenger door and tried to open it so I helped her and she got in. She said she wanted a lift home to Causeway Bay and despite me telling her I lived close in Kowloon I could take her to my place she insisted on going to Causeway Bay. As we were fast approaching the Cross Harbour Tunnel, I decided to drive her to Causeway Bay and she invited me up to her flat.

She said she worked at Club Volvo and was from Belgium and I said I was from England but worked in the police. She said she knew a few police officers and mentioned one by name GMm who I knew had been in Hong Kong a long time and was a Chief Inspector. She got me a drink and we started to kiss at which point she said she was hot and took off her dress revealing he white knickers and firm breast.

We kissed some more and I took off my T-shirt at which point she put her hand over my trousers over my groin and pushed down feeling the hardness. She then said she knew I wasn't married and she was quite tired and she gave me her number asking me to ring her on her day off. I gave her a last kiss and left to get my car. While driving back to Kowloon I couldn't believe what had happened and

I thought what a tease, threw the telephone number away and thought what would the guys say when I tell them!

Hit by a Freight Train in Ricks Cafe

One night in Ricks I had a few drinks and a local guy bumped into me after which he turned around and asked me to be more careful. I quickly let him know he walked into me and it was him who better watch where he was going. Things got a bit tense and as we were about to come to blows, I was hit from behind by what seemed like a freight train only to find out it was MDm from Kwun Tong Station who was trying to defuse things. The local guy left and MDm and I got talking with him saying I had been walking around like a bear with a bad head, which he put down to the pressures of my job. We had a couple of drinks and he explained that he had finished with the girlfriend I knew he was with adding the one that had got his name tattooed on her breast. He then told me she had met another police inspector who she married much later. He said he was making the most of Josephine who worked in Red Lips who would come back to his place in the New World Apartments and give him comfort, company and would also tidy up and iron his clothes so life was good. He told me to avoid going to CID KT DIV, as his boss was a wanker which I made a mental note of to avoid. Just before my leave in 1986 I heard that MDm had taken many CID case files on leave with him, which he posted back to Hong Kong from places he visited just to annoy his ex-boss who he hated.

7th Avenue Mong Kok

On a night during the middle of the week I ended up in Rick's but no one I knew was in so I drank by myself with the occasional dance. This was despite touching the nose of the camel half way down the stairs, which I always did for good luck. It had been about two weeks since I had seen anyone out socially and I felt the need for company and comfort. On leaving Rick's Café I walked passed the corner of Hart Avenue and Prat Avenue and the usual guy was there asking if anyone wanting girls could follow him to the 8th floor in the building he was stood in front of. This building had been raided several times often using expat inspectors as undercover agents. This meant that when the premise was raided most under covers had already had sex with the girl they had been allocated. The waiting list for this type of work was long so no matter how tempting I didn't take the bait. A few steps further on I saw a taxi jumped inside and stated to the taxi driver that I wanted some comfort and company and he took me to the 7th Avenue of Mong Kok just off Portland Street and directed me to go up one floor and knock and I would find what I wanted. I certainly did and what was provided lived up to the lyrics of the song "The Boxer" by Simon and Garfunkel. I returned home forlorn and feeling guilty!

Chapter 45

Work in SDS 1 KT DIST Continues

Work was going well but there were occasions that I could see drug addicts from a mile off which even my team couldn't. On one day I said to my team that we were not going off duty until we got a case. We drove round all the usual spots but nothing was found and no new information was received.

One of the team asked to be dropped off near Cha Kwo Ling with the team and they would search the area while I stayed with the van. After about 45 minutes the team came back with a thin haggard looking guy in his 50's already in handcuffs. On seeing me the team showed me a 10-gram packet of heroin and got in the van and I drove to KT Station. On the way back I saw the drug addict head butt the arresting officer however the only thing I could do at that time was shout at him not to move. On arrival back at KT Police Station I noticed the auxiliary officers were having an inspection, as it was their training night. I jumped out of the vehicle and ran around to the side sliding door and on opening it grabbed the drug addict and dragged him from the van. I then flogged marched him to the report room shouting at him the whole time which caused some of the auxiliary officers to look what was happening. The drug addict was processed and handed over to CID for the charge of assaulting a police officer, which resulted in the CID PC who collected him testing how strong his hair was when he grabbed it.

Chapter 46

Christmas Week Dinner in Food Street Causeway Bay

Christmas was fast approaching and as you could order cooked turkey and gammons hams from the Police Station Messes RJm and I decided we would have Christmas in the flat and invite a few of the guys round.

It was common practice that expats got Christmas off while the local officers got Chinese New Year while the expats worked.

As I would be off on Christmas Day and Boxing Day, I decided to treat the team to dinner before Christmas, which I would pay for as they were like my family at the time and it would be my treat.

On Saturday day the 22nd of December 1984 I took my team to have our evening meal break in Food Street Causeway Bay at a restaurant I had been to previously. When ordering our dishes, I asked for a beer the restaurant didn't sell but the staff said that was OK, as they would buy one from outside, which they did, and the meal went really well. I'm not too sure how much work we got done that day but I'm sure enough to document we had been working. The next day when talking to one of my team he mentioned the beer I had ordered that the restaurant didn't stock and went outside to buy it. In mentioning this he stated that if he as a Chinese had ordered the drink the restaurant would have just told him they didn't stock that kind of beer and offered an alternative, which the restaurant did stock. I found this hard to believe but the longer I stayed in Hong Kong the more examples I saw of this behaviour, which I found disgusting!

Christmas came and went and before you knew it was already January. In November I had seen a job advertisement for the Special Duty Unit (SDU) who would have a selection in January 1985 so I did more running, swimming and pushups and pull ups before going to work. On Saturday 5th of January 1985 there was the Dowman Road Race which RJm and I had entered and trained for noting the course would be the same as the year before from Man Yee South Dam to Sai Kung Sports Stadium. At the half way point on the course I told RJm I had plenty of energy still in the tank and ran faster finishing the 12 Kilometer run in 44 minutes and 45 seconds. In the afternoon I played rugby for the casuals and then went to work basically to catch up on paperwork for files we had to submit as the SDU Selection would last two weeks. The whole of Sunday was devoted to getting all my files updated and minuted to the DOO KT DIST who had originally tried to stop my attendance at the selection. The DC KT DIST had changed to SBm who had been the DC PTU HQ and he informed me that the SDU Selection would be the hardest thing I would do and that I should avoid getting injured. On Sunday I finished at about 22:00hrs and went home to pack all the gear I would need for the SDU selection and got some sleep.

Part Four
1985

Chapter 47

SDU Selection Monday 7th January 1985

On arrival at NT Depot, I parked up and got all my gear from the car and went to fall in at the SDU offices. There were about six inspectors and 30 PCs. One inspector, [BLm], arrived late on his motorcycle and being in VIPPU, he had to check his arms into the armoury. There was a judo expert [BWPm] from traffic, another new inspector [DNm], one other called [NMm], who was a triathlete and me.

We were all told to change to PE gear and then given a full fitness test similar to the ones we had at PTS. We then ran over to the Wo Hop Cemetery and did frog jumps up 10 steps, jumping using two legs, one step at a time. These increased to 20 steps and 30 steps, eventually getting to 100 steps. We then did some more sit-ups and pushups as well as star jumps and burpees, and somehow the whole morning had flown past. After a short break to get some water on board, we were given a 10-mile run to complete at 8 miles an hour pace. The next exercise was the assault course, and we had about five rounds of doing that before undertaking even more exercise. Later, we all had to run up what was named the A Course, which went to the top of Butterfly Hill behind PTU HQ at Volunteer Slopes. This was run by George Kwok, who had greeted me as 'The

Turbo' after my Dowman Road Race effort when I arrived at the start of the day. On the top of the hill was a chin-up bar, so it was as many chin-ups as you could do. Then we had to run back to NT Depot going down the A Course path, which was at best a dried-up stream bed. George set off at a very fast pace, and I followed him, taking note that if I stayed behind George, I couldn't see the streambed or where to put my feet. I eventually overtook George, who later only just beat me back to NT Depot. After all the guys on the course arrived back, [DNm] asked how far ahead I had finished in front of him, and I answered about five minutes. They then started a game of leapfrog going all the way around NT depot, and this went on for about two hours. After about 90 minutes, while jumping over [DNm], I fell and landed on my left hand, which seemed okay but then started to ache and was a bit painful. They then took us all up to PTU HQ to use the indoor gym, getting from one end of the gym to the other, and I was put in charge of one team. We basically had to connect a rope from one end of the gym from a high point and then climb to the other end of the gym to set up a line so we could slide down. I delegated the task to a member of my team who looked fit but was ultimately asked why I didn't do it, to which I answered I had banged my left hand and was using the team's strength.

This exercise eventually finished, and we were all sent on a run to Shek Kong camp and back. It was already 23:00hrs, and we were told to get a bite to eat and some sleep in a classroom at NT Depot. By midnight most of us were asleep, but a vehicle would skid to a stop outside the classroom every 15 minutes. Due to the number of mosquitos, I put my police issue jacket over my face and went to sleep. At about 02:00hrs, the door of the classroom was thrown open, and a flash bang was thrown in, followed by MP5 blanks being discharged. Everyone woke up and was told to get changed into PE gear and or tracksuits. I then noticed that my left hand was completely swollen up, and I couldn't see the knuckles on my fingers. I got help zipping up my tracksuit top and then fell in. We then did some planning exercises and even did a recce of a huge mansion off Ting Kok Road, in which we had one hour to write up a plan for covertly entering the house to rescue hostages. In the morning, we did another fitness test, after which we would do some free fighting, but when the Chief Inspector saw my hand, he told me to go to Fanling Medical Centre and get it looked at. This was despite me saying all I needed was some anti-inflammatories.

At Fanling Medical Clinic, they took an X-Ray and said I had fractured a bone close to my thumb and needed a half plaster cast, which they arranged to be done at Queen Elisabeth Hospital (QEH). That was basically my selection over and done with, and I left to go to QEH, get a half plaster and go home. [RJm] saw the hand, which was still badly swollen. However, I went to work the next day.

The DOO KT DIST was glad to see me and the DC KT DIST said he had heard what had happened, but I had been doing well before the injury. Two inspectors finished the selection, [BLm] and [DNm], who both got in SDU, while [NMm] left after about four days due to the physical effects the selection was having on his body, as did [BWPm].

Chapter 48

Back to OC SDS 1 KT DIST

Life went on in SDS 1 KT DIST, however, I was the only driver for the hire van, which had a gearshift near the steering wheel. I couldn't change gears with my left hand, but I could depress the clutch and steer.

I then found a willing member of the team who would change gear when I told him to, and I depressed the clutch. This caused some amusement in the team but was good team building.

During an observation in Tsui Ping Estate, I chased a trafficker and caught him just after he dumped a brown bag down a steep concrete slope. I grabbed him with my left forearm around his neck, which with the plaster cast I still had on under my jacket, almost throttled him.

I retrieved the brown bag, which had 30 small sticks of heroin contained in sections of drinking straws. I then debriefed him and lent on him with my left forearm, which caused him to get quite excited as he thought it was my muscular forearm.

He gave the team some good intelligence after I had moved away from where he was.

Lam Tin Estate Gang Fight & Possession of Offensive Weapon

Also, in January 1985, while travelling to Lam Tin Estate to undertake some bookmaking observations and raids, we pulled into the area near the bus station and immediately saw one gang of about five teenagers running holding melon knives. They were chasing after another gang of teenagers who were unarmed, so we immediately debussed and followed them, shouting that we were the police and that they should stop. Eventually, we caught two teenagers with melon knives and arrested them for being in possession of an offensive weapon. Lam Tin, at that time, consisted of H Shaped housing blocks with communal showers and toilets. The hillside where Lam Tin MTR Station is nowadays was all wooden squatter huts before.

The case eventually went to court, and on the trial day, the public gallery was full of the friends of the arrested persons. Many of which had dyed yellow hair (Gam Mo Tau's), had tattoos and spoke in an abusive manner. All the officers gave evidence, and the arrested persons chose not to give evidence after a case to answer was found against them. The evidence had to be translated into English as all the Magistrates at Kwun Tong Magistrates Court were European. Hence, the trial took a couple of days.

On the day of the verdict, the Magistrate found that the case had not been proved beyond all reasonable doubt. This was because the leading police officer chasing the knife-wielding teenagers stated that when they ran around a corner, he momentarily lost sight of them until he got around the corner and saw them again. The whole court erupted into loud cheers and claps from the unsavoury friends of the arrested persons. After they had left the court, I asked if I could speak to the Magistrate. This was allowed, and when I saw him, I questioned him about the 1 second of loss of sight and his decision to acquit. The Magistrate stated that he was correct, to which I stated that if I come across another similar happening, I would order my guys to open fire all because of his decision! A few weeks later, I was asked to see the Kwun Tong Deputy District

Commander and explain why the Magistrate had complained that I had harangued him after the court case. I explained what I had said and stated that it was said in a polite manner, and nothing more was said or mentioned!

Chapter 49

The Golden Dragon (Gam Lung) Ballroom Jordan Road.

One night when we finished duty at about 22:00hrs, the team asked me if I wanted to go for a drink, so they took me to the Golden dragon Ballroom situated on Jordan Road near Nathan Road. One of the team members knew a Mamasang called Winnie, who was quite cute, and she arranged drinks and female company to join in rounds of the hand game, All Open, All Closed and 5, 10, 15 fingers. It was a great way to relax and also get drunk. I took a liking to Winnie and went to see two local films with her, but that's as far as it went.

After the third occasion that we had been, I had noted a couple of the guys had left with girls, and so being drunk one night, I asked how about me. In no time at all, I was in a taxi with a girl heading back to Ming Court and once inside my bedroom, there was a lustful tryst. In the morning, there wasn't a hint of a tryst, so I got up as I had to go for physiotherapy on my left hand at Kowloon hospital. However, the girl who had come back was talking to her friend on the phone. Eventually, she got dressed and left with me as I told her I would get her a taxi.

A couple of taxis stopped and left, and it seemed that the taxi fare I was giving her wasn't enough. That's all the money I had on me, so I said I would go back to the flat to get some more. On arrival at the flat, I informed [RJm] what was going on and that I had to be at Kowloon Hospital for physio and was going to leave the building via the back door, and if the girl came back, he could tell her I had left. This indeed happened, but after 30minutes, he managed to eventually get rid of her. That was the last time I went to the Kam Lung Ballroom.

Chapter 50

Splitting KT into Two Districts KT & Sau Mau Ping (SMP)

By February 1985, it was announced that KT DIST would split into two Districts, and as I came from NTK Division, I would transfer to SDS 1 SMP DIST. However, I had already done my normal six-month tour. During an interview, I mentioned this and was informed that I would do two months in SDS 1 SMP DIST and then go to PTU. I was happy with this, however, there was some final action I wanted to take against a trafficker in Tsui Ping Road Estate.

Finally, my last day in SDS 1 KT DIST arrived, and I was determined to undertake an undercover buy for drugs in Tsui Ping Estate at the north end, tackling the main trafficker who was different from the one at the south end of the estate.

On this occasion, we would be trying to arrest an estate drug trafficker, and I had briefed my new SGT to dress like a drug addict and gave him some money to buy drugs. The serial number was noted on each bank note so that if it was used to buy drugs and ended up in the drug trafficker's possession, we could arrest him. The rest of the team were put into ambush locations, and I took charge of the observation post, which saw only me positioned in a flat in Wo Lok Estate, which overlooked Tsui Ping Estate. I was observing what was going on at the black spot and informing the team who were aware of the usual sellers of dangerous drugs, having already done two days of observations. On spotting a drug addict purchasing drugs, I tried to tell the team the description of the buyer. However, all the auxiliary police duties came on duty and were using the radio channel to sign on, so I could not convey the message. Having seen the premise the drug addict went into, I ran very fast to the location and made the arrest myself before he could consume the drug. It turned out he was a 70-year-old recipient of a Good Citizens Award and had been trying to kick his habit for years. The team was informed of where I was, and then we joined up and raided the drug trafficker's flat under a Dangerous Drug General Authorization (DDGA), which meant that if the door didn't open when we knocked, we could kick it in without a warrant.

Upon entering, we held everyone where they were and the phone rang, which I picked up to hear the caller say, "the Gweilo with the moustache is on his way", being stated in Cantonese. However, the warning was too late. Next, we got the list of marked money ready and then compared all the bank notes found in the flat with our list. On seeing this, the drug trafficker had a look of resignation that a marked bank note would be found. However, having checked twice, we didn't find any, to which the trafficker asked why we didn't take action against another trafficker in the estate that we knew. He then gave us his flat number and telephone number. Just after he announced this, one of my officers who had been checking shoe boxes found 50 straws of heroin which the trafficker looked surprised at but immediately pleaded guilty as he didn't want his wife to be arrested jointly. I told him he was under arrest and that I would go and see the trafficker at the south end of the estate and inform him that the trafficker from the north had advised me to do so.

That afternoon, we were going off duty for the last time as SDS 1 KT DIST, and I spotted [RJm] in the PTU barrack getting changed to go on duty. We had a bit of banter with him being on the fourth floor and my team and I being in the station compound. The next thing I saw, or more to the point my WPC saw, was [RJm] sticking his arse out of the window, giving us all a moon. However, he also revealed his meat and two veg hanging down, much to all our amusement.

Later, at a mess function held for the splitting of the District, I related the story of the drug trafficker to the ADC C KT DIST SP [CSMm], who, on hearing the story, informed me I was lucky that there hadn't been reports of wounding between the two traffickers. He did, however, see my point of view in the end but advised caution in the future.

Transfer to OC SDS 1 SMP DIST

I arrived at Sau Mau Ping (SMP) Police Station in late February 1985 and entered the SDS 1 SMP DIST office to find it completely empty. Not only was the office empty, but also there was no District Operations Officer (DOO SMP DIST) in place either. I answered immediately to the DDC SMP DIST, an ex-pat officer called [HAm]. He instructed me to set up the office, carry out operations and see him every morning to brief him on what my team and I had been up to the day before and what we had planned. This was because he would have to brief the District Commander (DC) SMP DIST, who was a Chief Superintendent and horse owner called [MTYm].

The office was sorted out within a week, even having time for observations in new areas in the newly formed SMP DIST in Shun Lee Estate Block 20, Jordan Valley and NTK Lower Estate. After about two weeks, I put together a list of suspects and locations that were active in the early morning and decided that it would be good to have a whole week starting at 06:00hrs. This led to a few arrests but was also good for my body clock as I was taking part in the Coast of China Marathon on the 6th of March, and I wanted my toilet habits to be in line with the marathon running time. This was quite hard work as we had been mainly doing afternoons and late nights. The new routine worked, and my body clock adjusted.

Chapter 51

Coast of China Marathon

On Sunday 6th March 1985, I got up at 04:00hrs and was at the start point at Pak Tam Chung in the Sai Kung Country Park by 06:00hrs, having had my shit, shower and shave, which sorted out my morning ablutions. The race started at 08:00hrs, and the first half of the marathon ran along Tai Mong Tsai Road to the roundabout at Tso Wo Hang. The route then went up to Kei Ling Ha and turnaround at the end of the road at Wu Kai Sha before returning to Pak Tam Chung, which was the halfway mark. I completed this faster than I wanted in a time of 1 hour and 24 minutes, mainly because I had been running with a British soldier who was running at an agreeable pace.

The second half of the marathon was quite hilly and ran to the High Island East dam near Long Ke and then back to the car park at Pak Tam Chung. This half of the marathon took 1 hour and 58 minutes as I hit the wall at about the 33-kilometre mark. I was very glad to finish and pleased with the time as it was more than 118 minutes faster than my Windermere marathon time, which I ran in 1982.

I went back to Ming Court, had a shower and then went to SMP Police Station as I had arranged to do an afternoon shift, basically checking licensed premises. During a check of a hotel that rented rooms by the hour, one room took some time to open the door. The male who opened it looked worried, so we checked him and his girlfriend's identity cards, but they weren't wanted. The thing that struck me was that the girlfriend, who was still in bed covered by blankets, didn't shake an eyelid despite four police officers being in the room. The look on her face wasn't normal as she looked to be in a state of ecstasy and in a different place which, when compared to her boyfriend, who was a nervous wreck, was almost surreal. The rest of the checks went well, but I was a little tired when having to walk up four flights of stairs as I was feeling the effects of the marathon. We did exactly eight hours and thirty minutes that day, and when I signed off duty, I went straight home and straight to bed.

Chapter 52

Sau Mau Ping Estate Block 20 Operation

Block 20 Sau Mau Ping Estate during March and April became a target location to get cases and also gather intelligence. This was because it was very active, and we could get cases, but we hadn't identified the organizer who had the drug traffickers working for him.

This location became more important because one day, I attended a meeting with the CIP Narcotics Kowloon Region [LDm] (CIP N K), who was basically the frontman for the Narcotics Bureau in Kowloon. He had asked all the OC SDSs in East Kowloon (SMP, KT, and WTS) for a briefing about a regional operation he was organizing and wanted us to give him the names and identity document details of three traffickers and their followers we knew about in our districts. He would then process the information, and after a week, he would ask us to concentrate on one main target to develop information on addict addresses and other figures in the trafficking organization.

After a week, I was told to concentrate on SMP Estate Block 20, and that is exactly what I did. I was also told that the Anti-Dangerous Drugs Operation would be held in three weeks and would also involve a **PTU COY** as backup. This was because **PTU** duties when patrolling some of the rougher housing estates had all sorts of items dropped from a height on them, ranging from small beer cans to batteries and used tampons. This confirmed what my flatmate [RJm] had told me, especially in SMP and Lam Tin Estates.

The organizer of drugs in Block 20 SMP Estate we found out was [FCm], and we knew where he lived and also that he ran two crews basically covering early morning to afternoon and also early evening to late night. We concentrated on arresting drug addicts for simple possession cases and, while processing their cases, asking them covertly about the modus operandi (MO) of their supplier and name as well as description. We very quickly produced a drug trafficking tree for block 20 and obtained at least 20 addresses for the block.

In the morning, we could see traffickers stashing their drugs in the small round concrete tubes that created air circulation gaps on staircases. The traffickers would meet a drug addict on the 18th Floor staircase, take his money off him and then descend or ascend one floor to retrieve the drugs before returning to the 18th floor to pass the drugs to the addict. On some occasions, this involved the trafficker and his assistant, so only the trafficker handled the money, and the assistant fetched and handed over the drugs.

After two weeks, we handed over all the information we had gathered and explained how the operation was run. The CIP N K [LDm] then analyzed the information, obtained search warrants and compiled an Operational Order.

Ten days later, we all gathered in Wong Tai Sin Police Station compound at 04:00hrs to be briefed and allocated a **PTU** platoon who would follow our raiding parties and break open metal grilles and wooden doors, if needed. On arrival, I saw [HNm] from my squad in PTU uniform in the middle of the station car park, standing by himself at ease but with a Remington shotgun behind his back. [RJm], my flatmate, saw me as he was in the same PTU

Sau Mau Ping Estate Block 20 Operation

COY and told me [HNm's] platoon would follow my SDS team but also advised me that [HNm] had been drinking most of the night. [HNm], while at PTU, had got himself into trouble because one night while at training at PTU HQ, he got drunk in the mess while still in uniform and checked an AR-15 out of the armoury, put on a CS respirator and ran the C Course all because he thought it was a good idea at the time. He was severely bollocked by his COY CDR, and a note was made in his record of service. This incident came on top of another incident while in UB WTS DIST where he chased someone he wanted to stop in a taxi to Mong Kok and when he stopped him, he drew his revolver. The rumour was that he might not be allowed to serve for a second tour even if he passed all his Standard Twos.

The operation commenced, and the first address we knocked at in SMP Estate Block 20 was the organizer. PTU knocked on the wooden door, which was behind a metal grille, and when the door opened, [HNm] stuck his Remington shotgun through the grille and ordered that the grille be opened, or he would open fire. This happened at many addresses, and the operation lasted four hours, with tens of people arrested and exhibits seized. The information obtained kept me busy for a couple of weeks, and the operation was judged to be a success across the East of Kowloon.

Chapter 53

Raid on Ngau Tau Kok Lower Estate & CAPO Complaint

At the end of March 1985, I raided a drug trafficker flat in NTK L Est., and despite a thorough search, found no drugs but plenty of telephone and pager numbers. During the raid, the trafficker was somewhat hostile, and I told him to watch his behaviour. We found some illegal firecrackers, so we seized them and intended to take them away when we finished the search for disposal.

During the raid, two groups of two people knocked at the trafficker's door. We let them in and searched them as well as checking their identities. Just before the search ended, as I only had my SGT, WPC and two PCs, the five males got a bit aggressive until I read them the riot act and let them know we were armed and prepared to use them if need be.

On finally leaving, we documented the raid back at the station and thought nothing more of it until two weeks later. At that time, I heard that the five males in the flat overturned and smashed furniture inside the flat and lodged a CAPO complaint immediately, and a CAPO team on reserve went down, took statements and photographs. Eventually, after investigation, the complaint was substantiated other than reported because I hadn't got the drug trafficker to sign a police notebook that we had seized the firecrackers. The complaint was signed off by no other than a [Mr. Bm] of the Standard Chartered Bank, who, holding a high position, had probably never been anywhere near NTK L Estate and most certainly never dealt with undesirable characters. I was going to appeal but was advised not to by my **PTU COY CDR** later on that year.

Chapter 54

Raid in Lei Yue Mun with CID Action Squad NTK

One Sunday at the end of March 1985, my SDS 1 Team and I called into NTK Police Station to document a raid we had done in Amoy Gardens. While in the report room, the OC Action Squad NTK Division, a guy called [SBHm] saw me and asked if we could talk. He said he had arrested a 16-year-old youth who, during his detention, had informed him that he lived in a house on its own walled-off grounds in Lei Yue Mun Kwun Tong Division. The youth also stated that there were drugs kept at the house by the owner, his gang boss.

[SBHm] informed me that he was going to do a house search at the house in Lei Yue Mun, but SDS KT DIST were off duty. He wanted to know if my team and I would accompany him and provide backup if drugs were found as he was holding the boy for a case of Unlawful Sexual Intercourse. I said I would but let me brief my team.

Upon seeing my team and explaining the situation, they informed me that the Duty Officer had informed them that the prisoner of the OC Action Squad had been in custody for nearly 44 hours and had not been allowed outside contact. The other rumour was that the 16-year-old boy might be the son of a police officer. They also mentioned that the OC Action Squad had a reputation for being gung-ho and not following the rules. They all stated that if we accompanied the OC Action Squad and his team, then they wanted to be under my control and in my team.

I then saw [SBHm] and explained I would go with him to Lei Yue Mun, but if there were no drugs, I would leave. He then gave a briefing to three teams as he had also enlisted the help of the NTK CID reserve team, and my team and I would be responsible for securing the South, East and West walls of the house's compound with the CID NTK reserve team. He and his team would go over the North wall and execute a search warrant at the house after they had kicked open the front door.

The approach to the property in Lei Yue Mun went according to plan because it was about 21:30hrs, and the dark of night covered our approach to the secluded house. On arrival, we climbed over the walls after securing them, and when approaching the house, I heard someone say in English don't move, or he would open fire. My officers and I dropped to the floor, and I shouted in English that we were SDS 1 SMP DIST. Apparently, [SBHm] had problems climbing over the North wall's gate, and this had delayed him. He then kicked open the door and charged in, getting all occupants to sit in the lounge. He then searched the room of the 16-year-old boy and then set about debriefing all the occupants. [SBHm] got enthusiastic when manhandling the occupants, so my team and I searched the house but found no drugs. [SBHm] had seized a Singapore Airlines life jacket, but no one stated they had stolen it.

[SBHm] then approached me and said he had to return to NTK Police station to bail out his 16-year-old arrested person and could I do all the paperwork at Kwun Tong Police Station in respect of the execution of the search warrant and finding of the life jacket, I said I certainly could.

On arrival at Kwun Tong Police Station, I entered the report room and compiled the first information report on a POL 159, making sure to state that the OC Action Squad NTK [SBHm], supported by the NTK CID reserve team and SDS 1 SMP DIST in that order had executed a search warrant at an address in Lei Yue Mun, resulting in the seizure of a Singapore Airlines life jacket, stating that eight people had been searched. On arrival at my office at SMP Police Station, my team and I spent two hours updating our notebooks, if only to ensure we didn't get into any trouble.

Later on, in the Autumn of 1985, while at PTU, I was called as a prosecution witness in the defaulter hearing of [SBHm], with the prosecutor being no other than [GKLm] aka The Emperor.

Information Report Form (IFR) Selling of Dangerous Drugs (DD) From Estate Rubbish Room

In actioning IRFs, I would, on occasion, find the information unbelievable, like the one of a young female selling drugs from the 10th floor rubbish room in one of the blocks in Sau Mau Ping Estate. On checking it out, I had already formed my opinion that the information was rubbish. On arrival at the rubbish room, my team and I spotted two males leaving. I sent most of my team after them to conduct a search and another PC, and I entered the rubbish room to find a young female, aged about 18, with drugs on a table in front of her. On seeing us, she went to kick the drugs, but I grabbed her, stopping her just in time. She turned hysterical, so I tasked my PC to go and get the team's WPC so a search could be conducted. When the PC left, the female grabbed me and started to push me, even trying to bash me with her fists. I told her to stop, but when I was struck in the face with a punch that had a lot of weight, I reacted and thumped her several times on her back. This had the desired effect, and she slumped to the floor. When my team eventually joined me, they thought I had been too violent, and I couldn't explain the super human strength the girl had, which was probably a result of the drugs she was using.

Chapter 55

Sighting of The Emperor, Shatin Inn

One weekend in early April 1985, I drove my MGC with some friends to have Indonesian food at the Shatin Inn. The weather was sunny, so we sat outside and on choosing a table to sit at, I spotted The Emperor sat not too far away with a young-looking woman. He spotted that I had seen him and fairly soon afterwards paid the bill and left as the guys I was with reckoned she was a female inspector, who they couldn't remember the name of, or where she was stationed.

Chapter 56

The End of being OC SDS 1 SMP DIST

In early April 1985, I was told that I would transfer to PTU G COY 4/85 on the 28th of April 1985. I would hand over to the new OC SDS 1 SMP DIST on the 7th of April, and I was allowed to take leave between the 13th of April 1985 to the 27th of April 1985.

Basically, I was on a rundown which gave me time to update all file work and statements as well as plan on going to the Philippines with my flatmate [RJm] and [HNm] between the evening of the 13th of April and the 25th of April, before coming back to Hong Kong to get ready for going to PTU. One night, during my handover week, I went out with [RJm] and, while in the Cavern Disco, ran into [BMm], who told me he was going to be my PTU COY 2 IC and that we would be based in Mong Kok Police Station, giving PTU support to the West of Kowloon.

I immediately answered him that he knew where he and I stood after dropping me in the shit with my ex-DVC NTK [RKm]. In speaking to him, I had already had a few beers, but he didn't take things too badly.

Signing Off Duty in SMP Divisional Station and arranging to go for a Drink with the Owner of a Dog that had Bitten Someone.

During my last week in SDS 1 SMP DIST, I was signing off duty when I noticed a good-looking girl in the report room. I quickly established from the Duty Officer that she was the owner of a dog that had bitten someone, so I went to talk to her. After a brief conversation, I asked if she wanted to meet up that night and when she said yes, I said I would meet her in the Bar Someplace Else, which was in the Sheraton Hotel in TST. We arranged to meet at 19:30hrs, so I went home, had a shower and got changed to go out. [RJm] was busy as his younger sister was in town and staying in the third bedroom. They were both out at the time sightseeing, but I expected that they would be home at about 22:00hrs.

I was in the bar Someplace Else at 19:15hrs in the upstairs section, which was at ground level as the main bar was one floor down. This bar was very popular to drink in at the start of the night as they always had a singer and gave popcorn with beers.

Exactly at 19:30hrs, the girl I had met in the report room of Sau Mau Ping Police Station arrived, and she looked stunning as she had made herself up and put on a dress. We ordered drinks, and just after they arrived, [SDKSf] walked in and spotted me and came across to talk. I introduced the girl I was with and informed her that I had been very busy workwise, but I had seen her from a distance at the Hong Kong Stadium where the Rugby Sevens had been held. I even recalled what she had been wearing and told her that I knew she had moved flat to Boundary Street, about a 10-minute walk from my quarters which I shared with [RJm]. She seemed surprised I knew, but I said I had my means and spies jokingly. After she went down to the next level, I couldn't help but think how bad the timing had been as she was someone I really wanted to get to know better. Anyway, back to my date, that didn't really understand all I had said to [SDKSf]. We had a couple of drinks and went for dinner at an Italian restaurant I knew and liked. We had several beers and a bottle of wine, and when dinner finished, I asked if she wanted to come back to my place, which she said she did.

On arrival at my quarters, [RJm] and his sister were back, so I made some tea, and we all chatted. Eventually, [RJm] and his sister went to their rooms, and I put on some music and got comfortable with the girl I had brought home. As things progressed well, I put the LP player on repeat and took the girl I was with to my room to get further acquainted. During the course of doing this, I heard someone turn the music off, but I was getting far too involved and eventually, there was a lustful tryst or two. The one thing I hadn't bargained for was that the lustful tryst was quite noisy, and in the morning after I had got the girl a taxi and her contact number, [RJm] had already surfaced and was having a cup of tea. He commented on the noise, and all I said was I couldn't do anything about it.

That night when I arrived home, [RJm's] sister was a bit frosty towards me. After she returned to the UK, [RJm] confided in me that he had got a stern bollocking off his sister when she got up the morning after I had brought the girl home. She said he was living a debauched existence, and his quarters were like a fraternity house from the movie Animal House. She even stated that if he didn't leave Hong Kong, he would slip into depths even she couldn't imagine.

After this, [RJm] started to concentrate on joining the British Army and attending Sandhurst at the end of his contract, although I know he was struggling with whether he should stay or go.

Chapter 57

The Philippines Vacation with RJm & HNm

In March 1985, [RJm] informed me that he would finish his PTU attachment on Friday the 12th of April, and he would take two weeks off before starting as the Police Duty Officer at POLMIL (Police/Military) Operations Room in Police Headquarters on Monday the 29th April. I found that to be a coincidence as I would finish SDS SMP DIST also on Friday the 12th of April and would commence PTU training on Monday the 29th of April.

We quickly decided to go on holiday, and [RJm] said [HNm] was also interested. After a meeting, we decided to go to the Philippines and spend some time in Manila and then go to Puerto Galera. As the holiday drew nearer, we booked flights with Cathay Pacific to leave on the evening of Friday the 12th of April and return on Thursday the 25th of April. It was also decided that we would stay at the Swagman Hotel, as it wasn't far from the strip, which had the famous Fire House nightclub. It was of note that [WFLJm] from mine and [HNm's] intake had hooked up with a girl from Fire House. We took a photograph of him to ask the girls in Fire House if they remembered him or not.

Friday the 12th of April arrived, and we had a very quick one-hour flight to Manila, after which we checked into the Swagman Hotel, unpacked and went to get some dinner. At about 22:00hrs, we went to Fire House. The place was rocking and much better than the girlie bars in Wan Chai. We quickly got a drink, followed by very many more drinks and also danced and talked to many girls, some of whom remembered [WFLJm] and the girl he had taken to Hong Kong. At almost closing time, [HNm] and I was hooking up with some girls after dancing, and when we went to leave, we told [RJm] to get himself a female to take back to the hotel for more drinks. We pointed out a girl wearing a tartan headband, and so [RJm] grabbed her, and we all went back to the hotel for more drinks. After about one more hour of drinking, we went back to our rooms to retire to nocturnal activities and then went to sleep. At about 03:00hrs, one of us stated he had a problem with the girl he had brought back as she was talking to herself and shouting. We quickly went to his room with the girls we were with, and they helped get the girl out of the room, at which time security arrived and escorted her to the ground floor. We all followed to make sure she left. On reaching the street, the girl started to strip off, at which time, [RJm], [HNm], and I watched her walk back and forth across the street naked until the police turned up. On returning to our rooms, we all discussed the matter and concluded she must have popped a few pills before leaving Fire House.

The next day, we gave our female company money to get a taxi home and buy a meal after breakfast as that day we had booked a trip to Pagsanjan Falls, which turned out to be a great and good way to sober up, ready for another night out. On Sunday, after a really heavy night of partying, we took a coach to Batangas, and I brought along the girl I met on Saturday night, as she knew the way and where to stay.

We arrived in Batangas quite late, quickly got a room and had a meal before hitting the disco in our hotel. Everybody thought we were Americans and didn't believe we came from Hong Kong, as we weren't Chinese. At the end of the evening, we danced to three plays of the song Born in the USA by the boss. On turning into our rooms, two Filipino males asked me for money for dancing with the girl I was with. [HNm] immediately talked to them and gave them a few hundred pesos each, and they left.

The next morning being a Monday, I gave the girl I was with enough money to get back to Manila and a good tip as she informed me that she had something really important to do. Hence, she needed more money. At about lunch, we got the ferry to Puerto Galera and, on arrival, went to White Beach and found a beach resort to stay at. We each got our own little shack. That night, we went partying again and found some more female company. In the morning, while discussing the night before, one of us stated that they were so drunk the night before while having a doggy lustful tryst that they slipped out after a few strokes but got right back in, only to be told they were in the wrong hole. On hearing this, it took them two strokes to realize they were in the thick and chunky peanut butter before they slipped out and right back into the silky-smooth peanut butter. We all found this to be unbelievable and a great presence of mind by the female, who was engaged in the lustful tryst. That day we did some sunbathing and had another late night with plenty of beers before retiring with female company.

In the morning, [HNm] was up early as it was his birthday, and we all said goodbye to the female company. About 10 minutes later, at about 09:00hrs, a crate of 24 San Miguel beer bottles arrived with a ton of ice, and we partied all day, albeit at a less hectic pace. That night we had an early night after dinner as we had booked a sight-seeing tour by boat the next day being Thursday, the end of our first week.

During the tour the next day, we met two female backpackers from Belgium who, after talking with them for a while, asked why we were not attached, as every Western male they had seen had been with a local girl. We quickly admitted we were not different but were having a quiet day. They then told us about the place they were staying at that had two rooms with one common roof in a beach hut. In the room next to theirs was an older German male who one night, while listening to the song "No More Lonely Nights", was heard to say to the local female he was with that as he had paid for it, he was going to get it, after which there was the noise of a lustful tryst. We had a civilized dinner with the girls, and after they left, I told [RJm] and [HNm] that I had to dry out, and the next morning I would try and get to Boracay, which I had heard so much about if they were interested. They said they would stay at White Beach until flying back to Hong Kong.

Early Saturday morning, I set off overland to Roxas, and when finding a place to stay, I asked a local male for directions, and he lost his temper thinking I was an American until I convinced him I was from England. On Sunday, I travelled by Banca boat across what I thought was a large expanse of water. After nightfall, I arrived on a beach on Boracay and checked into a nearby hotel called Fridays.

I must admit I was very taken by Boracay, because it was totally unspoilt and had brilliant white sand beaches and transparent seas. It was hardly inhabited and had quaint, palm-tree-lined paths that had signs for visitors to watch out for falling coconuts. It could be said, it was a piece of paradise on Earth at that time. (It was a shame to hear in 2018 that it would be closed to tourists for six months because of over-development, under-capacity and a failed sewage system. In fact, President Duterte described it as a "cesspool".)

I had two nights at Fridays, after which I moved into cheaper accommodation for a final day before taking the Wednesday ferry back to Manila.

The ship back to Manila set off about six hours later than scheduled and pulled into Manila Harbour at about 11:00hrs, just in time for me to see my Cathay Pacific Flight taking off to fly back to Hong Kong. After docking, I immediately got a taxi to the Cathay Pacific (CX) Offices and arrived just as they were about to close. I tried to explain my way in, but a security guard told me to come back in the morning and even gave me a flash of his gun as an incentive to leave. I then went to check into the Swagman, and that night when I urinated, I felt a bit of pain, so I decided that the less I drank, the less I would need to urinate. I went to bed early as I had an early start to get to the CX offices as they opened up for business the next day. I managed to get a new ticket for the afternoon flight and arrived back in Hong Kong at about 18:00hrs. On arrival back at Ming Court, [RJm] was at home and I told him how I missed my flight. I also mentioned the pain I was having when urinating. He gave me the name of a doctor all the guys used for similar complaints, and the first thing Saturday morning, I was at the Doctors, who was called [LCm]. I described my symptoms, and after a check, he said I had a urinary tract infection (UTI) and put me on a course of antibiotics, advising me to stay off alcohol for a week and that I should finish all the tablets. He said the pain would lessen almost immediately and he was correct, much to my relief. This was the first time I had used this doctor. After Dr. [LCm] treated me, I couldn't help but think about the girl I said goodbye to in Batangas who asked for a good tip as she had something important to do. I believed the reason why she asked for the tip was the cause of my visit to the doctor and wished she had been more upfront with me. About six months later, I heard Dr. [LCm] had taken his own life, but no one knew the reason why.

Chapter 58

PTU Company Training: First Day

Sunday the 28th of April 1985 was spent relaxing and getting everything ready that was needed to go to PTU HQ on Monday. This was for 12 weeks of training at Volunteer Slopes Fanling before being based in Mong Kok Police Station for the Kowloon West Regional attachment by PTU Golf COY 4/85.

Early Monday morning, I arrived at SMP Police Station and collected all my uniforms and kit bag, returning to the ground floor before 07:30hrs. The PTU transport arrived at 07:45hrs, having already picked up other officers as well as NCOs and headed straight to Mong Kok Police Station. Here we met the COY CDR [YSFm], the COY 2I/C [BMm] together with their COY HQs, including the SSGT, the transport SGT and orderly. We then went in convoy to PTU HQ Fanling, arriving at 08:45hrs, well before our 09:00hrs fall in time.

That morning flew by with collection of our PTU and IS uniforms and PTU training notes. We all had a short back and sides haircut, after which we were shown to our accommodation before changing into PE kit to undertake a fitness test. This was a normal test consisting of the usual shuttle run, pull-ups, sit-ups, press-ups and a

2.4km run. Just after I had done my 55 press-ups, the G COY 2I/C [BMm] said I hadn't gone down far enough, so he asked me to do them again. I did another full-on 55 press-ups and followed them up with three press-up jumps with hand claps just to let him know I wasn't tired. Indirectly, I was also sticking up my middle finger but in a polite physical prowess manner.

The 2.4km run came next, and we were told to follow a PTU HQ staff Training Inspector called [WSm] and not fall behind. He explained we would do the B Course around the villages and come back to PTU HQ through the back gate. This staff inspector set off at a fast pace, but after about four minutes, I followed him closely and then started to press him, so he went faster. On arrival at the rear gate to PTU HQ, [WSm] stopped at the rear gate after opening it and told me to run to the gym and wait for him to round the other inspectors up who had become spread out. I must admit I took him for word value, but he also looked like he needed to catch his breath. After the fitness test had been completed, we were allowed to get showered and then get into PTU HQ camp kit and go to the mess for lunch.

The afternoon went quickly, and most of it was spent sorting out the PTU training notes and doing some drill. At the end of the day, after another shower, as the drill session had been physical, we were told to meet in the mess for the lecture on mess etiquette, how to sign for food and order lunches. It was also pointed out to us that we could sit in the C PTU's chair, but if he came in and we didn't move, we would be fined a round of drinks for everyone in the mess. The bell (when someone talks bullshit) and the wagers book (bets on the number of pints drunk or who was fastest over the PTU HQ runs, etc.) were also explained. At the end of the briefing, the PTU HQ mess bought us a beer, but I insisted on having an orange juice. This caused the staff inspector [WSm] to comment that I must have caught something in the Philippines, otherwise, I would have a beer. I answered, "thank you very much, and yes, I would have a beer after my orange juice", which shocked the canny Yorkshire man. He had just bought me my first beer, much to the amusement of my fellow platoon commanders and some of the other PTU HQ staff inspectors who said Lancashire had just won the War of the Roses again! My Dr. [LCm] would not have been impressed as I was still taking my antibiotics.

After the beer had been drunk, the other platoon commanders from Alpha COY Hong Kong Island (HKI) entered the mess and joined us for a drink. By that time, the PTU HQ staff inspectors had left as well as our COY CDR and 2I/C conversation flowed more freely. It was noted by [ADm] (squad below me at PTS), [RMm] and [KJm] that one particular inspector of the PTU HQ staff [GDMm] was extremely strict and problematic on occasion, so much so that they had nicknamed him "Captain Bastard". We were advised to be careful around him as he could be a bit of a bully. We were also told that there was a good pub in Fanling, called the Better Ole, which was frequented by New Territories Police, and also British Forces, not to mention PTU HQ staff if they weren't in the mess. We were also told that the Special Duties Unit (SDU Anti-Terrorist Unit) based at NT Depot would have lunch at the mess as well as the occasional drink. Lastly, it was pointed out to us that Alpha and Charlie COYs were from HKI, and Foxtrot and Golf COYs would serve in Kowloon West. Bravo and Hotel would serve in Kowloon East, and Delta and Echo would serve in the New Territories. At about 20:00hrs, I caught the train back to Kowloon Tong, got home, and quickly got a bite to eat before going to bed for an early night as the day had been quite strict after my holiday and SDS attachments. In the morning, I had an early start as I had arranged a lift on the back of [FMm's] motorcycle, who still lived in HISQs. The pick-up was on Waterloo Road just near the Kowloon Tong Club entrance at 07:30hrs, which was only a three-minute walk from Ming Court.

Chapter 59

The Forming of PTU G COY 4/85: Officer / NCO Cadre Training

The next four weeks saw the inspectors from the company be given lectures by PTU HQ staff inspectors. This was essential as we would be responsible for giving the same lectures to our PCs when they arrived in four weeks for the full formation of the company. Lectures concerning such things as the wearing of kits, such as respirators, stop, question, search, and related powers, words of command, platoon structure and platoon form up, draw stores and attack were given. Other topics, such as anti-crime patrol, high rise cordon and sweep as well as operational order formats, emergency turnout, the work of a platoon briefing, and map drawing team, were also explained. The NCOs likewise were given similar lectures by the PTU HQ NCOs.

Every day would start with physical exercise, be it circuit training or a run or both. This was meant to get us fit so that in four weeks when the PCs arrived, we could keep up with them as they would be invariably younger but also so we knew just how hard to push them. This would be followed by lectures and the physical practice of platoon draw stores and emergency turnout.

The practical side saw all NCOs take the positions of the PC in a platoon that had 41 men consisting of four sections. Each section had eight men, and sections included: the arrest section, smoke section, wooden baton round section, and firearms section. In addition to this, there were three drivers as the platoon had three vehicles, two lorry guards, and the platoon headquarters, which had two inspectors, a platoon SGT and the platoon orderly.

The practicals would cover platoon attacks and how to give orders to bring different sections up with appropriate warnings. How to "Gi Woon" (reinforce sections), all-round defence, how to use and strip weapons, and the limits of each weapon as well as shields used were taught. These practical sessions were very physical, and orders had to be precise and clearly given. Range courses would be held, and use of weapons tests passed. No slacking would be tolerated.

The four weeks passed quite quickly, but for me, it was a challenge as I had been my own boss for nearly a year doing real operational work in Districts. It took some adjusting, but I warmed to the physical exercise and range courses and eventually the lectures. I relaxed at lunchtime by swimming 2000 metres in the 17-metre swimming pool that had been built by drug addicts for the camp.

During the cadre part of the course, there was some banter with staff, especially the Yorkshire man [WSm], due to the rivalry of my origins being Lancashire. One day, [WSm] walked into the mess styling a new haircut, which made him look like a monk with an all-rounded level fringe. I asked him where he had his hair cut as it didn't look like a camp haircut, and he admitted he had it done downtown over the weekend. Several other members of PTU HQ staff were present during the conversation, and then I told him he looked like a monk and, in fact, resembled "Friar Tuck" from the movie Robin Hood. He argued otherwise. However, his fellow staff said I had a point and burst out laughing, which he didn't take too well initially, but eventually accepted.

Soon the end of the cadre arrived, and on the last day, we all found out who our partner platoon commander inspectors would be. Out

The Forming of PTU G COY 4/85: Officer / NCO Cadre Training 277

of eight inspectors, consisting of seven one-pip inspectors and one senior inspector (SIP), I was paired with the SIP who came from Kowloon West named [CKKm] and the Platoon SGT [LMNm], who was from Mong Kok and very fit. I believed I was assigned the SIP as it was thought he would be able to counsel me, so I didn't go off on a tangent being a one-pip hardworking inspector. The rest of the four NCOs had various backgrounds from UB to CID, with one SGT coming from crime only just being reinstated to the police force on appeal after being dismissed due to a disciplinary case as a result of a restaurant he owned. I was sure we would all get on well, and after being paired up, we went for a coffee to discuss the arrival of the PCs the following Monday. We also discussed our style of command, being very strict initially until just after the "Slackening of Slings", which occurred at the end of demonstrating we could carry out a perfect platoon attack. This meant that the slings on our weapons would be slackened off for the start of flexible drills training. Hence, a sign we had achieved the basics.

Thereafter, it would be strict, as PTU was a very disciplined unit. [CKKm] and I discussed what we wanted in a platoon orderly. We would have to ask for volunteers when the PCs arrived and most probably appoint one on the first day.

Chapter 60

The Forming of PTU G COY 4/85

The day of arrival of the PCs to camp saw all platoon drivers take their Bedford trucks to various pick-up points in Kowloon police stations, accompanied by a platoon officer and the PLN SGT. The remaining platoon commander would be at PTU HQ setting up a table for a roll call to be taken for their own platoon PCs with an information sheet asking which section they would like to be placed in. On the arrival of the PCs, they were harried to march properly, and discipline was very strict. If a PC looked like he wasn't giving 100%, he was given press-ups or a run around the drill square as punishment.

For the rest of the first day, the PCs were assigned their barracks, collected their uniforms and kit and had a haircut. In the afternoon, there was platoon admin work to get out of the way. This was followed by a beast of a PE session by the PTIs, which, on occasion, was added by the platoon officers, especially during dumbbell sessions when all the platoon NCOs would demand 110% effort.

At the end of the day, we interviewed PCs for the position of platoon orderly and lorry guard. On finishing duty, [CKKm] took me to have a glass of iced honey water at a famous bee farm just outside the PTU HQ camp. We discussed who should be platoon orderly with us, and we both agreed that it should be [YDm].

The next two weeks saw us give all our lectures to the PCs, with PTU HQ staff inspectors checking up on what we were doing and giving feedback on occasion. I remember giving a lecture on stop, question and search, translated by the platoon orderly [YDm] and also covering frisk search, wall search and a full protective search, with me as the person being stopped. At the end of the protective search, when the PC stated he had finished, I asked him to go back to his seat. As he turned his back to me, I produced a meat chopper hung from a piece of string in the front of my shorts and went to attack the officer. This drew gasps of shock from the rest of the platoon PCs. I felt relieved, especially as I hadn't cut anything important during the concealment of the weapon. This point was never forgotten, and all PCs made sure they concentrated on the lectures.

Also, during the first two weeks, we did platoon attack training and draw stores. PTU HQ staff gave no leeway for lacklustre performances, and this was something we instilled in all our platoon members. During the cadre, and especially after the arrival of the PCs, I had become accustomed and knew I would be responsible for their training, welfare and level of attainment, with some spirited guidance from PTU HQ Staff. Bonding took place during classroom lectures, physical fitness training, range courses and platoon standardization drills where you learnt riot dispersal tactics using your four sections of eight officers, all with increasing levels of firepower. The drills became your life, and discipline was very tightly maintained as your life could depend on it. You had to demonstrate that you were straining every sinew in your body carrying out the drills and that your platoon members were doing the same. If this wasn't done, PTU HQ staff would conjure up a more intense physical respite so that you would concentrate the mind to demonstrate the exacting levels of attainment expected of you, as nothing else would be acceptable! At the end of COY week two, all four platoons in the PTU Company had to fully demonstrate their knowledge and proficiency in what were called platoon attack drills, better known as standardization, after which slings could be slackened as a sort of coming-of-age ceremony. The remaining six weeks of training took on more flexible drill training, not to mention three platoon exercises concerning dispersing rioting mobs and more bread-and-butter policing, such as high-rise cordon and sweeps as well as anti-crime patrols. This ultimately resulted in the PTU Company Exercise, where Company Headquarters arranged their four platoons (170 men) like chess pieces to control an area where law and order would become a problem, only redeemable by a company level Internal Security Sweep of rioting mobs so that they dispersed and were no longer a problem. In our case, we were also given a building to undertake a high-rise cordon and sweep. The COY CDR brought me on as one of his briefing team members, and during his briefing discussion with PTU HQ staff, I asked how we would communicate if COY HQ used a different communication channel. This was because if he didn't let us know what it was, this would be problematic. This was a small point but important, especially as there were no mobile phones in those days.

During a second COY exercise, we were given the Long Valley to cordon and sweep for illegal immigrants, with all troops being flown in by RAF Wessex helicopters. This was successful, as was the first exercise, and we lived up to our company T-Shirt motto, "Our Balls Go the Furthest". The only illegal immigrant spotted that day was a barking deer native to the area.

During our last week of COY training, I was waiting to go on a range course, but SDU members were using it first. When the targets were collected, there was no centre of body bullet holes, and initially, I thought they had all missed the targets until I looked at the head of the target that was pitted with many bullet holes. This was because they had been practising double-tap headshots.

That same week, I did a full platoon attack drill demonstration for some visiting British Army high-ranking officers. Near the end, [YDm] my platoon orderly informed me that I hadn't given the "Teng Gi" (wait) command for the use of the shotguns, which I immediately then did, after which I gave the order to fire with six Remington shotguns all firing together, sending an echo around the surrounding hills.

That same week, I stayed one night in camp with the platoon on a Commissioner of Police Reserve (CPs reserve), which meant that I was on duty with my platoon for 24 hours, and if anything happened that needed a PTU platoon, we would be called out. The COY 2 I/C stayed at camp with us, and we played a Chinese card game called "Chow Daai Di". By 01:00hrs, I was a few hundred dollars up when I said I was going to bed. The COY 2 I/C said he, as senior officer, would decide when the game finished. So, we played for another two hours, after which no one person had won too much, so we went to bed.

That week there was much drill practice for the Passing Out Parade (POP). However, that Wednesday, there was an inter PTU HQ training Coy sports day between our company Golf COY and Echo COY, which was an NT COY. This went well, but we lost the stretcher race and another event with only the football remaining. During the football match, both companies were sat in their platoons around the football pitch, and we were winning the football match. Our COY 2I/C [BMm] didn't like the Echo COY song being played full blast on the Echo COY jeep, so he told [FMm] and me to do something about it. A short time later, I grabbed the Echo COY driver while [FMm] grabbed the tape being played, and all hell let loose. Two platoons from Golf COY rushed down to the football pitch, and three platoons from Echo did the same, during which a huge fight took place. The PTU HQ PTIs joined in the fight, and I saw one physical training instructor punch and lay out one NCO from Echo COY. Eventually, the melee was brought under control, and during the prizegiving ceremony, the C PTU, who had been out of camp, mentioned the high spirits shown. It was of note that our Coy 2 I/C [BMm] told [FMm] and myself that he hadn't said anything about the music if we should be asked. [FMm] and I thought that was typical, but at the same time, if the fight had been reported involving two

Internal Security (IS) COYs at PTU HQs, who would they have called, the Ghostbusters?

That night there were a few beers in the mess, and during a conversation with the Echo COY CDR and the C PTU, I mentioned that I had seen [BLm] on the news attending the sight of an SDU raid, to which the C PTU, who was drunk, said that wasn't possible as he was still under training. I repeated what I had said as I had been on an SDU selection with him and knew what he looked like. The C PTU said that he was in charge of SDU and that a trainee wouldn't attend an actual raid site. He then said I had become boring and told me to fuck off. The ECHO COY CDR gave me a wink, and I left. On leaving, I couldn't stop thinking that the C PTU had earlier been at the bar when he pissed his shorts while engaged in conversation and that this apparently was commonplace. I couldn't fathom out the sense of needing to go for a piss being overruled by being engaged in conversation and resulting in pissing in your shorts.

The day of the Passing Out Parade (POP) arrived, and I took part in the morning PT session with Echo COY, after which I had a quick shower and got on my finest uniform for the POP. This saw my platoon win Best Sports Platoon, and I drove past, sat atop the Saracen Armoured Car for the salute to the Reviewing Officer, who, in my case, was the RC Marine [MJm]. In the afternoon, we packed up all our belongings and went to Monk Kok Police station to take over our barracks and COY offices. The 12 weeks of training had been great, and I was looking forward to the Regional attachment being away from frontline police work for 12 weeks. The next 20 weeks would see us take part in company and platoon strength operations tackling prevalent crime problems as well as licensed premise checks in Kowloon West.

Chapter 61

Kowloon West PTU Golf COY Regional Attachment Incidents

A Shift in TST DIV

A Shift in TST for PTU Golf COY platoon officers was normally quite quiet as it was full of nightlife entertainment premises. Most of the time, we were in uniform and occasionally plain clothes. The hotels in TST loved me not because if I wanted to go to the toilet, I would go to the Sheraton or the Peninsula. On entering in uniform, the hotel security would be all over me. However, I insisted on using their toilets, as they were always the cleanest and nearest. In the end, the hotel security just met me and greeted me but stopped asking me to leave and go elsewhere.

Another feature of A Shift in TST was the number of tourists walking around with map in hand, looking lost. They would see me and my orderly, and when stopping us, they would look at the backing behind our number or **RHKP** badge and ask my orderly a question in English, all because he had a red cloth backing and I had a black cloth backing. At the end of the conversation, I would say hello in English and ask how their holiday was going. Most tourists looked surprised that I could speak English, as I did not have a red backing to my **RHKP** badge. Usually, after this introduction, we would have a conversation for about five minutes, and I would give them pointers in respect of what to see while they asked where I was from and how long I had been in Hong Kong.

License Checks in TST DIV

Normally on B shift, the ADVC ADM TST DIV would draw up a list of licensed premises to check normally during an Operation Levington (Anti-crime). This normally went well until the first time I entered the cavernous Canton Disco for a license check because it didn't have a liquor license at that time.

On realizing this but noticing lots of drinks, I was informed they had been brought in from outside. I then just wanted to check the patron's identity cards and leave. During the check, we would get the lights turned on and ask the DJ to make an announcement that the faster everyone cooperated, the quicker we could finish the check and leave. On one occasion, the DJ extended the message and added that the police had ruined the atmosphere and that we were deliberately working too slowly. I quickly managed to stop the DJ from using the mike and warned him that he could be arrested. However, when I returned to the ID Card checks, some customers were stroppy. One particular customer used some choice words with one of my PCs and even commented on his number 1924, asking whether that was the year he was born because he looked so young. At this juncture, I slammed the customer against the wall and did a thorough search in front of all the other customers, at which point, he shrank. He shrank even further when I told him he was going back to TST Police Station as there was a problem checking his ID card, and I didn't want to inconvenience the other patrons while I checked his ID card.

Chapter 62

Problematic Police Division of Shek Kip Mei

Stolen Car Wheel

Usually, on arrival at Shek Kip Mei Police Division, we were given a tasking sheet that resembled a thesis. Their ADVC OPS, a female Chief Inspector called [LKWf], who I heard was problematic, had compiled this. On one particular A shift, I arrived back at SKM police station to check my officers before we left to go back to our Mong Kok base to go off duty when I found two PCs missing. I was informed that they were seeing the ADVC OPS SKM and were getting a bollocking. I knocked on her office door and entered only to see her shouting at my two officers. I asked if there was a problem and if there was, I should be present, but all she said was that they hadn't reported a theft from vehicle case in one of the car parks the officers were assigned to patrol. She then asked me to leave, which I did, and then went to check the car park concerned with an NCO who knew the location. The car turned out to be abandoned and one wheel was missing, but the bolts that would have held the wheel were all rusty. I immediately went back to the station and told my PLN SGT to take the rest of the platoon back to Mong Kok as I would see the ADVC OPS SKM. I knocked on her door and went in just as she finished bollocking my two PCs, so I asked them to leave while I spoke to WCIP [LKWf]. I informed her that I had been to the car park and the car was an abandoned car with rusty bolts at the missing wheel position. This implied it had been taken a long time ago, and if she bollocked my PCs, I should be present, being their immediate commander. I then stated that if she bollocked my officers, why didn't she bollock her own men. She then said she would speak to my COY CDR, so I said, "right, do that", as I would also speak to him when I went off duty. On the way out, I saw one of her patrol subunit commanders (PSUC) [BBm], and he told me she was loopy. On arrival back at Mong Kok Police Station, I knocked on my COY CDR's door and went in. He waved for me to sit down as he was on the phone. After the phone call ended, I told him what had happened and he then stated that the phone call was from the ADVC OPS SKM, who wasn't happy about my manner. I informed him that my manner had been both firm and fair, at which point he smiled.

4 lbs of Heroin in SKM DIV

On another A shift in SKM DIV, two of my officers spotted two males acting suspiciously near the boot of a private car near the Police Sports and Recreation Club (PSRC). They approached them, asked them for their HK ID cards and searched them. They then asked who owned the car, and after one of the males stated he did, they asked for the keys and said they were going to check the car. The males became very nervous, so they were controlled more, and when the boot was open, four one-pound bags of number three heroin were found wrapped in a brown bag. Assistance was called, and I arrived and managed the scene until CID took over. On going off duty, the COY CDR asked to see me and congratulated the officers for a great case. After they had left, he told me [LKWf] had rang him to complain that my officers should not have been at the location they saw the two males as they should have been two hundred meters away according to her beat time schedule. He stated that what she had said was truly unbelievable and that he would write a written compliment in the concerned officer's record of service for the case.

Rape and Murder Case

One day on afternoon shift, my platoon was reformed to report to Regional CID in Kowloon Headquarters to get a briefing on a rape and murder case in SKM DIV as we were needed to undertake door to door enquiries. A few ex-pat CID officers were present as well as their crime squad officers. On checking attendance, a superintendent started to brief about the location in Shek Kip Mei Estate on Woh Chai Street, even giving the block and flat number. At that moment, the door to the briefing room opened and in walked the **ADVC OPS SKM** [LKWf] in uniform, who excused herself for being late. The superintendent said an elderly woman of 70 had been found in her flat naked and tied to a chair, with her right leg tied to her upper torso. She had a plastic bag tied to her face so she couldn't breathe, but it wasn't known if this was done before or after she was raped. This was quite shocking, but the superintendent added some money was missing. It was believed the culprit was a drug addict as it was a problematic drug location.

At the end of the briefing, he asked if there were any questions before giving out duties. [LKWf] put her hand up and looked as though she had an important question to ask and was seeking an answer. She asked why the rapist had tied the right leg of the elderly woman to her upper torso, and the whole room went quiet, bearing in mind that everyone else was male officers.

A short time later, an officer said penetration, to which [LKWf] asked what he meant by penetration? He then explained that whoever raped the old lady with one leg out of the way could penetrate her vagina more so than normal. [LKWf] looked shocked and left the room, to which a few officers mentioned she should not have asked the stupid question if she didn't like the answer. I stayed a bit longer, and one of the crime inspectors let me know [LKWf] was known for being loopy and that she had been laid out by a female SSGT whose husband had become [LKWf's] boyfriend. A few years later, I heard that she had sought professional help for her OCD.

Chapter 63

Golf Company Life

Firecrackers in the Golf Company NCO's Barrack

One night, the whole of PTU Golf COY 4/85 was on CPs reserve, and when this happened, there was normally a COY daai sik wooi (big meal) in a nearby Chinese restaurant. This normally involved a lot of beer and a late night.

I applied for some time off the next day and, after going to bed in my office, set my alarm for 03:30hrs. When the alarm went off, I went to the main barrack block and took the lift to the eleventh floor, wedging the lift door open and then went to my NCOs barrack and tossed in a full packet of firecrackers which I had lit before legging it for the lift that was waiting.

In the morning at roll call, all the NCOs looked tired, especially mine. One of which was SGT [Bm], being ex CID, obviously hadn't seen the funny side of my prank. On reporting on duty the next day, I bought all my NCOs tea and everything was fine.

They told me they knew it was me as no one else would do such a thing.

Social Life and Physical Training

SDU selection was advertised for early September, and I applied. [MBm] and [SEPm], also from my intake, both applied upon hearing what I had said about my first attempt. Plus, we had made friends with all the younger unit inspectorate officers, who were good to be with on a night out. Physical training together and in our own time took place, but no fighting practice was done. All three of us were getting very fit as the two-week selection would require nothing less. On one of our joint training exercises, I popped a muscle in my shoulder, which [MBm] put back into position, much to my amazement and thanks. I will leave the SDU selection for a section later on. However, what I will say is that we all attended a medical at HMS Tamar by a navy doctor as the vacancy was for the SDU Water Team. During the medical, the doctor mentioned that my ears didn't equalize at the same time and asked whether I had ever fallen flat on my face. I thought a while and said that I had fallen off a bar stool in Hollywood East disco some two years earlier, knocking myself out after watching Swan Lake. He told me not to worry, as he would arrange for me to have an operation at the British Military Hospital to have my septum put straight, which would solve the problem. I gave the dates of the Monday after the end of the two-week SDU selection.

Panorama Restaurant New World Hotel TST

If I had Saturday night and Sunday off, I would stay out late and get up late and have a slice of toast and a cup of tea. In the afternoon, I would go to the Panorama restaurant in the New World Hotel for afternoon tea. One Sunday morning, I got a call from a girl who I thought was from the hardware shop in Ngau Tau Kok. After the conversation, I asked if she wanted to have afternoon tea at the New World Hotel, to which she said yes and would bring her friend, who I took to mean her sister. We arranged to meet at 15:00hrs, and on arrival, I noticed it wasn't the two sisters from the hardware shop but two girls who used to hang around KT police

Station that [RJm] and I knew. We knew them because they were chatty and we practised their English conversation. After we finished afternoon tea, I knew [RJm] would be home after his morning shift, so I asked the girls if they wanted to see [RJm], and they both said yes. On arrival at the flat, we gave them a drink, and after a conversation, they said they would like to go out some more. However, both [RJm] and I knew that they were both nearly 16 and that seeing them might not be a good idea as they both looked like they were looking for a boyfriend. We said we would call and got them a taxi home! Better safe than sorry.

Hill Walk with SDKSf and flat mate

In early July 1985, I got a phone call from [SDKSf], and after conversation, we decided to go for a hill walk with [RJm] and two of her friends. The hill walk went really well until near the end when [SKDSf] handed me a bottle of water to take a drink. When I put the whole bottleneck in my mouth, she said I could keep the bottle. She then mentioned something about pouring the water into her mouth rather than drink from the top. This irritated me no end as she had literally implied that I was not hygienic and I said as much, mentioning something may have been lost in translation. The rest of the walk went well, but the several months we had not seen each other or rang certainly put a gap between us that day, which you could say was not for the best.

SCMP Reporter and Friend

One day during the summer, [RJm] said he had met someone, and she had asked if they could go out on a foursome. I was up for that, and after afternoon tea at the panorama in the New World Hotel, we ended up back at our Ming Court flat. Eventually, after putting some music on, [RJm] and I were sat on our own sofas with one girl each when it started to go dark, which meant that body contact increased, as did playful kissing.

This progressed with the girl I was with to removal of clothing as the flat was very dark and the LP playing was on repeat. Eventually, a lustful tryst took place and after another half an hour and a trip to the bathroom for me and my new friend, I asked if anyone wanted a drink. The evening ended well, and we all agreed to see each other again.

About two weeks later, the two girls came round. While [RJm] was speaking to his reporter friend, I said to my friend that I had something to show her, and we quickly retired to my bedroom for a lustful tryst. Just after finishing, there was a knock at the door and we both came out. There then ensued a conversation about being boyfriend and girlfriend, and eventually, this finished and the girls left. I believe [RJm] saw his reporter friend a couple of times more, but my duty hours didn't allow me to join him or meet the other girl.

The Mysterious Ring of the Door Bell

One night I was home and the front doorbell rang. I opened the door and there was a reasonable looking girl at the door asking if I was [AAm], and I said I was. She asked if she could come in, so I said yes and made her a drink. She said that a friend of mine thought that she should contact me, but she wouldn't say whom, which left me somewhat bewildered. She said she was looking for a companion for everything but nothing serious, even stating she preferred comfort and company.

Thereafter, things progressed very quickly and a lustful tryst occurred, but she could not stay the night. This happened once a week for the next four weeks, and on the last occasion, we were both in the bath when I realized I knew nothing about this girl other than she had nipples that looked like button mushrooms.

I then told a white lie that a girlfriend was coming to visit me and this was the last time we could meet. I later learnt from a couple of inspectors that this had happened to them, and they thought it was down to the countdown to 1997 and or wanting to know how to interact more with ex-pats.

RJm's Answering the Call for More Experience

One night, I got up at about 03:00hrs to go to the toilet and [RJm] was just coming back from the kitchen. He said he had company and opened his bedroom door to show me a lithe body lying under the body-hugging sheets, revealing a female [CEf] who was fast asleep. He explained he met her dancing in a disco and that she was going to be married to another inspector soon, but she had confided in [RJm] that she hadn't had much sexual experience and would he mind helping her out. He jumped at the chance and brought her home for a few lustful trysts. The next day, after the girl had left, I told [RJm] that I had heard that this had happened on two other occasions. However, I didn't believe it until he enlightened me! I also mentioned that [RJm] looked like the girl's future husband.

25th Birthday Massage Present from RJm

On my 25th Birthday, [RJm] said I better be home as he had arranged for a female masseuse to come to the flat and give me a massage. The woman arrived and gave me a poor massage, so much so that after about 30 minutes, I said I would give her a massage just so she knew what a good massage should be like. About 30 minutes later, I said goodbye and when I saw [RJm], he was surprised there had been no hanky panky.

Scuttlebutt

In the summer of 1985, the trial of Inspector Jeffrey Davison took place for the killing of Inspector Graham Dallas in the summer of 1984. Both these inspectors had the same Thai female girlfriend. In 1984, there had been a knife fight in Davison's flat at the Kennedy Road Police Inspectors Quarters on Hong Kong Island when

Graham Dallas went to see him armed with a knife. At the end of the trial, Davison was found not guilty and was immediately repatriated back to the UK. A lot of interest was shown in the Thai female, but when she appeared, everyone was astounded as she was very plain.

TBm Conviction for Unlawful Sexual Intercourse (USI)

[TBm], the inspector junior to me at PTS and the one who said I worked too hard in SDS, occupied the post of an OC Crime HQ in HMT DIST. This allowed him to work mainly days and not shifts. He preferred this because he could moonlight as a stripper at night, dressed either as a Chief Inspector of Police or a traffic cop. He had a Japanese girlfriend who assisted him, who worked for Cathay Pacific, but he also played the field.

One of his other girlfriends was a student at King George the 5th School (KGV), and he found out her school PE teacher was making love to her and had given her a sexually transmitted infection (STI). He then crafted a letter using his office typewriter and sent it anonymously to the police. The girl was interviewed and admitted to having sex with her PE teacher, who was later arrested. She was also asked if there was anyone else, to which she mentioned inspector [TBm].

This resulted in [TBm] being summoned to the internal investigations unit. He turned up to see SP [PLm], who, on noticing his shoulder holster, told him that the interview was an official criminal interview and instructed him to go and check in the revolver. Eventually, he was charged with USI and went to court in early 1986, where he pleaded not guilty. Part of the evidence was his office typewriter, as the face of one of the letter keys was the same as on the anonymous letter. After intervention by his lawyer, he was brought up that same afternoon, where he changed his plea to guilty for USI and was convicted. However, he got an absolute discharge for stating that he thought the girl was 16 and taking credit for reporting the PE teacher. He was allowed to leave Hong Kong soon after, even receiving his gratuity, whereas the PE teacher went to prison. He was no longer allowed to work in the Royal Hong Kong Police.

Trip To Macau for Sight Seeing and Massage

In early October, one of [RJm's] friends came to Hong Kong who was about 22 years old and came from a farming family. We went out for a few drinks on a few nights, but as [RJm] was working, I said I would take him to Macau. On arrival in Macau, we did the normal sights and had some good food, after which we saw the Crazy Paris show before going for a massage. On arrival at the massage parlour, all the girl masseuses were sat down with numbers on their blouses, and we were asked which numbered girl we wanted for the massage. He picked a number, and he asked me if anything untoward would happen, and I said no and to just follow the lead of the masseuse. When he came out of the massage, he was a bit sheepish but soon brightened up, and we got the overnight ferry back to Hong Kong.

Fitness Training with RJm

[RJm] had finally decided he would leave the Royal Hong Kong Police and interview to become an officer in the British Army. This would take place in the New Year of 1986 as he would leave Hong Kong in December 1985. He wanted to make the most of his three months of vacation leave, travelling to India and enjoying Christmas in Scotland.

It was important that he stay fit, so every time we were off together, we would do some fitness training. This either involved circuit training at Tai Hang Tung Sports Recreation Ground on Boundary Street, the Police Sports and Recreation Club, Beacon Hill and Tai Po Road runs or, indeed, dumbbells at home and circuits at Kings Park Rise. He also had a fascination with the Filofax and had chosen that as his preferred subject of discussion. [RJm] also sought out as much information as possible while working in POLMIL at Police Headquarters. His preparation went well, and both he and I could see the difference that our joint PE training had on his fitness. [RJm] was successful and joined the British Army and attended Sandhurst in 1986.

Disciplinary Hearing Involving SBHm & The Emperor as Prosecutor

During the Autumn of 1985, I was informed that I would be a prosecution witness in the defaulter hearing of [SBHm], the OC Action Squad NTK. This was for his raid and execution of a search warrant at a house on its own grounds in Lei Yue Mun KT Police Division, supported by the NTK CID reserve team and my SDS 1 SMP DIST.

The only worrying thing was that as [SBHm] was a senior inspector of police and the prosecutor had to be one rank higher. The appointed prosecutor was none other than The Emperor [GKLm], who was now the ADVC OPS SMP DIV. I wrote out my statement according to my extensive notebook entry and sent it via dispatch to The Emperor. Nothing more was asked for, and eventually, I was informed of the date of the defaulter hearing.

On the day of the defaulter hearing, I was called as witness one, and The Emperor led the questioning. He asked me what my part was, and I stated that [SBHm] had seen me in NTK Police Station and had told me there might be drugs at the house that was raided and that I should come along, seeing as I was SDS SMP, which tackled drug problems. He asked me if I saw anyone being assaulted, to which I said I only saw people found at the premise being controlled. He then asked me if I had seen anyone draw a revolver, and I stated that when we raided the house, it was dark, and I had not seen anyone draw a revolver. I didn't add that I had heard [SBHm] shout at me not to move, as he would open fire in English, as there was no need to, as I hadn't seen any revolver drawn. He then asked me what was found and I said a Singapore Airlines life jacket. After which, he asked what I had done at the end of the raid, and I said I had compiled the police first information report form, which was a POL 159 back at Kwun Tong Station.

Then it happened. The Emperor stated that as I had compiled the POL 159, I was in charge of the raid and responsible for all the occurrences during the raid. He went on further to say that it was a drugs raid really and not just a prisoner house search. While concluding, he stated that I, as the OC SDS 1 SMP, operating outside my own police district, was also in violation of my terms of deployment, which was to tackle drugs in SMP District. It was obvious he was trying to blame me and hang me out to dry. He finally asked if I agreed.

I then referred him to the POL 159 I had compiled, which clearly stated that I had only assisted the OC Action Squad NTK DIV and the NTK CID reserve team in that order. I also pointed out that the POL 159 had also mentioned that the OC Action Squad NTK DIV led the raid. On pointing this out, he asked me one more time if I was responsible, and I stated I was not, while all the time thinking, what a bastard he was for trying to blame me. I was then done with giving my evidence, and the Appropriate Tribunal, who held the rank of Superintendent, thanked me for the evidence I had given in an assured manner.

Unfortunately, this was not the last time I would have to foil the Emperor.

Three Armed Robberies in One Day in Kowloon West

One Friday, while on mobile patrol in Kowloon West, I said to my PLN SGT that I had a gut feeling that there would be a report of armed robbery during our afternoon shift. The PLN SGT looked perturbed and informed me that it was bad luck saying such things and hoped that there would be no such reports, and the shift carried on. However, about an hour later, we overheard a report of an armed robbery at the junction of Nathan Road and Jordan Road at a Hong Kong and Shanghai Bank. I told the PLN SGT that we were not far away, and despite the Emergency Unit Kowloon West

(EUKW) being tasked, we should go. I even instructed the driver to get there as quickly as possible but not to use the sirens or lights. The PLN SGT broke out the BRVs, handed me one, and even slid another one over the shoulders of the driver. Activity in our mobile patrol car was frantic, checking revolvers and even the orderly, making his AR-15 ready. On arrival at the junction of Nathan Road and Jordan Road, unusually, there was no traffic, which added to the suspense. We debussed a short way away from the concerned bank and, being first on the scene, approached cautiously. Once inside the bank and making sure it was clear, we informed RCCC K that the report was false and everything was normal. We waited for EU KW and UB YMT to turn up and then left.

During the rest of the shift, there were two similar reports, which we went to, but again, nothing was found. The PLN SGT stated that this sometimes occurred when the "bad guys" wanted to see how long responding units would take to respond and in what manner. To say the shift was strange would be an understatement, but it was certainly exciting and one not for the faint-hearted.

Chapter 64

Special Duty Unit Selection Again

This SDU selection was set down to be held from the 2nd of September 1985 to the 14th of September 1985, if you managed to survive that long. Even if you did survive the whole selection, there was no guarantee that you would be selected.

On the morning of Monday 2nd of September 1985, approximately 12 police inspectors and 60 PCs fell in at New Territories Depot (NTD) Fanling, which was the home of the Special Duties Unit. We were all assigned an area to keep our backpacks and belongings. After this, we were given a bib with a number to wear over our PE kit or jungle greens if we wore them. I had arrived with [MBm] and [SEPm], both from my intake, in [MBm's] car. I had brought an Esky box in which we could put cold drinks that already had ice in it and was stacked full of cold hydrating drinks.

We were immediately told to get into PE gear and given five minutes to fall back in before we did a fitness test. This was the normal fitness test but done twice, during which I managed 27 chin-ups, twice. After the fitness test, we went for a run to Wo Hop Shek Cemetery. On arrival at the cemetery, a huge set of steps was pointed out to us, and we were split into smaller groups. Each group was headed by an inspector, and we were told to do two-legged jumps up each step until we got to the 10th step, then run down and do the same, increasing 10 steps at a time until we reached 50 steps. This was very hard work, especially in the heat of September being 33°C and 80%+ humidity. Once all the groups had done this, we ran back to NT Depot for more dumbbells and circuit training. More circuits in the indoor weights room followed this, while the rest of the attendees did more circuits outside.

The physical exercise was relentless, and the only saving grace was that we were given regular water breaks at the end of each scheduled activity, albeit very brief ones.

Midway through one of the circuits, a SDU inspector accused [SEPm] of not giving his all and asked him to follow him to the indoor weights room. Once in the indoor weights room, he was given a bar with 200lbs of weight on it and was asked to do squats. [SEPm] managed to survive 10 minutes of this and then rejoined us. The physical tasks continued, switching between runs and circuits with the odd session in the indoor weights room thrown in. At about 18:00hrs, we were given 30 minutes to eat and or change PE gear.

At 18:30hrs exactly, we were given another three hours of physical exercise and then told to change into jungle greens with running shoes. On falling back in, it was apparent that we had lost about 20 PCs and two inspectors, either quitting themselves or succumbing to injury. The PCs who were not dressed in jungle greens were allowed to leave that night but report back early in the morning at 07:30hrs.

The remaining police inspectors were told to board two Ford Transit trucks and go to the Tai Po Industrial Estate, debussing on the Sha Lo Tung Road. Just after we debussed, two police transits stopped near us. We then heard two loud slaps on the ground, and on looking around, we saw two large punch bags. We were told to pick up the punching bags after we had been placed in two teams of five inspectors. We were instructed it would be a race to the top of the hill, and four inspectors would carry the punch bags, with the 5th

inspector replacing an inspector carrying the punch bag on the instruction of an SDU inspector.

The two teams set off, and even from the start, they were both harried by SDU members to go faster, with some even pushing inspectors physically to do so. The top of the hill didn't come quick enough, but it was under 10 minutes. Once at the top, we were told to drop the punch bags and take some water quickly and then navigate to Hok Tau Reservoir without torches. Just before we got to Hok Tau, we were gathered together and instructed to do a covert recce of the dam where there was a criminal gang discussing a bank robbery and to try to get as much information as possible but not get caught. Each inspector took their own routes, and while doing the recce, I heard a large splash in the reservoir, after which a SDU inspector shouted it was unsafe to go in the water and that whoever went in had better get out. This exercise lasted for about two hours, after which we were all debriefed separately.

We then walked to the Hok Tau Road, during which we all did press-ups, sit-ups, star jumps and burpees, not to mention a massive dumbbell session when we met the vehicles. Once this had ended, we heard the punch bags hit the deck, and we went back to our teams of fives and were told to run with the bags to Sha Tau Kok Road. On arrival, we all boarded police transit vehicles and drove to Luk Keng. On arrival at Luk Keng, we were told we would do a race walk, setting off at two-minute intervals, accompanied by a member of SDU. Running was not allowed, but if we were caught up, we would be eliminated. Finally, we were all given a 10-foot wooden pole weighing about 30lbs, which we had to carry the whole time. If we put it down for any reason, we would be given 50 press-ups to do before resuming the speed walk that would end at PTU HQ. I was assigned [TSKm], a CIP who would later become a CP, and I set off at a very brisk pace. The only thing stopping me from going any faster was the 10-foot pole. On occasion, [TSKm] would also update me that the person behind me was catching up and that I should walk faster. Near Ping Che, my left running shoelace came undone, and I was told if I fastened it and the pole touched the ground, it would result in 50 press-ups. I took the penalty and fastened my shoelace, and reached PTU HQ in just over two hours, a distance of about 13km.

On the arrival of all inspectors at PTU HQ, we were allowed 30 minutes to get something to eat and fall in at the gym. That morning, I fought three inspectors, including [EGm], [RMm] and one other. The other one was much bigger than me, but I had learnt from my brother, who fought for England at Tae Kwan Do, to keep close, so a full swing couldn't be thrown. The bout with [EGm] was evenly split but very physical, resulting in a few clashes of heads and bruises. In the final one with [RMm], I believed I had the better of him, despite him being taller and more wiry.

The next exercise was down at Shek Kong Army base, where we did the assault course and the high heights climbing frame. Once at the top, we were blindfolded and given an AR-15 to hold while we stood astride with our feet on two bars that had a 30-foot drop between them, while we were pushed and pulled to see if we maintained our balance. Immediately after this, we did a 2.4km run around a track that took [SEPm] and me 8 minutes to complete. We were then given a break near the Naafi, where I got myself a meat pie but was seen eating it and was told the break had been for water only. We were then given another 2.4km run, which we did again in 8 minutes, and I was lucky not to throw up my meat pie. Subsequently, we were set off in 5-minute intervals to run to the Fire Services Training School (FSTS) for phobia tests. The weather was extremely hot, and by the time I got to the FSTS, I was overheating and breathing very heavily. I was then given a respirator to wear that had cloth over the air intake, with blackout eye goggles and then put in a tunnel. This was made of wood in the hot room and had false ends as well as up and down sections. I was told to find the end of the tunnel, but as soon as I entered, I noticed I wasn't getting enough air, as the respirator rubber would compress on my face every time I took a breath. I controlled my breathing and eventually set off. The heat in the hot room got to about 45°C, which made everything hard work.

Once this exercise was over and everyone had completed the tunnel, we were taken to the abseiling tower and instructed to run to the seventh floor. On arrival, we put on an abseil belt and got ourselves ready to abseil, taking one step down from the departure ledge. On reaching this point, someone on the ground floor took hold of the abseil rope, and we were told to let go of the rope and lean backwards. This was putting your life in someone's hands that you didn't know, and we were then instructed that whatever happened, to not grab the rope. The person at ground level laid out 20 feet of slack rope and flipped it, meaning that I fell like a stone, and after about 15 feet, I grabbed the rope. On reaching the ground, we were told to run back to PTU HQ as fast as we could. I soon established a lead, and somewhere near the Golf Club, I was told to sit down behind a police transit and tell the other inspectors I had given up to see their reaction. Once at PTU HQ, we went to San Uk Ling for a range course where we also stripped down The SDU preferred handgun, which was the Browning and then reassembled it, initially without a blindfold but later with a blindfold. After this, we were split into two teams and played murder ball with a medicine ball, which got very rough for an hour until the ball went down the sides of the hill into a restricted area. At about 21:00hrs, we were told to go home and report back at 07:30hrs to NT Depot in PE kit.

The next day, we did more circuits, including the weights room and [SEPm] was again accused of not putting in enough effort and taken to the indoor weights room. This time, the session went past the 10-minute mark, and as he thought there would be no end to it, he threw the weights bar onto the deck, stating he was done and left. This was a shock to the other inspectors but an incentive not to be seen slacking.

Next, we were taken to Tai Lam Chung, where on debussing, we were taken for a run to the reservoir and back to the Marine West Base. We ran straight off the pier into the water and one of the inspectors, [TPm] freaked. This was because, as soon as he hit the water, he clung to the pier because he wasn't a strong swimmer. This was the end of the selection for [TPm] but not for the rest who were taken out to a cargo ship and made to climb mountaineering ladders to the ship's deck.

Once on deck, we climbed to the highest point and jumped off with one SDU member demonstrating how to do it. He was wearing a wet suit but didn't jump with the wind, which caught him, and he hit the water from 35 feet sideways on. I didn't make the same mistake even though we did the exercise three times. Next, we went back to PTU HQ and were allocated a locker to store our kit, but by that time, we had shrunk to just five inspectors. While changing and storing our kit, [WSm] told us his wife was pregnant, and we shouldn't mention it as SDU would use it against him. That night, we climbed out of Shek Kong from the Fan Kam Road, walking up the side of a hill and not on a trail, as we were told we shouldn't be seen.

Once at the top of Pak Tai To Yan, a height of 480 metres, we set up camp, which we had to defend. One of the SDU NCOs [KGm], who had been complaining about the weight of his backpack, unpacked it to find a 20lb rock that had been stashed by his colleagues. That night, we were kept busy and eventually, because a Typhoon 8 was likely to go up during the day, we headed back to PTU HQ. Upon arrival, after a 2-hour walk, we were told we could go home but be back at PTU HQ at 07:30hrs the next morning. Once in the barrack, we began to get changed, and someone switched on the TV set, which had an aerobics programme on, being demonstrated by [SDf] the now [PDf]. There were some choice words about her body being sex on legs and what the lads would like to do to it. However, I took the opportunity to get some firecrackers I had brought and set them off.

Immediately, the firecrackers went off, and the four remaining inspectors turned around at me, thinking they had been played by SDU and were not going home. When realizing that it was only me playing a prank, they were mightily relieved but not best pleased. That night, I went to Jimmy's Kitchen for a steak with [MBm], but halfway through the meal, we decided to go home and get some sleep. This was mainly because our stomachs had shrunk, and we had been sleep deprived.

The next morning while getting changed, [WSm] informed us that he wanted to quit, to which I immediately said he could quit when we said he could. This shocked him, but I quickly added that he had done five days and if he left, that would be wasted, and the remaining four inspectors would get more attention.

The next four days went very quickly, doing rural recces in the NT and even going through bogs, up to our heads in putrid water, trying not to be seen while SDU PCs ran about shouting that they had seen a snake, just to see how we would react. The putrid water did little for the scratches and cuts we had, even turning some scratches septic. Also, during the four days, another highlight was racing with punch bags again, but this time from NT Depot to the Police Cadet School near the now North District Hospital, first thing in the morning before I had time to fully hydrate myself. During the run, my tongue stuck to the top of my mouth, my throat was that dry. My stomach began to overheat, and on arrival at the Cadet School, we were given water from a plastic jerry can that was filled halfway with pure ice. I took several drinks of this ice-cold water to not only hydrate but depth charge my stomach to cool it off to ensure I didn't get heat stroke.

After a few runs over the assault course, sometimes with stretchers, we ran back to NT Depot with the punch bags again. On arrival, we were given our worst session of circuit training, which towards the end meant doing press-ups, and hundreds of them. Towards the end of the session, I couldn't lock out my arms and instantly was under the spotlight with the SDU staff. I was shouted out, ridiculed, and sworn at for about five minutes while holding 90% of the press-up I was trying to achieve. When the exercise stopped, I collapsed to the ground and rolled over, rubbing my arms, trying to get rid of the lactic acid, just in case we were given more press-ups. I was absolutely drained, both physically and mentally, and the closest I had been to dropping out. After the four days, we heard we had a two-day camp in Lantau. Only we wouldn't be camping, we would be exercising.

On arrival at Tung Chung, I led the way up to Ngong Ping on a non-recognized trail, even discovering a cobra that the SDU guy with us quickly dispatched. On arrival at Ngong Ping, we were told that we were late and were directed to get to the top of Lantau Peak for further instructions. Once at Lantau Peak, we were directed to Tong Fuk, down a ridge that had very steep sides and set up an ambush in the rocks near the beach. At about 03:00hrs, we were stood down and told to fall in at 06:00hrs. So, as I had been paired with [WSm], we found a coach, broke in, and got three hours of good sleep.

At 06:00hrs, we were instructed to go to the top of Sunset Peak and collect instructions but were ambushed approaching the Tung Chung Road. [WSm] was asked what he wanted to do, and he said he would call for an air strike while I said I would try to outflank the attackers. At the top of Sunset Peak, we set up another camp that we had to guard overnight. While [WSm] and I were filling out canteens from a small stream, we saw one of the selection PCs dressed in his pyjamas, pissing into the same stream just above us. We weren't impressed, as we had to empty our canteens and refill them. At 04:00hrs, we were stood down and informed to be up at 06:00hrs.

The next morning, we walked from Sunset Peak to Hung Fa Ngan. We ran out of water on route, luckily finding a really small stream after three hours of no water. After refilling our canteens, we headed to Mui Wo Police Station and got the Lady Moraine (The Governor's Boat) back to Kowloon. While on the boat, we had to answer the order of which items of 10 tools would we get rid of first. Once back at PTU HQ, we were allowed to go home and told to report the next morning at 09:00hrs.

On Friday the 13th of September 1985, we were all given two topics that we had to talk about for two minutes each. I got salt and toothpicks, but being mentally and physically drained, I couldn't think of saying much, even though afterwards, I found myself in abundance. The third topic given was introducing yourself, which was a lot easier to do after the first two topics. At about 11:00hrs, we were all interviewed and asked how we thought we had done so far. On being asked who I thought had done the best, I answered [MBm]. They then asked how I rated myself, and I said the same as [MBm]. At 12:00hrs, we were told selection had finished, but it took some convincing for us to believe them. Once we were on board with the idea, we were treated to lunch at the Deluxe Café in Luen Wo Hui and allowed to go home.

Chapter 65

End of SDU Selection Dinner

We all agreed to meet at the Kempinski Hotel in TST East and have a thorough roman bath with a Shanghai rub down and massage, which didn't have any hanky panky. While waiting with [WSm] for the other three finishers to arrive in the hotel lobby, an old-looking guy walked past us with a young Chinese girl and gave us a dirty look. [WSm] immediately stated that if he looked again, he would lay him out.

During the sauna, the guy that was giving the Shanghai rub scraped pounds of dirt and dead skin off us, so much so we were asked what we had been doing. During the massage, the girls couldn't get over how solid and rigid our muscles were, much to their amusement. We then had dinner at Jimmy's Kitchen, and while going into the Cavern Disco, the bouncer stopped us and asked us to pay. This came at a time when we had quite a bit to drink and [MBm] told him to take a hike, lashed out a little and left. This was not surprising, seeing for the last two weeks, we couldn't say no to anything. Hence, when we were told no, there was a reaction. We all met up later at Rick's Cafe, which was much better, albeit we left at about 01:00hrs to go home and sleep.

Chapter 66

British Military Hospital for Nose Operation

I was admitted to the British Military Hospital on Monday, the 16th of September. This was because, on the following day, I would have an operation on my septum to have it put straight. This was a consequence of the issue I had with my ears. They didn't equalise at the same time, and I needed them to do that for scuba diving.

On arrival at the hospital and upon being given a bed, I pointed out to the British military nurse that my left knee had a cut from a selection I had just finished and had become infected. She looked at the kneecap and said yes, it was infected and had become septic and looked just like a miniature egg tart. She then took me to the treatment room, had me lie down on a treatment bed and said she would sort it in no time. She then left the room and came back with a packet of surgical blades as I could read the label. I kept thinking that I wished I couldn't read, and then she took a blade out and said this might be a bit painful. As she cut into the egg tart like infection, I passed out, and when I came to in a struggle, she held me tight and explained where I was as I adjusted to becoming conscious. She said I had passed out but wouldn't say anything if I didn't. She also explained that while I was unconscious, she had cleaned out the infection, which was as deep as the first knuckle on my small finger.

I then went back to the ward and noticed there was another male patient in for a similar reason to me as he had his sinus problem corrected. It turned out he was also a civil servant, and he would be operated on immediately after me the next day.

The next morning came, and we were not allowed any breakfast as we would be given general anaesthetic. At the same time, I was given my pre-operation injection and was told not to walk about. I also had thin gauzes packed into both nostrils. About two hours later, I was taken to the operation theatre and given my general anaesthetic. Once I was operated on, I then woke up in the recovery room where I was asked what my name was, only to complain that it was f*cking cold. I was then taken back to my ward and allowed more sleep. At about 17:00hrs, I was allowed a little bit of food, but it was difficult eating as I had a tampon like dressing under my nose collecting any blood or mucus that might be discharged.

In the evening, [RJm] came to see me with a couple of friends, but as I was still groggy, they didn't stay too long, allowing me to have an early night. In the morning, I woke up, was given some tea and asked to sit at the end of my bed on a metal-framed chair as the doctor would do his rounds soon. The other male in the ward was asked to do the same while my nurse took off the tampon like dressing from under my nose and used some hot water to clean the area. The nurse then explained that I had a piece of dressing stuck to the bottom of my nose and that she would pluck it off with a pair of tweezers. Unbeknown to me, both my nostrils had been repacked with thin gauze after my operation. The nurse then used the tweezers to grab the end of the gauze and yanked it out of my left nostril. This was very painful, as the gauze had become stuck to my nose by blood and mucus. When I opened up my eyes, the nurse said, "it makes the eyes water". She then yanked on the gauze in my right nostril, which caused me to hold onto my chair like I was on a white-knuckle ride. I opened my eyes very angrily, but all I could see was the face of the other patient who was next, and he looked horrified. This caused me to think that I was lucky that I went first. After lunch, I went home and got ready for work the next day.

Chapter 67

Return to PTU Golf COY 4/85 KW

The rest of the PTU attachment went as normal. However, I was informed by the COY 2I/C that I hadn't gotten into SDU when I was in the toilet one morning. No formal interview took place and I was not allowed to see the notification. My intake friend [MBm] was the only one selected, and a few months later, I heard [EGm] was leaving the Force. [RMm] only did one tour and returned to the UK to become a doctor. [WSm] stayed in Hong Kong like me and was satisfied in knowing he had completed SDU selection.

About four weeks after finishing selection, I was running for PTU HQ in the Henry Shield 4-person relay run around Aberdeen Reservoir. I was the anchor leg, which meant that I had to run the 4th leg of the course, just over three kilometres. Halfway around the hilly and challenging course, I felt completely drained, both physically and mentally, and I put this down to not having fully recovered from my exertions at the SDU selection.

In mid-October, [HNm] was going to have his leaving party in Macau, and my COY CDR heard of this and advised several PTU inspectors on Golf COY not to go. This actually turned out to be good advice as [HNm], after a night out on the beers, fell off the balcony railing of the flat he was staying in, fell one floor and smashed his head wide open. Nearly everyone said that this was an accident, but others had different explanations, with some saying that he had done a handstand on the balcony railing and threw himself off.

Chapter 68

Visit of the last of the Three "A"s from Peking KAf

Just after the SDU selection, I got to know that [KAf], one of the original three A's we had met at PTS, would be in Hong Kong for one night on the 26th of September, so we agreed to meet up for a meal. The evening went well, and as she was staying in Wan Chai, we stayed there to eat, drink and dance at the clubs. At the end of the night, the last two songs played in the club we were in before it closed were our favourites, namely "Through the Barricades" and "True" by Spandau Ballet. We danced really close and hugged each other like there was no tomorrow. As the last song finished, [KAf] said the evening would have been perfect if I had picked her up and carried her off. I gave her a bear hug and a peck on the cheek and said I knew, feeling regret that the moment had passed. I walked her back to her hotel, gave her a warm embrace and wished her well on her journey to Washington DC.

Chapter 69

Sighting of SDKSf and Invite to Her Flat October 1985

Out of the blue, I got a phone call from [SDKSf], and both [RJm] and I were invited to her flat when she heard [RJm] would be leaving Hong Kong. On arrival at her flat, [SDKSf's] flatmate was also present, who she introduced to us. Just before we left, she stated that her friend in Germany had gone off the radar, and she pointed to a half-drunk bottle of whiskey, which she said she had drunk when he told her that things were over. I said to her that she should have rung me, but she said she was still adjusting and that she would be all right.

Chapter 70

RJM Leaving Party and Leaving Night

At the end of October (Halloween), [MBm] and I had arranged to take [RJm] out for beers, and we hit all the hotspots in TST after a curry. On arriving at Hot Gossip, we got the DJ to put on some good songs, which we could dance to on our own. During the songs, [RJm] and [MBm] spotted three girls and started dancing with them. As the music ended, they said they were going to The Cavern. After about two minutes, we left to go to the Cavern and spotted the girls entering. Once in The Cavern, [RJm] and [MBm] danced with two girls while I rested up. The third girl came to the table I was standing at, ordered a drink, and we got engaged in conversation. We stayed in The Cavern for about an hour, and when we said we were leaving, the girl [SBRf] asked where I lived and said she could drop me in her taxi. [RJm] and [MBm] got their own taxi, and while going along Princess Margaret Road, our taxis were side by side. [RJm] was gesticulating to me, asking what was happening. I got dropped near the Coffee House on Prince Edward Road and on leaving the taxi was given a telephone number. Once back at Ming Court, [RJm] asked me what happened, and I said I wasn't sure.

On the night that [RJm] flew out of Hong Kong in early December 1985, I had contacted all his mates, and we had drinks in Someplace Else at the Sheraton Hotel in TST. Many people turned up, and many drinks were drunk, so much so we had to pour [RJm] into the taxi to the airport. He was heading to India first to see [LAf], who by now had transferred from Peking to Bombay. Upon going through immigration, he realised he had left the cheese for [LAf] at the Sheraton, but at least he hadn't missed his flight. I returned to the Ming Court Flat knowing I would be doing the same in four months as I had extended my tour by three months to take my final Standard Two paper.

Chapter 71

End of PTU Golf COY 4/85 KW & Transfer to MESUC SMP DIV

PTU attachment finished for me in early December. Initially, I was going to a PSUC job in SMP DIV until I saw the DVC. I informed him about how I had been treated by [GLKm], aka The Emperor, who then held the post of ADVC OPS SMP DIV. The DVC said I would go to MESUC, and he would ensure that [GLKm] would not bother me. Just prior to finishing PTU, the COY CDR [YSFm] informed me that as I had accumulated 17 CAPO complaints on my first tour, CAPO had asked whether I was the sort of inspector that attracted complaints. The DC KT [SBm] had answered the memorandum stating that I was not but had undertaken posts that dealt with people who made complaints purely for the sake of making them or for a tactical reason.

The end of PTU was a sad moment as we had all worked together for nine months, which was unheard of in normal police Divisions at that time. During PTU, many friendships were forged, and we all became more useful to our original formations due to our PTU training and exposure to operations.

I didn't take any leave other than one week's worth of time off at the end of PTU, mainly to do hillwalking or exercise. This was because I wanted to save my casual leave for a trip to Thailand in early March (8th to 25th). I was planning to go with [SEPm] before going on my first tour vacation leave, which would occur between the 1st of April and the 11th of August.

Chapter 72

Social Activities November 1985 to April 1986

During November, I rang [SBRf] a couple of times, and she even came to see me play rugby at the PSRC on boundary Street. After rugby, I took her back to Ming Court and made quiche from scratch, which surprised her that I could cook. I began to get to know her quite well as we went out with her friends [BNm] and [Af]. [BNm] and I had an interest in cars, so we got on quite well.

In respect of the Ming Court flat, I talked to [MBm], who agreed to move in with me after February 1986 as he wouldn't go on leave until August/September 1986 because of his new posting to SDU. This way, I could leave all my gear at the flat, and he could do likewise when I came back from leave.

Christmas 1985 was spent at the flat with [MBm], [SEPm] and [PJm], [YWCf] and [SBRf]. We all chipped in for the food and its preparation as well as ordered things from our station messes, such as gammon ham. I believe the movie of choice was The Duellist, which was set in France and starred Keith Carradine, Harvey Keitel and Albert Finney.

The New Year Fireworks saw me deployed in a composite company from the East of Kowloon, doing crowd control at the East TST waterfront. [SBRf] had been watching the fireworks and said she had seen me but didn't say hello as I looked busy.

Part Five
1986

Chapter 73

Last Standard Two

January was dedicated to studying for my last Standard Two paper, which, when I took it, I knew I had passed. [SEPm] was also doing his last paper, and he was confident knowing our leave and future employment depended on the result.

Immediately after the Standard Two exam, I somehow caught dysentery and was off work for about four days. [SBRf], who sometimes stayed at the flat, was in my flat when the Department of Health came around to check who lived at the flat and collect stool samples. I thought this was hilarious as well as embarrassing. I reckon that the Dysentery was down to the cherries that [RJm] had left behind when he left Hong Kong in December 1985, which I had used to make a cocktail.

In February 1986, on hearing of my passing of the Standard Two paper, planning started for our two-week trip to Bangkok, Phuket and Koh Samui in March. We also had to fill in our vacation leave papers and appointed Plan Travel to organise a world trip, planning visits to India, Nepal, Maldives, Sri Lanka, UK, USA (New York, North Carolina, San Francisco, and LA), and Japan (Tokyo, Hiroshima and Kyoto). Things progressed well with [SBRf], and we became very close, with me even sending her an anonymous Valentine's Day card signed with my thumbprint! [MBm] and [YWCf] moved into [RJm's] old room in Ming Court in mid-February, and plans to retain the flat on my return from vacation leave were in play.

Chapter 74

Two-Week Holiday in Thailand

Bangkok

[SEPm] and I headed to Bangkok on Saturday the 8th of March, staying in a cheap hotel on Sukhumvit Road. On arrival and getting to the hotel through heavy traffic, we checked in and got ready to go out. We had a drink at the reception, with me having a Singha beer while [SEPm] ordered a half bottle of Mekong Whiskey. I had a glass and then a few more beers. [SEPm] had become a little drunk as he had finished the bottle of whiskey. Just before we left, [SEPm] asked me to look at two girls who had just walked into the bar that were standing at reception. Upon looking, I informed [SEPm] that the two girls were, in fact, ladyboys, which he took some time to realise.

We went out for a long night and hit some nightspots that [SEPm] had received recommendations about, including one nightlife area where the girls served drinks naked. Eventually, we got to the hotel on a tuk-tuk and had a good sleep. On Sunday, [PJm] arrived and we hit the town again, eventually leaving [SEPm] in a bar as he was chatting to one of the girls. On arrival back at the hotel, we had an extra bed put in our room for [PJm] to sleep in and went to bed. At about 04:00hrs, [SEPm] came back to the hotel absolutely drunk and, while getting into the room, almost took the door off. On entry, he kicked me out of my bed, so I moved, and he immediately slept. In the morning, we were up early for the floating vegetable market trip, after which we did the Palace sightseeing. Getting [SEPm] up in the morning was a miracle, but at least he sobered up soon enough.

Phuket

Monday, we flew to Phuket and stayed in a hotel in Pa Tong, which was then a small little village cum town. We did lots of sunbathing and boat trips to the Phi Phi islands and other places. We had all bought Walkman tape players, and my favourite tape was Sade, which I listened to non-stop. I must admit I was missing [SBRf] quite a bit and had sent her several postcards. One evening, we went to see the movie Out of Africa and were surprised when all the locals stood up for the National Anthem before the movie started, which caused us to stand as well.

Koh Samui

On the 15th of March 1986, we flew to Koh Samui by a short take-off and landing aircraft (STOL) as the runway in Koh Samui was short. We stayed at a beach resort on White Sand Beach and did some more sunbathing. There wasn't much nightlife, so we hired motorcycles as we had done in Phuket and explored the island, which was a lot smaller.

One day [SEPm] and I went diving, albeit I was a little sceptical, as I hadn't finished my diving course due to my SDS KT attachment. In fact, I had only done half the course, but [SEPm] told me not to worry. He advised that I should just do the same as him, but a second slower so I could see what he was doing. I had brought my diving gear, including the horse collar life jacket I had bought second hand. Kitting up went well, and then we got taken to a dive site that had a depth of 30 feet. Once at the bottom, I couldn't get neutral buoyancy as I couldn't put air into my life jacket. [SEPm] thought my valve was stuck and hand gestured me to blow into the valve. This I did, but the valve didn't work even after I had blown into it. At this point, I was running out of air and didn't know how to put my regulator back into my mouth without swallowing a lot of seawater.

I made a command decision that I needed to get to the surface and swam upwards. It seemed like it took a long time to get to the surface, especially with my weight belt still on, and as I got closer, the sky got brighter. Just before I surfaced, every orifice in my body was twitching to get some air because I was swimming upwards on empty lungs. As I surfaced, I took big gulps of air, and then [SEPm] surfaced and asked me what the problem was. After my explanation, he said that was f*cking stupid and immediately taught me how to purge air in order to get my regulator back into my mouth. The rest of the diving went well as we also fixed my life jacket valve.

On the 23rd of March, we flew to Phuket and then back to Hong Kong, having got a brilliant tan and plenty of rest after the Bangkok section of the holiday.

Chapter 75

Return to MESUC SMP DIV

On return to work on Monday the 24th of March 1986, I noted I was on a one week count down to the beginning of my end of tour vacation leave. During that time, I would do a review of all outstanding death case files prior to [FGm] coming back from leave to take over my post on the 28th of March 1986.

[SEPm] and I read the book, Trekking in the Nepal Himalayas by Stan Armington, as we intended to do the Annapurna Circuit when in Nepal. We had got all sorts of gear, including Berghaus jackets, a good camera, medicine including Diamox for altitude sickness and iodine to make water clean. This took some time, as well as obtaining visas to Nepal, India and the USA.

I saw more of [SBRf], and we got even closer than we had before my trip to Thailand. I gave her the dates of when I would be in the UK and asked her to visit me during my leave. She then said she would rearrange her flight to Manchester when I was in the UK.

Chapter 76

Last Sighting of The Emperor as MESUC SMP DIV

Just prior to finishing as MESUC SMP DIV, there was a squatter hut fire in part of the SMP squatter area, and the DVC SMP asked me to report to The Emperor, who was still the ADVC OPS SMP DIV. Upon seeing me, he instructed me as the Miscellaneous Enquiry Subunit Commander to investigate the cause of the fire and take over from his Patrol Subunit Commander. Luckily, he also supplied a list of affected residents and said his patrol subunit would still guard the area. He then asked me to leave, so I did and set about undertaking my new task. In examining the meeting, I judged that The Emperor was wary of me because I was now confirmed in rank. He was glad to hand over the investigation, as it would prove less work. That was the last time I saw The Emperor, which I was thankful to the DVC SMP for.

Chapter 77

Vacation Leave: India

We left Hong Kong on Monday 31st March 1986 and flew to Bombay to stay with and see [LAf]. She had moved to Bombay to work at the British Consulate after finishing in Peking. The only thing she wanted us to bring, other than ourselves, was plenty of cheese that [RJm] had forgotten.

Prior to leaving Hong Kong, I had spent the whole of Friday and Saturday with [SBRf], and we had a great time knowing we would meet up in Manchester during my leave. If I am honest, there was a sort of understanding between us that had developed at that time.

On arrival in Bombay, [LAf] picked us up from the airport and took us to her flat in Breach Candy on Cumballa Hill, in downtown Bombay, not far from Chowpatty Beach. We had four days in Bombay, and [LAf] showed us all the sights, including Elephanta Island, Crawford Market, the Gateway of India, and other parts of Colaba. We dined in some good restaurants, serving excellent curry, both at street level and in hotels. We even had afternoon tea at the Taj Mahal Hotel, which was the hotel that was targeted in the 2008 Mumbai attacks. We also visited Mahatma Gandhi's house and swam at the Breach Candy pool as well as at a private members club while [LAf] was at work. During the four days, we booked our train to New Delhi, leaving Thursday night so we could meet [LAf] on Friday as she was also flying to Delhi on Friday. [SEPm] insisted on getting an air-conditioned car, although I said 2nd Class reserve would do. On Wednesday night, we went to Chowpatty Beach at sunset, and we were also shown the red-light area, which, I must admit, looked absolutely grim.

Thursday night arrived, and [LAf] drove to Victoria Terminus, a very beautiful railway station more like the House of Commons. We said goodbye, and as agreed, we would meet her at the British Embassy in New Delhi. She had a friend living in quarters there who would put us all up for the weekend as well as Monday and Tuesday.

Once on the train, [SEPm] ordered the night meal, and I did as well but was careful of what I ate. [SEPm] asked why I had left half the food untouched if I thought that Indian train food was good, to which I stated that I was referring to boiled eggs, tea and toast. He then asked me if I would have eaten what he had, and I said I would have left the cheese and the Dhal.

During the night, [SEPm] started to sweat profusely and shiver and said he wasn't feeling too well. He insisted on moving to a non-airconditioned car for the rest of the trip, and we were lucky that we could swap seats. On arrival at the Old Delhi Railway Station, [SEPm] could hardly lift his backpack, and while leaving the station, he said that I shouldn't walk so close to him, just in case he collapsed. We walked a couple of hundred metres, and I persuaded him to take a rickshaw to the embassy.

On arrival at the embassy, we met [LAf] and her friend and put our bags in her quarters. [SEPm] insisted on going straight to bed, and [LAf's] friend got a doctor who prescribed medicine for [SEPm's] fever.

That weekend, I was shown around places I hadn't seen on my first trip, and [SEPm] stayed in bed recuperating. On Sunday, [SEPm] surfaced and had some toast and tea and said he would be okay to go to the Taj Mahal with [LAf] and me on Monday. The next day, we sat in 2nd class reserve on the train and reached Agra within three hours. We went straight to the Taj Mahal to sightsee, and then we went to the marble shops afterwards, where [SEPm] and I bought a small tabletop and drink coasters, all inlaid with semi-precious stones. We had time to go visit the abandoned city of Fatehpur Sikri, which, although not as beautiful as the Taj Mahal, certainly had its own beauty. In the evening, we sat in 1st Class on the train to ensure that [LAf] was not always looked at in a lustful manner because of the way she was dressed, showing a minimum amount of skin but wearing shorts. She admitted that in Bombay, walking around the street was a problem and that she had been groped a couple of times. Tuesday saw us do more sightseeing, and in the evening, [LAf] flew back to Bombay while we took an overnight coach to Srinagar in Kashmir, which had Bollywood films and air-conditioning. We got the coach from Connaught Circus, to which we had reserved seats. Upon boarding and setting off on the trip, the coach stopped 30 minutes into the journey and picked up more people who sat on the central aisle. They were obviously extra passengers that the coach driver got paid for, but it was annoying as they sat on their bags and disturbed the once peaceful coach. The one next to me kept insisting on leaning on my armrest until I bluntly put him straight.

We arrived early morning in Srinagar and got a taxi to the houseboat we had booked, having heard so much about them. On arrival, the accommodation was poor, and the lake water was dirty. We dropped our backpacks after some breakfast and went sightseeing. On visiting an ancient fort, I couldn't help but note that some of the women tourists were rather good looking. The next day we went to the ski resort of Gulmarg and were quite pleased to see snow, something we hadn't seen in four years. We had a good curry back in Srinagar, and the next morning, we took a coach back to Delhi, where we changed coaches after dinner at Gaylords Restaurant in Connaught Circus, now heading to Lucknow. During the travel to Delhi, we noted how steep and dangerous the road was to Delhi, something we hadn't noted on our previous overnight trip to Srinagar when the coach was severely overloaded.

On arrival in Lucknow, we decided to hire a taxi for the whole day and go around all the old sites listed in our Lonely Planet guidebook. Most of the sites were not very well kept, and while travelling around, we couldn't help but see the difference in income, with some school kids going to school in posh uniforms by rickshaw. We stopped for a bite to eat in a reasonable restaurant, but when I went to the toilet, the squat toilet foot placements were well splattered with shit. I balanced on the end of the foot placements, but when I pushed to have a big job, I lost balance and fell forward, catching myself just in time. I didn't hear a plop, so I looked down at my running shorts and saw that it had landed in the lining. Luckily, it was dry, so I shook it out of my shorts, wiped my bum, and left the restaurant, thankful that my deposit hadn't been wet. Upon leaving Lucknow, we got the coach going to Kathmandu, which entered Nepal at the border town of Gorakhpur. We arrived early morning and got our passports stamped and our visas checked. We arrived in Kathmandu midafternoon and checked into a guest house.

Chapter 78

Vacation Leave: Nepal and the Annapurna Circuit

On the 17th of April, we arrived in Kathmandu, and the next day was reserved for getting our trekking permits for the Annapurna Circuit Trek. Once all this was done, we did some sightseeing and booked tickets for the next day to go to the start of the trek at Besi Sahar, arriving there late evening on the 19th of April. The 200km trek started on the 20th of April, and even though Stan Armington said it was a 21-day trek, we knew we could walk longer each day to try and reduce the trek to between 12-14 days. It took us six days to get to Manang, where we had to undertake an acclimatisation day. During the six-day hike, [SEPm] had been farting like a trooper, producing smelly egg farts. He also felt rough every three days since the commencement of the train journey to New Delhi. Luckily, in Manang, there was a first-aid post, so we decided to see the doctor, who turned out to be an American whose hobby was climbing. I went with [SEPm], and when he was asked what his symptoms were, he mentioned feeling rough every three days, and I mentioned the smelly egg farts that I had been chomping on while walking behind him. This convinced the doctor that [SEPm] had Giardia, which is acquired by eating human shit, so the cook on the train to New Delhi must have had dirty hands when cooking. Most probably after wiping his arse with his hand, which then wasn't washed thoroughly. The tablets worked almost immediately, and [SEPm] felt much better. The day in Manang went well with a walk up to the nearest glacier, keeping with the theme, walk high and sleep low. In the evening, while listening to the BBC on my Walkman, I heard that there had been a nuclear incident in a place called Chernobyl and that the whole of Western Europe could be enveloped by a cloud of radiation. This story would be listened to for new developments as we would be in the UK in June, four weeks later. That night, I was on the rooftop of our Bhatti teahouse and got talking to a girl from California who, on hearing that we would be in San Francisco and LA, advised we take Highway 101, which hugged the coast. It was good talking to the girl as it had been some time since I had an in-depth interaction with the opposite sex. Plus, she was good looking.

On the 27th of April, we set off for Thorong Phedi, the last rest house situated at 14000 feet, before going over the Thorong La Pass at just under 18000 feet. I had a rough night in Phedi as I had a severe headache due to altitude sickness, so I took some Diamox to see if it would help, but I still had a terrible sleep. At 06:00hrs, we left for the pass, which took [SEPm] four hours, while it took me five hours as every three steps I took, I had to stop to catch my breath. I also needed to have a big job two hours into the walk, which was much easier said than done, but I eventually managed. As I approached the pass, the trail left by the other trekkers began to be covered by snow. It was lucky that [SEPm] appeared to have seen where I was as I heard him shout. At the top, we got a hot tea and then walked on to Muktinath and spent the night, having ascended 4000 feet and dropped down 6000 feet.

The rest of the trek went very well as the food was much better on this side of the pass, as stated in the guidebook. We took two days to get to Tatopani, where we stayed the night to enjoy the hot springs before climbing up to Poon Hill, which involved another 4000 feet increase in height. We stayed the night and got up before dawn to take photos of all the mountains in the area. It then took us three days to get to Pokhara, where we stayed the night before going back to Kathmandu for two days of sightseeing. On one of the stops going to Pokhara, we stayed at a guesthouse where one of the walkers had got his funds for his trek from a security fraud in the UK. Another trekker at the guest house found out we were in the Royal Hong Kong Police and kept using the term 'Asia's Finest' in a derisory way, so much so that I wanted to punch his lights out, but [SEPm] told him to f*ck off, which he did.

On our last night in Kathmandu, we went to a good restaurant to have good food and a few beers. I had a steak and a salad that had been soaked in iodine water, so it wasn't dirty. In the morning, I felt very rough, and as it was [SEPm's] turn to sit next to the window, I asked if I could, just in case I vomited, to which [SEPm] said it was his turn. After about 30 minutes, I lent across [SEPm] to his open window and vomited, so [SEPm] immediately switched seats. I put this down to having digested too much iodine in the salad.

Chapter 79

Vacation Leave: Return to India

On the 6th of May, we again entered India at Bihar State and took an overnight train from Patna to Calcutta. When the train arrived, the 2nd class reserve carriage, in which we had seats, was too full to enter, so we eventually upgraded to 1st Class and arrived in Calcutta in the early morning. We took a rickshaw over an impressive looking bridge over the River Hooghly and stayed in a guesthouse near Mother Teresa's. We spent two days in Calcutta and then took a two-day train to Bombay in 2nd Class reserve, arriving on the morning of Sunday, the 11th of May. We went straight to [LAf's] flat and woke her up. On opening the door, she directed us to go have a shower and change our clothes. I took the opportunity to shave and felt much better, for this was our first real shower in nearly three weeks.

That day was fairly quiet, [LAf] made a really good Sunday dinner, and we had an early night. During dinner, she said, as Monday was our last night, we would go to the Oberoi Hotel and have drinks in their disco. We offered to buy her a meal at the hotel before going to the disco, and she accepted.

Monday was spent washing and drying our clothes and packing our backpacks. After which, we were ready for an overnight stay in Colombo near the airport on the 13th of May before flying out to the Maldives on the 14th of May to stay at Bolifushi Island. Dinner went really well, although [SEPm] had a whole bottle of wine and a few beers. In the disco, [SEPm] fell asleep at the table we had after about an hour, so [LAf] and I danced the night away. There were some British Airways Stewardesses in the disco, so our dancing became a friendly challenge of who could dance the longest. It was really enjoyable as I hadn't had female company for nearly six weeks. In fact, I didn't want the night to finish, but [SEPm] eventually woke up and wanted to go to bed, telling me I should turn the air-con off when I came to bed. Once at [LAf's] flat, we had tea, and despite not wanting the night to finish, I went to bed for a dead man's sleep until I was woken up by [LAf], who would drive us to the airport.

Chapter 80

Vacation Leave: Maldives Bolifushi Island

Life on Bolifushi Island was great but very expensive compared to India and Nepal. We wanted to go to the Maldives for the watersports, which this island had plenty of, including windsurfing, Hobie Cat Catamarans and diving. During the week, I went sailing on a catamaran with a guy who worked in Bahrain, only to capsize the boat with the mast snagging on the island's sewage pipe. [SEPm] went windsurfing, only to be blown away from the island and had to be rescued. We did three dives after the female dive instructor checked me out as I said I had forgotten my diving card. She found me good enough to join the dives and even tested if I knew how to purge, which I now most certainly did. On one of the dives, we went to shark point and [SEPm] was my buddy. On getting into the water, we spotted many sharks, went to the bottom as instructed and watched the dive instructor feed the sharks, thinking she was absolutely mad. It wasn't fun when we reached the surface only to have to wait to board the boat, as sharks were everywhere. The last dive I went on was a 100-foot dive to a sunken post ship, which required a decompression stop on the way up at about 20 feet. [SEPm] was my buddy, but after about 20 minutes, he came to me and signalled that he was low on air, but I refused to go to the surface with him and joined another diver. On seeing air bubbles coming out of the post ship, we went to investigate but found nothing. On the way up, I couldn't dump air quickly enough and had to be caught by the leg at the compression stop before I stopped rising. Once the decompression stop finished and on getting in the dive boat, a few people were not happy with me, especially the female dive instructor, who told me that if she hadn't stopped me, I could have got The Bends. That night, we all had a meal, with [SEPm] and I having Lobster thermidor, which cost us an arm and a leg but tasted amazing. Afterwards, we had beer games which I lost very badly, so much, so I had to go and throw up everything I had consumed. All of which was caused by a middle-aged Yorkshire Jeweler who was an expert in playing the game, who thought it was a great laugh, especially when he saw me in the morning waiting for the boat back to the airport with a huge hangover.

Chapter 81

Vacation Leave: Sri Lanka

We arrived in Sri Lanka on the 21st of May for a 12-day stay, taking in Kandy and the whole of the South coast. On arrival, we hired a car with a driver who could also act as our guide. After about three days, we arrived in Kandy, and while seeing the temples, we bumped into two other inspectors who were also on leave, including a rugby player called [MRm]. We had dinner in the evening and then switched into Hong Kong mode, going from one place that sold drink to another until we ran out of places to go to other than our hotels, where we continued drinking. The next morning it was hard to wake up, but we did. We then went to Nuwara Eliya in the tea country to stay for one night. On one stop on the south coast at Hikkaduwa, when shown a hotel room that had one double bed, we complained that we wanted separate beds, which came as quite a surprise for the hotel staff until we said we were straight. We eventually got a room with separate beds, and the next day at the swimming pool, we saw two gay couples, and we then concluded that it was a gay-friendly hotel.

On our last night in Sri Lanka, we stayed at the Browns Hotel in Negombo near the airport as we had an early evening flight to London on the 1st of June 1986. During the day, we stayed around the swimming pool, and I was heavily into reading a book, so much so that [SEPm] wasn't impressed when waiting in the lobby to call a taxi. I took this as a sign that our nearly nine weeks together had taken their toll and that now was a good time for a break in the UK prior to flying to the USA on the 27th of July 1986.

Chapter 82

United Kingdom: 7 Weeks Leave

On arrival at Heathrow Airport, I said goodbye to [SEPm] but agreed we would meet up sometime before we flew out to the US. I then caught my connecting flight to Glasgow to meet my friends [WNm] and [WKf]. I had arranged to purchase [WNm's] Moto Guzzi Spada motorcycle so that I had some mode of transport in the UK. However, for the first week of my stay, the motorcycle was being prepared. I spent the week getting my photos developed and some of them made into slides, especially the ones of Nepal, as both my hosts were keen mountaineers. During the two-week stay, I went climbing with my hosts, and they taught me the basics of climbing on rock faces in and around their home of Blanefield, mainly in the Trossachs and elsewhere. As all good things must come to an end, I left to go back to Manchester to see my mother and family.

The fact that I had not been on a motorcycle or in the UK weather for three years came to haunt me on a windy day on the trip back down to Manchester. Before I joined the motorway, I was nearly blown off the motorcycle when a huge articulated truck drove past me in the opposite direction. This was because I hadn't fully gripped the handlebars, and the pressure wave the truck created gave me a big shock. Later, going down the M6 just after Shap, the weather really closed in. At one point, when I was having difficulty deciding what the tarmac was from the overcast horizon on the motorway ahead of me, a gigantic westerly gust of wind blew me from the fast lane to the slow lane. The backpack that I had on my back acted like a sail, and I was only saved from being blown off the motorway by leaning over an at angle of 45°, all while doing 90mph.

I arrived in Manchester safe and sound and did the usual round of family visits before going down to Catford in London to see my friend [MIm], who I had been the best man at his wedding in 1984. I spent eight days with them and did windsurfing for two weekends on the south coast near Brighton. I then headed up to Manchester as [SBRf] came to visit me for three days, and it was surprising how well we got on and how comfortable we felt in each other's company. During the stay, she said that she had got all my postcards and that life in Hong Kong was not the same without me being around. Sadly, her visit ended, and I said I would be back in Hong Kong on the 11th of August, which was just over six weeks away.

After [SBRf] left, I travelled up to Newcastle Upon Tyne to see the Dilston boys, all of whom were now practising doctors. I spent about four days with them, after which I went to Edinburgh to see [ERf], who was living with her boyfriend. The weekend was crazy as we blitzed the city and all its tourist spots and enjoyed its nightlife, having 10 pints on the night before I left.

I then went down to Southend-On-Sea to see [SEPm] and his family for a couple of days. During the visit, [SEPm's] mother asked what portion of food she should give me, to which he said the same size as their family dog, which wasn't very big. On the weekend, we went to their second home in Wales and were joined by [LAf], with all of us walking up and down Snowdonia in bad weather. The highlight of the weekend was that after a night at the pub, where we had many beers, my tiredness caught up on me, and when that happens, I snore like a trooper. At the time, I was in a two-bed bedroom with [SEPm]. However, in the morning, he was nowhere to be seen until I went downstairs and found him asleep on the sofa. I never heard the last of it.

On leaving Snowdonia, I travelled back to Manchester to see my mother, who had decided to separate from my father. My brother, a few other family members, and I helped her move out midweek to rented accommodation, and I rang my father up to inform him that she had left. I spent the rest of my time in Manchester, helping her settle down. However, after 10 days, it was time to meet [SEPm] at Heathrow Airport on the morning of the 27th of July to continue our leave on the homeward leg back to Hong Kong.

Prior to leaving Manchester, I managed to sell the Moto Guzzi despite wanting to keep it, but with the new domestic arrangements, there was nowhere to park the motorcycle. Hence, it had to be sold. The time in the UK had, on occasion, gone quickly, but on others, it had dragged. I felt a need for some routine and knew the next 20 days of our remaining vacation leave would fly past, giving us only a fleeting glance of the places we would visit.

Chapter 83

Vacation Leave: USA

On arrival in New York, we checked into the YMCA near Central Park and immediately went sightseeing at the Statue of Liberty, which was freely open in those days, unlike now. We also checked out Ellis Island and then went for a night out, checking out some lively nightspots. The following day, we went up the Twin Towers. However, travel was all done by subway, and so we only saw New York when we surfaced from the underground subway, unlike now when you can go on Big Bus rides. On arrival at the Empire State Building, I told [SEPm] to go up himself while I made a phone call to [SBRf] in Hong Kong, speaking to her for about an hour, which used all my coins up. The call was all a matter of 'so near but so far', which is probably the best way to sum it up.

The next day, we were going to fly to see [SEPm's] brother in Raleigh in North Carolina. However, we had time for a run in Central Park. During the run, [SEPm's] speed used to get faster every time a good-looking female was nearby and slower when there were no women about. Anyway, the run took longer than we anticipated, and we only just made our flight.

The two days in Raleigh went well, and we experienced drive-through fast food joints for the first time ever. While at a BBQ, we were both called "Jocks" by some girls attending after seeing us swim in the pool someone had in their back garden. The two-day stay ended, and the next thing we knew, we were on the plane to San Francisco.

On arrival in San Francisco, we hired a car for six days, with the first day spent seeing the Golden Gate Bridge and Alcatraz. We then set off on Highway 101, the Pacific Coastal Highway and drove as far as Monterey. We had six days to drive to LA and then back cross-country through the Sequoia National Park to San Francisco. As our budget was tight, we decided to sleep in the car all six nights and take turns driving one day at a time. The first night, we stayed near Monterey and slept near a service station next to some bins. In the morning, when we woke up early, we found out that the driver's seat was bigger than the passenger's seat, which made for a night of better sleep. The next day it was my turn to drive. However, the speed limit of 55mph meant that most of the time, we broke the law and travelled at 65mph just to cover the distance. The towns on the highway were like a list of songs from the 1960s, with lunch spent at Morro Bay and dinner in Santa Barbara before sleeping in Ventura as well as Monterey the night before. The third day was spent in LA visiting Venice Beach, Hollywood Boulevard and Universal Studios before travelling through Bakersfield to Sequoia National Park, taking note of Danger Bear Signs before we slept next to a tourist information centre. In the morning, we were amazed at how big the trees were and when we were ready to move, I found [SEPm] sitting in the driver's seat. It was my turn to drive, but he wanted to drive because the road was winding, which he liked. The situation took about an hour to resolve until I was allowed to drive. That night we slept near Fresno, and in the morning, I was allowed to drive as [SEPm] wanted to drink when we got to San Francisco.

On arrival in San Francisco, we parked downtown on a sloping road and went to get dinner. [SEPm] ripped into the drink, like it was going out of fashion, and we ended up in a nightclub where we met a few people and were invited to a house party, eventually arriving back at the car at about 02:00hrs. [SEPm] asked me for the car keys, and when getting into the car, he lowered the windows down a little to let some air in, but in doing so, he broke the ignition key in the ignition. Anyway, we went to sleep and in the morning, as our flight to Tokyo was early at about 10:00hrs, I managed to get someone to fix the car at about 08:00hrs.

San Francisco Airport is a long way away from downtown SF, so I drove, breaking all the speed limits, arriving at the airport. I dropped [SEPm] off with both backpacks, passports and tickets. This was done so he could check in while I handed the car back. Before I could hand the car back, I had to fill it up, and when I got into the airport terminal at 09:30hrs, I asked where the Tokyo gate was. The person I asked, who was airport staff, just laughed. He informed me that I was in the domestic terminal and the Tokyo gate was in the International Terminal, about 1km away and pointed me in the right direction. I ran as fast as I could, but on reaching the gate, I saw [SEPm] just about to disappear down the passenger ramp. I shouted his name, and he came back to me and handed me my passport and ticket. He then asked me why I had taken so long, to which I asked why was he boarding with my passport. [SEPm] said he had checked the bags in and that someone had to be in Tokyo to pick them up. The airline staff asked me where I wanted to sit, so I asked [SEPm] where he was sitting and then told the staff that I wanted to sit on the opposite end of the aircraft, away from him, pointing at [SEPm].

Chapter 84

Vacation Leave: Japan and back to Hong Kong

On arrival in Tokyo on the 6th of August, we found a hotel and fell asleep for about 12 hours, waking up in the morning in Japanese local time. We went to a coffee shop for breakfast, ordering coffee and thick toast, and on paying the bill, we were shocked it had cost nearly $500 HK (£60 BPS). We then spent the rest of the day sightseeing, and the next morning, we took the bullet train to Hiroshima, arriving in mid-afternoon, being almost late for the train again because of the language barrier. On the 8th of August, we went to the Atomic Bomb Dome and left our thoughts in their remembrance book. [SEPm] wasn't impressed at what I had written, mentioning all the deaths suffered by other countries in World War II. Our visit was just two days after the anniversary of the bomb being dropped on the 6th of August 1945, so the memorial was very busy with Japanese Nationals paying their respects.

On the 9th of August, we travelled to Kyoto again by bullet train to see the temples and admire the scenic city. On the 10th of August, I had my birthday, so I bought [SEPm] a steak, which he devoured as he couldn't afford to feed himself with the prices in Japan. He was about twice the size of me, and I could see him visibly shrinking during the six days we had in Japan.

On the 11th of August 1986, we travelled by bullet train back to Tokyo and made our flight in plenty of time to catch our Cathay Pacific flight back to Hong Kong. We arrived early evening to very hot and humid weather, which when we disembarked, we both found almost unbearable. Once in the airport terminal, we went to the police post, and I found out my next posting would be UB Mong Kok. I then checked into the Hong Kong Hotel for three nights. During this time, I arranged my quarters, which I only just managed to retain as [MBm] had been made a Senior Inspector. This meant he was no longer eligible for Departmental Quarters and had to move to Non-Departmental Quarters. The three days in the Hong Kong Hotel were made all the more enjoyable because I got to see plenty of [SBRf], and things were as if I had never been away for eighteen weeks! I had a love that was both beautiful and sweet, and things were perfect! I wondered what the future would bring and what the next 36 months had in store for me.

End of Vacation Leave Hong Kong Hotel, 1986

Lantau Peak, 1986

Uniformed Branch MK Police District, 1986

Acknowledgments

I would like to thank (CBm) for asking me to write articles in respect of events I had been in charge of while in the entertainment industry in my position of Head of Security. This took me out of my comfort zone but tempted me to write an article about several events I experienced in a previous career.

On the back of this article, I believed I could write a book documenting my Probationary Inspector years. In exploring this, memories came flooding back from 40 years ago, so clear and distinct, it was like they occurred yesterday. This was especially so in respect of some of the characters and events which had an effect on my life at that time.

In writing this book it has been written from memory aided by reference to passport date stamps and a list of postings from my record of service. I would also like to thank my better half for allowing me to lock myself away for long times over the course of nine months. Further I'd like to thank (LAm), (SEPm), (RJm) and others for allowing me to use their photographs. I would like to thank Tori for proof reading and checking the book, Simon and Sofie for their valuable advice and suggestions. Lastly (CPm) for the proof reading with a fresh pair of eyes and comments given.